Further Praise for The Buying and Sellin
ing a System of Schools for All Childrei

"Susan Zelman and Margaret Sorensen have written the education book that America needs. Public education, built to ensure predictability and stability for adults, is struggling to innovate and adapt to COVID-era students' needs. It's also walled off from community assets like social service agencies, socially conscious companies and private schools. Enrollment declines and teacher shortages are evidence that things are not working. Zelman and Sorensen show how schools can have the mix of freedom and incentives to innovate, and how schools can be held publicly accountable whether they are chartered, private, or run by school districts. The system of fair funding, parent choice, school control of hiring, openness to new schools and public oversight based on specific school missions can transform and rescue post-Pandemic K-12 education."

—**Paul T. Hill**, Arizona State University; author of
A Democratic Constitution for Public Education

"For the general public and teacher education students who want to learn about how education works in America, Zelman and Sorensen's book offers a thought-provoking account about curriculum and instruction, making teaching a more honorable profession, school choice, community engagement, school finance, and governance. The authors provide an interesting model though not perfect that can stimulate our thinking to reimagine new systems of schools that can provide ALL students and their parents with more options for better schools that address their unique needs. This is a must read for all who want to see the current system be more equitable and eliminate the culture wars that tear America apart."

—**Richard Ross**, former superintendent, Reynoldsburg school system; former state superintendent, public instruction; member, Board of Trustees, Bowling Green State University

"In this comprehensive overview of efforts to improve American education, past and present, Susan Tave Zelman and Margaret Erlandson Sorensen offer readers a useful guide to the major issues in the field. While advocates will find plenty of specifics with which to quibble, Zelman's and Sorensen's commitment to the promise of American education comes through loud and clear."

—**Micheal J. Petrilli**, president, Thomas B. Fordham Institute and visiting fellow, Hoover Institution

"Drs. Zelman and Sorensen suggest we seize the opportunity to grow a new foundation based on respect for our democratic principles for public education. This book advocates for creating a vigorous national dialogue to stop making public education a political tool and create systems that balance societal needs with those of all children and their families. Examining both past and future perspectives about the structural barriers that have mitigated against efforts to reform public schools, Zelman and Sorensen strike a chord as they analyze the lens with which we plan for schooling, centering the dialogue around student-centered culture building, and not the needs or desires of adults in the general public. Their key questions are important for anyone interested in schools to reflect upon, during a most crucial time in the history of our nation."

—**Kirk Koennecke**, CEO—Superintendent, Indian Hill EVSD

"American education is at a crossroads and all those invested in its success need to understand the dynamics that have made schooling a commodity that has been cheapened by political myopia. Zelman and Sorensen insightfully document the way education has been bought and sold by political self-interests and how a new pluralistic model that engages a wide range of stakeholders is essential for fostering new and more effective paradigms of practice."

—**Thomas J. Lasley**, interim CEO, Learn to Earn Dayton; professor and dean emeritus, The University of Dayton

"Zelman and Sorensen have crafted a lucid, important primer at a moment when, as Lincoln once said, 'the dogmas of the quiet past are inadequate to the stormy present,' Read on for an education."

—**Ronald Richard**, president of the Cleveland Foundation

"As schools across the country emerge from the COVID-19 pandemic and other major educational disruptions, the United States has a unique opportunity to create a new system of education. Zelman and Sorensen examine our country's nearly 200 year old school systems and then uses that historical knowledge to offer a point of view about how to leverage this unique moment in time to think anew about American education. This book can serve as a primer for policymakers and school leaders alike as we seek to create more fair, just, and good systems of education for America's youth."

—**Eric Gordon**, district superintendent of Cleveland Metro Schools

"Zelman and Sorensen have provided vital resource for educators, parents, legislators and the general public as, together, we grapple with how to address inequities laid bare in American school during the COVID-19 pandemic. Beyond its concise and illuminating history of public education over the last two centuries, the authors provide a rich understanding of the manner in which policy continues to impede progress in our most disadvantaged

schools, forcing us to rethink our approach to American education now and in the future."
—**Christine Fowler Mack**, superintendent, Akron Public Schools

"While the public schools of our nation are responsible for starting our young people on the path to becoming bold and creative thinkers and caring and concerned citizens, the authors articulate a wide range of challenges that are currently undermining efforts on the part of school educators and administrators to achieve these vitally important goals and priorities. What makes the book such a compelling read for all stakeholders is that it then goes on to provide innovative and practical ways to transform these threats and challenges into opportunities for success!"
—**Howard Mandell**, social justice professor; former board chair, Southern Poverty Law Center

"Susan Zelman and I worked very closely together during the years when the education policies incorporated in the federal legislation known as No Child Left Behind were being considered and later implemented. But now we've entered a different era. People who are largely involved and invested in special interests have fought to weaken the reform movement and have left the edu-system ossified and less capable of effectively educating students. As Zelman and Sorensen's book makes clear, there's a great deal of work ahead. The angels will be in the details. But we do have here a vision and a general roadmap. And it's one well worth reading, understanding, and pursuing."
—**Sandy Kress**, former Senior Education Adviser to President George W. Bush

"Advocating for the child to be the center of learning, culture and educational structure, Drs. Zelman and Sorensen review the history of educational decision making and look to the future of a pluralistic education system. Understanding the past and the future of changing student learning needs to influence decision makers centers Dr. Zelman's and Dr. Sorensen's thoughtful and insightful perspective. Examining the past and future through the lens of what works best for all student learners is the discussion of our time."
—**Eleanor Smalley**, President and CEO of JASON Learning, a nonprofit dedicated to STEM for all children

"These authors understand the history of public education in our country and are strong advocates for improving 'life choices' for all students regardless of zip code or other demographic characteristics. No place is there greater need than in the rural area in which I have served for 35 plus years. Zelman and Sorensen are true champions for public education and the students they serve.

This book, their work, serves as a valuable catalyst to consider the education reform needed in our country to better address individual learner and systemic needs as we move deeper in the 21st century and beyond.
—**Dan Leffingwell**, Executive Director of Special Projects and Student Supports, East Central Ohio Educational Service Center, Buckeye Association of School Superintendents, 2022 Superintendent of the Year

"Calls to reform or reinvent the U.S. education system are heard far and wide. Serious efforts at reinvention, though, will require a thorough understanding of our country's education context – both its current state and the history that brought us to it. Without this deep contextual understanding, even serious reinvention efforts will fail. Zelman and Sorensen provide this desperately needed contextual understanding with extensive historical underpinnings and granular descriptions of the workings of our current system and its many nuances. They build a much-needed foundation for serious consideration of reinvention proposals and conclude with strong proposals of their own. I hope this book is widely read and thoroughly discussed."
—**Susan F. Lusi**, PhD, President & CEO of Mass Insight Education & Research and author of The Role of State Departments of Education in Complex School Reform.

"The Buying and Selling of American Education" offers a bold model for revamping the entirety of our mediocre status quo K-12 education system, which is necessary; and although I disagree with the authors' proposed funding mechanism and some conclusions, my disagreement validates their point – there exists a multitude of competing definitions of *public education* which, if honestly examined using their pluralism model, could produce much-needed purpose-driven improvements in the delivery of K-12 education in America."
—**Leslie Davis Hiner**, Attorney at Law, Vice President of Legal Affairs, Director, *EdChoice Legal Defense & Education Center*

The Buying and Selling
of American Education

New Frontiers in Education
A Rowman & Littlefield Series

Edited by Dr. Frederick M. Hess

Rowman & Littlefield Education series provides educational leaders, entrepreneurs, and researchers the opportunity to offer insights that stretch the boundaries of thinking on education. Educational entrepreneurs and leaders have too rarely shared their experiences and insights. Research has too often been characterized by impenetrable jargon. This series aims to foster volumes that can inform, educate, and inspire aspiring reformers and allow them to learn from the trials of some of today's most dynamic doers; provide researchers with a platform for explaining their work in language that allows policymakers and practitioners to take full advantage of its insights; and establish a launch pad for fresh ideas and hard-won experience.

Whether an author is a prominent leader in education, a researcher, or an entrepreneur, the key criterion for inclusion in New Frontiers in Education is a willingness to challenge conventional wisdom and pat answers.

The series editor, Frederick M. Hess, is the director of educational policy studies at the American Enterprise Institute and can be reached at rhess@aei.org or (202) 828–6030.

The Buying and Selling of American Education

Reimagining a System of Schools for all Children

Susan Tave Zelman and
Margaret Erlandson Sorensen

ROWMAN & LITTLEFIELD
Lanham • Boulder • New York • London

Published by Rowman & Littlefield
An imprint of The Rowman & Littlefield Publishing Group, Inc.
4501 Forbes Boulevard, Suite 200, Lanham, Maryland 20706
www.rowman.com

86–90 Paul Street, London EC2A 4NE

British Library Cataloguing in Publication Information Available

Library of Congress Cataloging-in-Publication Data

Names: Zelman, Susan Tave, 1946– author. | Sorensen, Margaret Erlandson, 1953– author.
Title: The buying and selling of American education : reimagining a system of schools for all children / Susan Tave Zelman and Margaret Erlandson Sorensen.
Description: Lanham, Maryland : Rowman & Littlefield, [2022] | Series: New Frontiers in Education | Includes bibliographical references and index. | Summary: "Traces the history of American education as a foundation to examining persistent weaknesses in education today"—Provided by publisher.
Identifiers: LCCN 2022031042 (print) | LCCN 2022031043 (ebook) | ISBN 9781607096405 (Cloth : acid-free paper) | ISBN 9781607096412 (Paperback : acid-free paper) | ISBN 9781607096429 (epub)
Subjects: LCSH: Education—United States—History. | Education—Evaluation—Research—United States.
Classification: LCC LA209 .Z45 2022 (print) | LCC LA209 (ebook) | DDC 370.973—dc23/eng/20220831
LC record available at https://lccn.loc.gov/2022031042
LC ebook record available at https://lccn.loc.gov/2022031043

My family has always been a source of inspiration for social justice and personal support. I dedicate this book to my husband, Allan, who has always been my best friend; my three children and their spouses: Alisa and James; Rachel and Peter; and Lara and Joshua. I adore my seven grandchildren whose accounts of their schooling motivated me to write this book: Ryan, Nathan, Andrew, Sammy, Joey, Max, and Dena.

Susan Zelman

As a parent, pushing my way through too many IEP meetings, there came a realization that nothing could ever truly get better for my child until it was better for all the children. My children are grown now (and have fed me and kept my house running so I could write). With gratitude for the love and support of my own family, I offer this book for all the other children.

Peggy Sorensen

Contents

Foreword   xiii

Preface   xv

Acknowledgments   xxv

Introduction: An Overview of American Education: The Importance of American Education History   1

1   School as We Know It   33

2   On Teachers   65

3   School Choice   105

4   Engagement   151

5   School Governance in America   181

6   A New System of Education: Starting from Scratch   213

Appendix A: Pertinent Court Cases   249

Appendix B: Discussion Questions   253

Index   261

About the Authors   275

Foreword

Elementary and secondary schooling is so frequently in the news that it seems that everyone has an opinion about how to "fix" public education. While everyone is entitled to their opinions, they are not necessarily entitled to their own facts. In *The Buying and Selling of American Education,* authors Susan Zelman and Margaret Sorensen give us the facts, concisely and plainly written, including how education in America is organized, paid for, conducted, governed, and the results these various kinds of schools produce. With these facts in mind, the authors guide us to thinking how we can get from where we are to where we need to be in providing our children the education that they and our society need.

The authors tell us how ideas and trends have affected American education over the past century or more, the research that scholars have produced to evaluate these ideas and trends, and what we as a society ought to do to shape the future of a system so badly in need of repair that—despite its many bright spots—is hardly worthy of being called a system.

Not surprisingly the authors conclude that we should start over. Well, at least, we should start with where we are and rebuild education that is focused foremost on meeting the needs of all the children. The children's predominant need is for good teachers, and the schools need adequate resources. The authors' proposal for state financing, for instance, is not to move away from the property tax but to make it a statewide tax, distributed equitably, along with state aid and other resources, so that each child would have access to education and attendant support that meet his or her needs.

Parents and families would have choices about where and how their children are to be educated in a system the authors describe as "pluralistic." Each child would have a "backpack" of resources that he or she would carry to the school. The state would impose standards; support teacher education; and provide regional administration of school districts, which would be guided by local advisory councils. This new system, it seems to me, would get teachers, parents, and administrators working together sensibly toward the common goal of maximizing the educational opportunities for all students.

The complexity of its subject often drives interest groups and pundits to proclaim they have the one simple "answer" on how to fix American education. They don't. They might find some thoughtful answers to their individual concerns with the help of *The Buying and Selling of American Education* and the multitude of sources that it cites.

The complexity that often drives observers to despair is not insurmountable. Like other complex systems American education in any given state can be fixed with a series of interrelated and simple changes. The challenge is to keep focused on the big-picture goal while attending to simple steps forward so as not to be discouraged by the resistance that a 200-year-system can offer. It is a long and ofttimes difficult journey; *The Buying and Selling of American Education* is an excellent and understandable guide.

Michael A. Wolff
Judge and Chief Justice, retired
Supreme Court of Missouri
Former Dean and Professor Emeritus
Saint Louis University School of Law

(Prior to his appointment to the Supreme Court of Missouri in 1998, Judge Wolff was special counsel to Missouri Gov. Mel Carnahan dealing with issues of public education.)

Preface

From the authors' front row seats, witnessing changing policies and programs in American education from different points of view, it is not difficult to see that American education is at a critical point. COVID-19 and other disruptions have exposed systemic weaknesses and inequities in many areas of our society, including health care, the workplace, and education, the focus of this book. Members of the public as well as policymakers have an opportunity, as well as an urgency, to create a new system of education and address the structural and policy issues that have been inherent in an almost 200-year-old public education system.

RECENT CRITICAL DISRUPTIONS IN EDUCATION

A disruption is a sudden and profound interruption. Disruptions can create uncertainty and chaos. Standard routines and expectations are gone. New ways of thinking are required to solve problems created by the disruption, and to establish new routines and expectations. Major disruptions can be disastrous or fortuitous, depending on how stakeholders react to them. In education, these major disruptions give us an opportunity to dramatically improve our education system.

In the past few years, American education has faced three major disruptions that dramatically impacted the American education system.

COVID-19

Throughout the pandemic, public school students experienced a range of educational events. Beginning in the spring of 2020, some schools were completely shut down for periods of time. Other schools held intermittent in-person classes. Some administered online classroom experiences, with a huge range of results. Controversies over school vaccine and mask mandates erupted across the nation.

COVID-19 may have accelerated a loss of respect for the public education system. In the past, while parents might not have supported public education generally, they have typically supported their local schools. The political turmoil of schools' openings and closings led many parents to lose faith in the stability and safety of their neighborhood school.

To meet the challenges of educating children during the pandemic, many parents had to stay home with their young children and supervise remote lesson. Some chose to homeschool or to find suitable alternatives to keep their children engaged in learning and connected with others.

With increased online learning when schools were closed, parents got a firsthand view into the complexities of teaching and learning. And although public schools may have closed, some charter schools, parochial schools, private schools, and learning pods remained open during COVID-19 and have increased their enrollment. As a result, many state legislatures across the country have increased support for charters, vouchers, and private scholarships that use public education dollars to fund these programs.

Black Lives Matter

During the time of COVID-19, the killing of George Floyd in May of 2020 brought the Black Lives Matter movement to the forefront in many communities. As the movement, and their cause, became more visible, state and local school boards passed resolutions to address racial and equity concerns. These resolutions were often used as a political tool by political operatives to inflame parents and advance other agendas through the election of local school board candidates.

Staff Shortages

Exhausted by COVID-19 and concerned about their health, as well as other challenges such as learning how to use new technologies, feeding and keeping track of students, and dealing with school politics, veteran administrators, teachers, and school staff, especially those over fifty years with a greater risk of serious disease, have retired in record numbers.

CHALLENGES

Throughout its history, the American education system has faced significant challenges. The disruptions faced over the recent past have exacerbated these challenges. Schools are currently dealing with staffing shortages, socio-emotional issues of students and educators, COVID-19 achievement loss, and the desire of some to return to business as usual. Addressing the current barriers and inventing solutions, with the help of new emerging technologies, have the potential to foster an education system that builds upon the strengths of all students and promotes the cognitive and socio-emotional growth of students, parents, and the community at large. This can provide a stronger economy and civic culture that will maintain our democracy and promote our economic prosperity.

The challenge for the future is to help policymakers, educators, and the general public modify their mental models of school and urge for development of new models that better serve our students. We can help bring about evolutionary change. But this requires that we advocate for a more efficient and effective public education system. This advocacy requires that we understand the present issues facing the system. It requires us to be well prepared to ask provocative questions that challenge policymakers at federal, state, and local levels. Our advocacy must include developing roles for research, innovation, and development of alternative education models, which can meet the needs of all learners.

The major challenges that must be addressed for twenty-first century education include the following:

Inequality

As we rebuild following COVID-19, we have the opportunity to examine structures, roles, and responsibilities to provide the political and psychological will to evolve to a new system of education by honestly confronting issues of racism and inequity. While there have always been inequities in education, these inequities were highlighted as schools pivoted during the pandemic. Various temporary learning situations have the potential to set the stage for learning in the future. In this book we hope to raise public awareness of the inequities that are present in our current system and present ideas that will enable educators to make sure all children can reach their full potential.

Technology

Evolving technologies have revolutionized the world of work but have only gradually impacted education. The COVID-19 crisis is giving technology a much-needed platform to demonstrate its capacities. Educators and the general public need to look forward, with a knowledge of history, to learn from the COVID-19 disruption. New technologies can be a positive influence on the fulfillment of the promise of American education. As a result of COVID, most schools now have technical devices for all students, and educators have had some professional development in using them. We should not underestimate how new technologies can help us redesign public education as we know it.

Distance Learning. As in health care, which had previously dabbled with online appointments and diagnostics, so has education previously dabbled in online education. However, with social distancing requirements as a result of the pandemic, our small and frequently experimental efforts at online education were, ready or not, pressed into immediate service. Effective distance learning protocols can be employed to address all kinds of educational needs.

Individualized Instruction. Digital tools are now available to help teachers individualize instruction for their students. As technologies develop, they offer incredible opportunities for both students and teachers to understand how and what they are doing in real time. Technology enables highly personalized responses to student need. But we also need critical thinking to evaluate the current storm of data and opinion as well as the storm of product salespersons bombarding teachers and educators. New technology can enhance education, but it can also simply reinforce the current system and magnify currently existing inequities.

There are many obvious pitfalls to the reliance on new digital technology in schools. Use of web-based programs has produced highly unreliable results—from success in some niches to accusations of fraud in others. An inherent danger to highly personalized education is that it may simply exacerbate existing inequities. Not only does it require greater care to ensure socialization of students, but "self-pacing," may simply widen existing achievement gaps and reinforce hidden bias.

Effective Instruction and Assessment. As we move into a marketplace of digital tools, we need to assure that educators are making decisions that will advance their development as well as their students and offer opportunities that will engage students and enhance their learning. Tools should be selected for their ability to foster deeper learning as well as providing ongoing feedback to students and teachers to monitor progress and effectiveness. Given the advances in artificial intelligence and the creation of informative data bases, we now have the capabilities to answer questions such as what works for which students and under what context and individual circumstances. To ensure we develop and fully utilize effective educational materials, we need to make substantial investments in education research and development.

Staffing

Education is dependent on human resources. Educators are human resource developers of their students and must be constantly supported in their professional endeavors. Our schools are the microcosm of political, social, and economic realities of the community they serve. The system's problems are historical, political, and economic. Because of human variability, best practices can be hard to scale. With the vast number of retirements and staff shortages, as a result of the pandemic, staffing all aspects of school life with qualified personnel has become a major challenge.

Governing School Choice

As a result of COVID-19, the issue of school choice has been exacerbated. Private schools, charter schools, homeschooling, and a myriad of responses to public school options have turned K–12 education upside down. By understanding barriers to reforming our system, we can invent new systems that move us to more accountability of publicly funded schools that offer more choices to parents to meet the needs of all children. Critical examination may lead to new ways of funding schools and the supportive services, revisioning public schools as central hubs of education for all in the community to use beneficially.

Fighting the Status Quo

Over the past several decades, politicians, policymakers, educators, and interest groups have worked hard to craft strategies to reform our existing education system. But change is very difficult. In spite of the tireless efforts and small accomplishments of education reformers in America, not only have there been no major decreases in achievement gaps between high- and low-performing students on international assessments, but our students also compare poorly with students from other developed countries. At times it seems that education is bogged down by a culture of mediocrity.

It is difficult to reform a system that has many vested interests. In this book we describe seven educational stakeholder groups which we call the seven Ps.

Professionals. This includes academics, teachers, and administrators.

Parents. All parents, including those whose children attend schools outside of public school system and included in this group.

Producers. Designers and sellers of hardware, software, and online programs, which impact public education, who have the potential to contribute but may be more interested in short-term profit than effectiveness.

Publishers. Before technology, we had textbooks. Textbook publishers have not gone away but continue to publish homogeneous textbooks and curricula based on the requirements of large states. Modern publishing can also provide alterations as needed for other states but lack the agility to pivot to emerging technologies that focus on meeting needs of individual students.

Politicians. Both parties want an accountable system to provide human capital for our economy and national defense. The players include term-limited politicians who have a fixed time line to make their mark and enact solutions. This tends toward quick legislative fixes, often reversed by future politicians.

Plutocrats. Some have power derived from their wealth. They have a stake in maintaining the status quo to ensure that their families will continue to have power and wealth. Plutocrats have access to the top of the quality education heap and may use their political contributions to influence educational policy for their continued benefit. Plutocrats tend to oppose inclusive social innovations that may affect the division of wealth and status in our country.

Partisans. These are strong supporters of a party, cause, or person, including unions, foundations, business, political operatives, and social media experts. They may see education as a political tool to support their strong beliefs.

These Ps form a complex set of interrelationships that help to create a current public education system in a status quo of constant flux, with constant struggles between competing interests and ideas and power relationships.

Curriculum, too, is mired in a status quo. Curriculum has long been influenced by the available textbooks or, today, curriculum "packages" that include online lessons and other teaching aids. From a sales perspective, curriculum is often defined by what is safe and what will sell to decision makers, who include educators, local, and state school boards. It is comfortable for policymakers and educators to purchase the familiar rather than the challenging that may require substantial change. This tends to affirm existing biases and support shallow understanding, rather than developing knowledge and skills needed to envision a more positive future.

OPPORTUNITY

Because our education system must be revived after the COVID-19 disruption, we have a unique opportunity to take advantage of our accumulated knowledge and experience in order to chart a future that equalizes opportunity for all our children. Not only must our students develop effective skills in reading and mathematics, and social and scientific literacy, but they must also garner an awareness of their roles and responsibilities as citizens of the United States. The quality of our children's education is the key to their future success as individuals, as citizens in a democratic society, and their ability to earn a living. With a strong educational foundation, our population will not only be employable, but our nation will also be competitive and vital for years and years to come.

In America, we believe that schools should educate students to be good citizens in a democracy. They must also have the knowledge, skills, and dispositions to participate in making the American economy strong and vital. A strong system of public education has long been regarded as foundational to the economic prosperity of any country. Today's American classrooms must cultivate future citizens who will work to preserve our democracy and be able to sustain and reinvent our economies. An American dream of a democracy that promotes social mobility, equity, and appreciation for diversity requires that teachers are able to engage and nurture students from many backgrounds and abilities.

To prepare our children for the future, we'll collectively need to reinvent our education system in ways that address the needs of the community based on some fundamental principles that prepare students for:

- confronting a future we cannot predict or imagine;
- being critical thinkers and innovators;
- establishing the psychological dispositions to be able to relearn new knowledge and skills in their professional lives and to assist in the economic growth of the nation;
- becoming lifelong learners;
- valuing American democracy and civic culture;
- practicing good stewardship of our planet, protecting it for generations to come;
- using technologies to benefit and not harm humanity;
- appreciating human values, including honesty, loyalty, integrity, civic engagement, civility, kindness, caring, and sharing; and
- appreciating diversity.

PURPOSE

The purpose of this book is to spell out in plain English the policies and issues that confront public education in America. This book is a call to break down barriers and recognize a legitimate role for families, the business community, and a wide range of related services in American education.

Our goal is to promote meaningful two-way communications between parents, the public, policymakers, and educators concerning five important education issues from the perspective of past and present efforts to improve our current system that need to be understood as factors to improve education quality. Each chapter provides background for answering critical questions.

Curriculum and Assessment. What and how should we teach?

The Teaching Profession. How can we make teaching a more valued and honored profession?

School Choice. How can our education system hold choice options accountable for the provision of high-quality education?

Community Engagement and Civic Participation. How do we build structures that seek out, include, and build on the strengths of our families and communities?

School Governance and Funding. How can education governance be more coherent and funding be more equitable?

A New System of Education: Starting from Scratch. What can schools of the future be?

Each chapter in this book will define and explain the historical roots of an issue, its current status, and observations about unsolved problems and challenges. In our final chapter, we call to stop tinkering with the system and focus on the actual work of educating children by creating a new system to support student and adult continuous learning.

Responsible change requires doggedly pursuing data, identifying the research into what works, and building community support to be heard. New avenues of media make more information than ever before readily available. What are needed now are tools and forums to evaluate the integrity of data, and conscious and unconscious bias of information being presented.

Given the right investments, we can create new systems that will commit to continuous improvement and lifelong education for all. In our efforts to create a new system, we must be clear about these key challenges.

- Specify the purposes of education.
- Employ methods to have civil dialogue to address our differences.
- Decide what we are for rather than what we are against.
- Include families in building structures to meet student needs, recognizing that needs may differ.
- Use technology to meet the needs of education in the twenty-first century.
- Choose solutions based on what is best for our children, knowing that they will be living in a more complex world than previous generations.

This book is intended for a broad audience of educators, policymakers, and families, including those who are highly educated and well situated in life, as well as those who advocate for better education in poor, rural, and urban communities. We recognize that various people experience education in widely differing ways based on how the resources are distributed, and how various students are seen by their teachers. But the future health of our country depends on a strong education system across all such barriers. These are all our children and attention must be paid to the inner workings of American public schools.

Educators and the general public need to look forward by understanding the lessons learned from the COVID-19 situation in a historical context and see how the new technologies can be a positive disruption that can fulfill the promise of American education. As we rebuild, we have the opportunity to examine structures, roles, and responsibilities to provide the political and psychological will to evolve to a new system of education. By addressing the current barriers and inventing solutions, we will build upon the strengths of all students, parents, and the community at large to provide a stronger economy, democratic civic culture, and a commitment to continuous learning.

In our efforts to create new systems, we hope we can come together to address our differences and use our imagination, ingenuity, and courage to ask the question, "Is this good for our children?" Instead of advocating revolution, we advocate long-lasting change and continuous improvement so that we can adjust and benefit from technology changes we will experience as a society to ultimately get us to the outcomes we want.

Let us hope we can create a new system that provides more options for children and parents to mitigate against the culture wars and structural deficiencies, which are described in the following chapters. We call this book, *The Buying and Selling of American Education* because we believe the past and current system has been designed around the needs of adults and not children. This does not mean that well-intended reformers are not committed to education for all children, it means that the system is broken.

The purpose of this book is not to bash educators or well-intentioned policymakers but to communicate to parents, the general public, and current and future educators about the educational issues from the perspective of the past, present, and future of attempts to improve the current education system. In addition, it is to encourage readers to understand that the structure of our current system has been with us since the last half of the nineteenth century and has vested interests that work against major reform.

Along with Appendix A, which provides a sampling of school funding cases that were resolved in the court system to provide further information for chapter 5, Appendix B offers a list of questions to begin discussion among stakeholders about the issues and proposals we raise in this book.

We hope that this book will create the political will to encourage a moral and savvy group of individuals concerned about preparing the next generation to live in these uncertain times and those that we cannot yet imagine.

Acknowledgments

We stand on the shoulders of a long line of women, beginning with the Mother's Clubs of the Progressive Era, working as unpaid volunteers to develop the system of public education, broadly conceived to include healthy environments, access to books, nutrition, and safe places to play. We each have had personal mentors and growth experiences bringing us to this point—recognizing that the needs of our children, despite a changing world, remain much the same—health, intellectual challenge, and especially safe places.

The authors gratefully acknowledge the work and support of others who share this vision: Dr. Susan E. Hodge, Dr. Heather Boughton, and Beverlee Jobrack who were willing to read and edit drafts of the book. We are also grateful for the work of Amy Palmer in scribing, and much of the technical work in developing and assembling drafts.

Introduction: An Overview of American Education

The Importance of American Education History

American education has evolved continuously throughout our history. To stand on the shoulders of those who came before, we must understand and avoid their mistakes and be sensitive to warning signs they may have missed. As we consider the controversies faced by education today, we may be comforted by considering how these same issues have been confronted (or not) in the past. Problems once regarded as resolved often rise again in a new context.

This introduction provides a brief overview of the history of American education from the colonial era to the present day. This provides a foundation to participate actively in considering how best to provide high-quality education to all students using a mental model of our past education reforms, successful and otherwise. An understanding of history is an important foundation to understanding our current system and the source of regional differences in education systems. A better understanding of the geographical, political, social, and economic contexts of the issues that we define as problematic can help our country improve both quality and equity in education.

By almost any measure, the American population today is more literate and better educated than at any time in the past. In 1850, for example, before the Civil War, 56 percent of White male children, while only 2 percent of Black children and those of other races, were enrolled in school. Illiteracy rates were near 80 percent for nonwhite populations. Today, according to the 2020 U.S. Census, the literacy rate across the entire population was 86 percent. The average American reads at the middle-school level (Brown, 2019). In 1920, only 17 percent of students graduated from high school. In 2019, 90 percent of U.S. high school students graduated. Of those graduates, 65 percent enrolled in postsecondary education within a year. In 1960, approximately 8 percent of the American population had graduated from college or had a postgraduate degree. In 2020, 35 percent of the U.S. adult population has a bachelor's degree or higher (Education, 2022).

Other measures, however, suggest a need for critical improvements. In 2022, based on the National Assessment of Educational Progress (NAEP), two-thirds of eighth graders were not proficient in math and reading (Education, 2022). American education must also change to respond to new technologies, research, and societal needs. To make intelligent changes, a study of the history of American education is instructive.

The following history is divided into different time periods. Each period is defined by significant movements in American education.

Before 1600: Native Americans before European Settlements
1607–1776: The Colonial Era
1776–1830: Education in a New Nation
1830–1865: The Common School and the Civil War
1865–1890: Reconstruction, Industrialization, and the Gilded Age
1890–1946: Education Reform and the Progressive Era
1947–1964: The Cold War
1965–1980: Equal Educational Opportunity
1980–Present: Nationalized Education Reform

Subsequent chapters will expand on this history with details for specific aspects of the educational system. The Learn More section at the end of each era identifies specific references to information that is expanded in each chapter.

BEFORE 1600: NATIVE AMERICANS BEFORE EUROPEAN SETTLEMENTS

Native Americans lived in America at least 20,000 years before any European settlements. At the time when the first White people came in the fifteenth century, there was an estimated 10 million people living in what would become America. Although little is known about their education systems, they clearly educated their populations in language, science, agriculture, economics, sociology, and government, among many other subjects (Urban, Wagoner, & Garther, 2019, pp. 1–10).

1607–1776: THE COLONIAL ERA

Among early European settlers, reading the Bible was the primary incentive to teach children to read. Available sources from the time indicate that, especially in New England, schools were organized and funded at the village or town level and provided a basic education for the community's children. The Puritans, in particular, obliged parents to educate their children. Educational options included religious schools, Dame schools, homeschooling, and private tutoring.

Legislation

Enslaved people, in many cases, were prohibited by law from learning to read and write. The first public school was created in Massachusetts in 1635 as the Boston Latin School, which still exists today. Massachusetts passed the Old Deluder Satan Act in 1647, laying the basis for public schools in America. In 1647, in Massachusetts, a law required towns of more than 100 families to hire a teacher and establish a school (Urban, Wagoner, & Garther, 2019, p. 32).

Major Reforms and Initiatives

Religious Schools

Massachusetts, one of the original thirteen colonies, was founded by both Pilgrims and Puritans. The Puritans highly valued literacy. They believed that all individuals should be able to read and interpret the Bible for themselves. Because the Puritans were fearful that their community might assimilate into the New World, they required religious participation by its congregants of all social classes, including slaves, to attend religious education seven days a week.

Dame Schools

Dame schools, which lasted until compulsory education was introduced, were privately run schools for young children. For a fee, children were taught reading, writing, and arithmetic, by a local woman. Girls were also taught sewing and knitting.

Educational Materials and Curriculum

Among educational materials available in the colonies were works of literature (such as Chaucer and Shakespeare) brought from England. Primers were available to teach reading, along with "horn books," or wooden paddles with the alphabet and verses written on them. The New England Primer was published in 1688, adapted from a British version. Also available, and in use, were Bibles and locally published circulars.

Teaching Profession

Parents and religious leaders bore the primary responsibility for the education of children. Different religious denominations established the first colleges to train ministers, including the Colonial Colleges, namely, Harvard, Yale, Princeton, Columbia (King's College), University of Pennsylvania, Brown, Dartmouth, William and Mary, and Rutgers (Queen's College).

Equality

In addition to Native Americans, the middle colonies were populated by Presbyterians, Baptist, Catholics, Dutch Reform, Jews, and Quakers. Religious schools taught basic literacy skills and religious doctrine.

The South was more rural and had large plantations and small subsistence farming. Although plantation owners arranged for private tutors for their own children and sent their children away to school, they did not support public education. There were some field schools, developed to teach literacy and numeracy skills. Some of these developed into private academies. The landed gentry in the South used private tutoring and/or private academies in Europe and at home to train the next generation.

Access to Education

Enslaved people were forbidden to learn to read and write, so their literacy rates were very low. In addition, it is estimated that half the women born in 1730 were illiterate. Women, taught at home to read were frequently not also taught to write and did not have access to school (Perlmann & Shirley, 1991). Daughters of wealthy Colonialists, however, were well educated by the standards of the day, which is demonstrated by the correspondences they sent (Norton, 1996).

Learn More

Deeper information about education in the colonial era is found in chapter 1, "School as We Know It," which describes the religious origins of educational curriculum and instruction that was established before the Constitution was ratified. Chapter 2, "On Teachers" discusses the characteristics of the people who took on the role of teachers in the early days of the nation. Chapter 3, "School Choice," traces the different educational opportunities available for free White males. Chapter 5, "School Governance in America," discusses the role of churches in the nation's early education efforts.

1776–1830: Education in a New Nation

America's Founding Fathers were greatly influenced by the Enlightenment, a movement during the 1700s that emphasized science and reason and the separation of church and state. During this period, prominent people argued for freedom from authority and that change would provide a better future and promote progress. Historians have commented that while Europeans invented the movement toward Enlightenment, Americans actualized it by establishing a government based on its principles (Urban, Wagoner, & Garther, 2019, pp. 52–56).

During this time American ministers, teachers, merchants, lawyers, landed gentry, and farmers had access to vast markets of printed books that explored and experimented with new ideas. After the American Revolution, Thomas Jefferson dreamed of a state system of education in Virginia for everyone who had talent. However, Jefferson's plan never got through the state legislature. He did help establish the University of Virginia in 1819 and stimulated small circulating libraries in many counties in Virginia.

Legislation

In the Tenth Amendment to America's Constitution, ratified in 1791, those rights not granted to the federal government were left to the states. While there was some discussion of a grand national system of education, it was never realized. Under the U.S. Constitution, education was and is the responsibility of each state.

Educational Materials and Curriculum

The Enlightenment inspired new literature that documented a balance between reason and nature (Urban, Wagoner, & Garther, 2019, p. 52). The tradition of religious education was kept in churches but was in large part replaced in schools with science, literature, and mathematics.

During this period, U.S. textbooks became popular and replaced European textbooks. U.S. textbooks were widely used in Dame Schools and local academies, which began to see tremendous growth. Textbooks during this time included geography texts and the McGuffey Readers. Noah Webster, known as the "Father of American Scholarship and Education" and for Webster's Dictionary, introduced the Blue-backed Speller that taught generations of children how to spell and read.

Teaching Profession

Although men sought better-paying jobs, literate women became teachers in the colonies, then the states, especially in New England. Dame Schools became coeducational schools as feeder schools to Latin grammar schools. Seeing education as the road to social mobility, poor towns paid for these teachers to teach their children. This period saw tremendous growth in local academies in New England, the middle states, and North Carolina.

Equality

The Quakers, which began as a Christian movement in the 1600s in England, were very influential in educational reform, as well as movements for abolition of slavery, peace, and equal rights for women. Pennsylvania was founded in 1682 as a place for Quakers to practice their faith. During the Revolutionary War, Quaker abolitionists opened schools for free Black children. By 1800, these Quaker schools appeared in Philadelphia, New Jersey, New York, and Boston. They taught several hundred free Black children how to read, write, and figure. Although there was opposition in these states to the racial integration of the Quaker schools, Quakers used their own resources to buy slaves' freedom in both the North and South.

Although Black students living on plantations were trained for manual jobs, Black schools during this period never opened in the Southern states. Some churches in the South started the African American Sunday School Movement and White plantation children may have taught their Black friends basic literacy skills, but Black education continued to be prohibited in Southern states by state law (Urban, Wagoner, & Garther, 2019, pp. 39–40).

Formal education in the New England and middle states became available to the lower classes, who could afford private academies, and in towns willing to pay a teacher to educate their children.

Benjamin Rush, one of the signers of the Declaration of Independence, as a leader of American Enlightenment and many reforms, promoted public education and advocated for broad education for both women and men. He believed that education would prevent women from believing in superstitions. He held that women should learn English grammar, handwriting, arithmetic, bookkeeping, history, biography, travel, astronomy, and natural philosophy, as well as music, dancing, poetry, moral essays, and Christianity. Education of women was seen as "Republican Motherhood." Mothers would be asked to send their sons off to defend our nation and, if educated, women would understand and support this (Urban, Wagoner, & Garther, 2019, pp. 60–63).

Access to Education

After a slave revolt in 1831, most slave states passed laws that made it illegal to teach slaves to read and write. As a result, the Black illiteracy rates were 80 percent.

By the end of the eighteenth century, Colonial girls were more literate than previous female populations in history (Perlmann & Shirley, 1991). Among White children, it was estimated that most could "read, write, and cipher" (Nemours, 1812).

Because of the emphasis on religious education, by 1800, it is likely that free Whites in the United States were the most literate population in the world. The United States had more advanced education than most other countries because it had many primary schools, which was not the case across Europe (Nemours, 1812).

Learn More

Chapter 1, "School as We Know It," describes early curricular materials and instruction in the early years of the nation. Chapter 2, "On Teachers," gives an overview of limited training and resources available to teachers. Chapter 3, "School Choice," details the lack of educational opportunities for females and enslaved people. Chapter 4, "Engagement" reveals how communities worked to develop educational systems. Chapter 5, "School Governance in America," provides information about the early efforts of states to develop educational systems under the Constitution.

1830–1865: The Common School and the Civil War

After the Revolution and before the American Civil War, agriculture was changing from subsistence farming to production of cash crops. This period was characterized by Andrew Jackson, the first president who was not one of the Founding Fathers. Jackson, who served from 1829 to 1837, was by no means a poor man but was nevertheless seen as the champion of the common man.

Jackson introduced the spoils system, also known as patronage, in which the winner of an election rewards their supporters and relatives with government jobs. At this time, a new political party, the Whigs, were formed to support a federally funded national growth of railroads, turnpikes, and canals. All these changes represented benefits to some forgotten groups of citizens, rather than just the elites and expanded educational opportunities to them (Urban, Wagoner, & Garther, 2019, pp. 80–83).

Legislation

States first established boards of education during this period. The position of state superintendent of schools also dates to this period.

In 1852, Massachusetts passed the first compulsory education law, requiring every town to have a grammar school. By 1890, twenty-eight states followed Massachusetts's lead by passing compulsory education laws that curbed child labor. By 1918, all states in the United States had compulsory education.

Major Reforms and Initiatives

Common Schools. Whigs advocated for what was called a Common School. They supported education for all, not just for the elites. The Whigs sought access to school for all young children with high school as a capstone of the American educational experience. Although these schools were free to most children, Black children and immigrant groups, regardless of social class, were not welcome. Small towns and villages supported Common Schools through local property taxes. This was supported by the Protestant moral establishment as a moral responsibility to contribute to the next generation. It also offered prestige to towns that supported elementary and high schools. Bureaucracy at the state level evolved to oversee the quality and quantity of education in each state.

Horace Mann is known as a leading champion of the Common School. A Boston area lawyer, former Massachusetts senator, and senate president, Mann became the first Superintendent of Public Instruction. He was able to convince the Commonwealth of Massachusetts to support a system of Common Schools by presenting different arguments to different interest groups. He appealed to the wealthy by convincing an emerging class of industrialists that an educated labor force would make better workers who could be better controlled. Mann argued to the working classes that the Common School was available to all and would help to prevent European rigid class structures. "Education, then beyond all other devices of human origin, is the great equalizer of the conditions of men—the balance wheel of social machinery" (Urban, Wagoner, & Garther, 2019, p. 91).

In his tenth annual report of 1846 to the Massachusetts State Board of Education, Mann stated that the Common School did not necessarily support the individual but benefited the whole community (Cremin, 1957; 1961). In Mann's view, property owners were at best stewards of "nature's treasures," and it was their sacred duty to provide benefits to the next generation. Many property owners, however, opposed the Common School for reasons that affected and continue to affect education equity today. People without children or people who already raised their children felt no obligation to support the institution that they would not personally use. Families who sent their children to private schools did not want to be taxed.

One-Room Schools. Throughout rural portions of the United States students at all grade levels met in a single-room school building. Students generally walked to school. One teacher taught basics to several grades of elementary school children. Standards depended on the expertise of the teacher and many teachers were former students. Many of these schools served as community meeting houses and local chapels at other times.

Educational Materials and Curriculum

The Common School reflected the pedagogical practices of the day: recitation, memorization, and drilling on facts and figures. American textbooks blossomed during this time to provide resources for curriculum.

Teaching Profession

Mann was influenced by Prussian philosopher Pestalozzi's pedagogical methods, known as *object* teaching. The object was to engage with the student and bring the child into the world of the teacher. This pedagogy supported the elimination of corporal punishment, the role of the teacher as holder of knowledge, and the teaching of whole word reading methods rather than phonics. Mann advocated this pedagogy before the State Board of Education in Massachusetts, but he became embattled with the educators who ran the Boston Latin Grammar Schools. Unfortunately, he lost this battle, and the Common School movement promoted the traditional pedagogy of its day (Urban, Wagoner, & Garther, 2019, p. 92).

Horace Mann also established in Massachusetts the first *normal* school for teachers (Kantrowitz & Larson, 2003). Normal schools, or teacher colleges, were teacher training institutions to teach teachers about curriculum, or what to teach, and pedagogy, or how to teach. The term, normal school, refers to reinforcing "norms" in students. These norms included basic skills, behavioral norms, and social values. The first American normal schools were founded in New England. Many public universities today were established as normal schools.

During the Common School era, unmarried women were preferred as teachers to save money on salaries and to foster a home-like environment for instruction in the younger grades.

Equality

Mann's work spread throughout the northeast, parts of the Midwest, far west, and in North Carolina before the Civil War, but did not take root in the South, which relied on private segregated academies. The Common School movement gained support from both political parties. The quality of the Common School varied greatly across locations. This was true during the Common School era, and it remains true today.

The relationship between the Common School ideals and racial, ethnic, and social class politics was complex. One year after Mann left the State Board of Education, a Black citizen filed a lawsuit against the Board of Education because his daughter was required to go to a Black school, even though White schools were closer to their home. The suit was unsuccessful. The court ruled that separate but equal segregated schools were acceptable. Although some laws were passed to attempt to integrate schools, they were never enforced (Urban, Wagoner, & Garther, 2019).

Access to Education

By the 1840s, primary school enrollment in the United States was greater than that in Germany. U.S. literacy rates were high among the free White population. At the end of the Civil War, 11.5 percent of Whites were illiterate, but 80 percent of Blacks were (National Assessment of Adult Literacy (NAAL), 2022).

After the establishment of Common schools in the 1840s, unenslaved girls and boys were generally educated for the same periods of time with as many girls as boys attending and graduating from high school (Goldin, 1999).

Learn More

Chapter 1, "School as We Know It," describes the development of curricular materials and teaching conditions as public schools became established. This leads into the overview of early teacher training in normal schools found in chapter 2, "On Teachers."

Chapter 3, "School Choice," details barriers to access to public education for various groups. Chapter 5, "School Governance in America," provides information about the growing state responsibility for education.

1865–1890: Reconstruction, Industrialization, and the Gilded Age

America began to modernize after the Civil War. This period, popularly known as the Gilded Age, saw a new class of wealthy citizens as an outgrowth of the Industrial Revolution. The growth of industry in the Northern states spurred migration and urbanization. The growing and modernizing country confronted social unrest, anti-immigration attitudes, and an unequal pooling of wealth, contrasting with urban poverty and violence (Putnam, 2020).

At the same time, the federal government imposed Reconstruction on Southern states. But in the South, a strong sense of localism, dispersed populations, traditional class and racial divisions, lack of transportation networks, and market economies worked against the establishment of a Common School system.

Reconstruction had a tremendous impact on education in the South. Before the Civil War, it was illegal to teach slaves to read and write, but after the

Civil War, there was an explosion of energy in Black communities to create schools, not just for children but also for adults and the elderly who had been deprived of access to education.

Backlash against Reconstruction was ferocious among White citizens. Fearing loss of privilege, many established terrorist groups to fight against racial integration in schools and society, voting rights for Blacks, and the autonomy of Black individuals and communities.

Legislation

Higher Education. The federal government enacted the Morrill Acts of 1862 and 1890, which provided financial support to create institutions of higher education that would not exclude classical, scientific, or military studies and that would teach agriculture, mechanical arts, and home economics.

School Funding. In the South after the Civil War, many states supported state funding for public education. However, there were still separate schools for Black and White students, and teachers from the North were replaced by Southern teachers.

Child Labor. Individual states began, in 1844, enacting laws that restricted child labor.

Major Reforms and Initiatives

Freedman's Bureau. The Freedman's Bureau was a government agency designed to help former slaves. The agency's greatest accomplishment was in education. Before the Civil War, most Southern states prohibited even free Blacks from being educated. The Freedman's Bureau appointed a school superintendent for each Southern state, who was responsible for developing a network of schools to provide vocational education and basic literacy. In 1870, there were more than 4,300 schools with about 250,000 students. They provided transportation and room and boarding for teachers, many of whom came from Northern states (Cimbala & Miller, 1999). The Freedman's Bureau also worked with philanthropic and religious organizations to develop a network of Black colleges and universities.

Immigration. During this period, urban school bureaucracies grew to accommodate an influx of immigrant children.

Educational Materials and Curriculum

In addition to the efforts to educate all people in the former Confederacy, schools across the nation began to offer industrial-related curricula.

Teaching Profession

Teaching quality and qualifications varied from state to state. There was no effort to establish a national system of textbooks, fees, or teacher qualifications.

When Reconstruction ended in 1877, two prominent Black educational figures emerged, Booker T. Washington and W. E. B. Du Bois. These important figures have very different views on Black education. Washington, founder of a secondary school and a teachers' normal school that became Tuskegee University, emphasized the need for Blacks to have marketable skills and valued skilled trades. On the other hand, Du Bois, the first Black PhD awarded by Harvard University, viewed Washington's position as surrendering to lack of equality and advocated a strong liberal education to provide leadership to resist rather than accommodate racism.

Equality

In the South, for those not part of the upper class, basic literacy and numeracy skills and religion were still taught in home settings or neighborhood schools of varying quality. Private academies dominated the South for middle- and upper-class White families with great variability in quality. Some field schools from the pre-revolutionary and revolutionary periods in the South turned into academies with specific functions such as military training, vocational skills, and female education. State-supported colleges and universities were for the upper-class Whites.

Access to Education

From 1860 to 1890, school enrollment increased from 49 to 69 percent of school-aged children (Urban, Wagoner, & Garther, 2019, p. 150).

Learn More

Chapter 1, "School as We Know It," and chapter 2, "On Teachers," describe the impact of industrialization and Reconstruction on curriculum, instruction, and the development of the teaching profession. Chapter 2 also includes a consideration of the impact of expanding populations of immigrants and former slaves on the growth of the profession. Chapter 3, "School Choice," also looks at the challenge of school systems over time to meet the needs of different populations of students. Chapter 5, "School Governance in America," provides additional specifics about state departments of education that were established and strongly influenced by social and political movements.

1890–1946: Education Reform and the Progressive Era

The 1890s and the first half of the twentieth century was called the Progressive Era. Progressivism can be thought of in two categories: conservative and liberal. Conservative progressives looked for efficiency and transparency of government reforms. They advocated elimination of political spoils or patronage-based systems. They promoted implementation of civil service systems with city managers and commissioners appointed by mayors. These managers were trained in management efficiency in normal schools and other higher education training institutions that expanded in the Progressive Era.

Liberal progressives advocated more voice for voters through political referendum and recall. They focused on curriculum reforms and school funding. Reacting to the plight and blight of urban children, they promoted the enactment and enforcement of child labor and compulsory education laws, which by this time had passed in every state. They advocated for temperance and women's right to vote. Liberal progressives also advocated for extracurricular activities, child-centered kindergartens, and junior high schools to ease the transition to high school (Goldstein, 2014, pp. 68–69).

This era was also filled with social turmoil that affected education. In the 1920s, for example, the Red Scare was a reaction to labor strikes and large groups of immigrants and Blacks arriving in American cities. Lower-class Whites and Blacks had not benefited from the booming economy of the 1920s, which also saw the rise of the Ku Klux Klan, with additional discrimination against Jews and Catholics. There was widespread inequality in educational access and quality as a result.

Legislation

Catholic Education. In 1875, Republican President Grant called for a Constitutional amendment to mandate free public schools and prohibit the use of public money for schools run by religious institutions, reinforcing the Constitution's separation of church and state. Although many states had already enacted similar policies, Republican Congressman James G. Blaine proposed the Blaine Amendment to the Constitution. Blaine would prevent public funds being used by parochial schools. The Blaine Amendment, however, failed in the Senate and never became law.

The Supreme Court overturned a law in Oregon that required all citizens to send their children only to public schools. This would have invalidated the existence of Catholic schools.

Plessy v. Ferguson. In 1896, the Supreme Court ruled that racial segregation laws that had been were passed in Southern states after the end of

Reconstruction were constitutional as long as the facilities were equal in quality. It became known as the "separate but equal" decision and allowed for continued discrimination toward Black students. By 1917, education expenditures for Black students in the south averaged only $0.29 for every dollar spent on White students (Schneider & Berkshire, 2020, pp. 26–27).

Scopes Trial. In 1925, John T. Scopes, a high school teacher, was tried for violating a law in Tennessee that made it illegal to teach human evolution in any state-funded school. The trial garnered national attention. In the end, Scopes was found guilty, but the case was later dismissed on a technicality. The law itself was repealed in 1967. This case highlighted the controversy that continues to rage between strict creationists and scientists over the teaching of evolution.

Major Reforms and Initiatives

Centralization. Conservative progressives helped to establish large school district bureaucracies, which established school superintendents as managers of staff, addressing curriculum and instruction, transportation, finances, human resources, union negotiations, food services, and facilities and grounds. The new bureaucratic structure resembled a factory organization, where there were now grades K–12 for students to pass through and tests, including intelligence quotient (IQ) testing, to sort students by ability and put them in different tracks. Local school boards changed from ward-based representation to city-wide representation.

Junior High and High Schools. Another new institution that emerged in the Progressive Era was the junior high school as a bridge between elementary, or grammar school, and high school. This period also saw the growth of high schools in smaller communities.

Extracurricular Activities. Many youth development extracurricular organizations such as the Boy and Girl Scouts were emerging and spreading across the United States during this time to make productive use out of school time.

Behaviorism. In the 1930s, B. F. Skinner founded a school of research psychology that championed operant conditioning, reinforcement, and response. He showed that if consequences to a behavior are bad, it likely will not be repeated. Similarly, if a behavior elicits a pleasant response, the chance that a behavior is repeated will increase. This had a major impact on American education (Skinner, 1938).

Educational Materials and Curriculum

In 1893, the Committee of Ten headed by President Charles Eliot of Harvard was established with a concern about routes to college admission. At that time, most students who entered higher education were tutored or went to private academies. The Committee of Ten report advocated for teaching core academic subjects. In response to the report, in 1906, the National Society for the Promotion of Industrial Education was founded. This organization argued for the creation of vocational schools, and in some states, separate vocational boards were created (Urban, Wagoner, & Garther, 2019, pp. 176–178). The Smith-Hughes Act in 1917 provided federal dollars to states to promote precollegiate vocational education in agriculture, industrial trades, and home economics.

Curriculum, the core business of education, was centralized and no longer the primary responsibility of superintendents. The new so-called efficient structure reduced principals' and teachers' control over curriculum and instruction (Cremin, 1961).

Liberal progressives advocated for psychology to be the underlying rational for pedagogy. They also reacted to the essentialist tradition of core academic subjects: recitation, memorization, and strict discipline. Liberal progressivism is associated with the writings and works of John Dewey, a philosopher who taught at the Universities of Michigan and Chicago as well as Teachers College, Columbia University. His written works can best be understood by the establishment of the Laboratory School at the University of Chicago (Wingo, 1965).

Dewey believed that the training of elementary school teachers promoted breadth of content over depth. His Laboratory School featured separate teachers for each subject, even at the elementary level. It was divided into kindergarten; the social sciences, including history, natural science, and mathematics; domestic science; and industries, manual training, art, music, and languages (French and Latin). Staff planned their activities together, and communication channels were essential.

The Laboratory School was ungraded. None of the requirements of a graded school system, such as meeting minimum promotion standards for each grade, was present. This allowed teachers to better meet the individual differences of every child, and students were flexibly grouped by interests. In Dewey's school, the themes focused on household and occupations, progress through invention, exploration through discovery, local history, and European backgrounds. These units departed from the ways of the traditional school experience and constituted a liberal protest to the essentialist traditions imbedded in traditional schools of the day (Wingo, 1965).

Teaching Profession

In this period, most administrators were male, and teachers were female. Many female teachers felt that the male administrators stifled innovation. At times, teachers formed coalitions with parent and community groups and lobbied against board and superintendent policies.

This period saw the growth of teacher unions. The American Federation of Teachers (AFT) was born and became popular in large urban areas, and the National Education Association (NEA) began to recruit members actively and place union teacher leaders in schools. At the end of the Progressive era, the NEA moved its headquarters to Washington DC to have a strong lobbying presence. The AFT became the union of choice in large urban areas. Unions pushed for more federal aid to education, a cabinet-level department of education, and better salaries comparable to other professions.

Equality

The Common School movement faced opposition from different factions. Catholic immigrants, on the one hand, opposed Protestant practices in public schools, such as reading the Protestant version of the Bible. German immigrants, on the other hand, demanded that schools teach the Protestant Bible and provide instruction in German. Although the Blaine Amendment to ban public support for parochial schools failed to pass in Congress, many states put the language of the amendment in their state constitutions. Because they could not influence public schools as they wanted, the Catholic bishops in 1884 required all parishes to establish Catholic schools, which enrolled approximately 50 percent of Catholic students (Fraser, 2000).

Access to Education

By 1940, 51 percent of American students graduated from high school (Goldin, 1999).

Learn More

Chapter 1, "School as We Know It," describes the impact of the progressive philosophy on curriculum and instruction, while chapter 2, "On Teachers," gives an overview of how progressive approaches to education affected teacher training and practice.

Chapter 3, "School Choice," looks at the consolidation of school districts, particularly in the North. Chapter 4, "Engagement," follows the growth and development of women's advocacy groups and their impact on many features of public education: libraries, playgrounds, and school lunch programs.

Chapter 5, "School Governance in America," provides information about how state governance responded to the need to enforce attendance and the pressure to ensure minimum standards and address special needs of students.

1947–1964: The Cold War

Following World War II, there was a period of optimism and hope. The postwar baby boom required double sessions in some schools to accommodate the growing population. Suburbs were growing along new commuter lines, and there was mass suburban housing development. Labor unions were strong, and there were fair wages so that many people could buy homes and televisions.

In 1950, more than 3 million students attended Catholic parochial schools. Parents paid tuition for these schools and also paid taxes to fund public education. The conflict over separation of church and state turned on whether the government should support private and parochial schools.

There were many critics of the postwar life. Reisman, Glazer, and Denney in *The Lonely Crowd* criticized a society in which middle-class individuals gravitated toward cookie cutter suburbs and sought approval of the status quo instead of fighting for change (Riesman, Glazer, & Denney, 1953). William Whyte wrote the *Organization Man* (1957), critical of a culture that valued materialism and wealth. Ralph Ellison's work, *The Invisible Man* (1952) described the pain experienced by Blacks. Federal and state housing loans discriminated against Blacks. The era also spawned the Beat Generation, characterized by a group of authors who rejected standard values, explored different religions, and rejected materialism (Urban, Wagoner, & Garther, 2019, p. 258).

Legislation

Brown v. Board of Education. In 1954, the U.S. Supreme Court handed down the landmark case, *Brown v. The Board of Education of Topeka*, which was one of the most important cases to this day. The National Association for the Advancement of Colored People (NAACP) had challenged the 1896 Supreme Court decision in *Plessy v. Ferguson*, which had endorsed separate but equal public facilities. Despite *Plessy*, both the North and the South remained both segregated and unequal. States and districts largely responded to Brown by ignoring the order to desegregate, "with all deliberate speed," and only began to integrate when suits challenging their noncompliance rose to the federal courts.

National Defense Education Act. In 1958, the National Defense Education Act (NDEA) was passed to gear up for the space race with the Soviets, following the launch of the Sputnik satellite. The NDEA provided federal funding to meet U.S. national defense needs. While these appropriations were not sufficient, the law did set precedents for future legislation and finally legitimatized a federal role of aid to the states for education. Some education lobbying groups, such as the Chief State School Officers and the NEA, did not support this legislation because it emphasized math and science over other subjects.

Engle v. Vitale. In this 1962 landmark and controversial case, the Supreme Court ruled that school-sponsored prayer violated the First Amendment of the Constitution, which establishes freedom of religion and the separation of church and state.

Major Reforms and Initiatives

High School. In the early 1960s, James Bryant Conant wrote two major books that influenced the American high school in the late 1950s and 1960s (Conant, 1959; 1961). As president of Harvard, he was concerned that the top 15 percent of students who attended higher education have access to high-quality rigorous academic subjects, such as science, English, mathematics, and foreign language. He supported enriched education for gifted and talented students and urged rigorous entrance exams for college admissions. He advocated college admissions based on merit rather that family background. In his *Slums and Suburbs* (1961), he describes the racial isolation in both slums which housed Black students and the suburbs that were dominated by White students. He supported the notion of comprehensive high schools, with rigorous academic programs as well as vocational training for suburban students who could not meet the rigor of an academic track.

International Competition. With the Soviet launch of Sputnik, particularly when the Soviets launched their second satellite, and the Americans could not launch its first, attention was riveted on the quality of American education. Many educational reports came out about how American students compared poorly to Soviet students in reading, writing, and math skills. There was a strong belief that the Soviet Union was superior in science and technology and that America needed to catch up. Even Southern senators supported this act because they realized that they needed more federal assistance in the quality of their schools (Urban, Wagoner, & Garther, 2019, pp. 258–259).

Cognitive Development. In contrast to the behaviorist school, works of psychologists, such as Jean Piaget and Lev Vygotsky became more and more influential in American education. Published works on learning theory and cognitive development emphasized the stages of childhood development and reasoning, intelligence, language, and memory.

Educational Materials and Curriculum

The National Science Foundation (NSF) was funded to support K–12 curriculum development rather than the federal office of education. States received money to improve education in science, mathematics, foreign languages, audiovisuals, and media services. Funds to improve guidance and counseling and education of technicians were also appropriated. With the support of the NSF, scientists and mathematicians began to develop new curricula groups such as the Physical Science Study Committee, the Biological Science Committee, and the Mathematics Study Group. There were several versions of each curriculum, based upon different academic tracks.

New math, science, and social studies curricula were developed and turned into textbooks and education materials. These new curricula were based upon the work of Jerome Bruner (1960). Bruner believed that students could master concepts of a discipline if it is taught in developmentally appropriate ways. His theories were based on the research of instructional and educational psychologists.

Tensions between progressives and essentialists in the 1940s were intense. George Counts, a disciple and then critic of John Dewey, proposed that education through social reconstruction should create a new world order. He argued that students should be educated for a future transformed by science, industry, and technology. In contrast, educational essentialists argued that education should preserve, not change, society. But Counts's ideas failed to take hold and were linked to communist and socialist tenets (Urban, Wagoner, & Garther, 2019, p. 235).

This period also saw the reorganization of high school curriculum. Among many changes, English and social studies were combined into two periods called blocks and there was an increase of vocational subjects. Life skills education, based on the principles of teaching students skills to adjust to life in a democratic society, became part of the curriculum, as educators attempted to base school subjects on social utility.

With the goal of increasing graduation rates among those not going on to college, business math and business English for middle of the road students were developed in the high school curriculum. These courses became part of a general high school curriculum track. The general curriculum track had very low expectations for student achievement and constituted about 60 percent of American high school graduates.

These lower standards for some students had many unintended consequences. In response to these changes, anti-intellectualism of American life was greatly criticized by many college presidents. Television programs exposed that some students received high school credit in wholesome relationships and lessons in leisure time. Many people were angry that high schools took away the primary function of teaching academic subjects.

Teaching Profession

At this time, the growth of unions spurred teacher strikes for higher wages and better working conditions. The AFT became very strong in American cities across the country.

The Red Scare of the 1950s inspired politicians to target public school teachers and college professors and make them sign loyalty oaths or be suspended or fired. Many argued that their academic freedom and Constitutional protections were under attack.

While some professional development was given to teachers to teach the enhanced science and math concepts promoted by the NDEA legislation, many of these materials would be seen, untouched, in teachers' closets in 1970s and 1980s. The new approaches to teaching science and math failed because teachers did not understand the nature of the discipline and its major principles and concepts. John Dewey understood this phenomenon when he criticized the education of elementary educators for its lack of depth in subject matter. Teachers did not understand and embrace new curriculum, and the academics who created it did not understand the day-to-day operations of schools.

Equality

The *Brown v. Board of Education* decision ushered in the civil rights movement of the 1960s. But the South was defiant, and in 1957, the Little Rock school board opposed desegregation. Federal marshals escorted nine Black students into Central High School. This event was televised and exposed the South's violent objection to integrated institutions. Four states removed the requirement of public education from their state constitutions. Many states implemented state-supported private school scholarships to be used for segregated White academies.

Many urban areas postponed integrating their schools in the North and Midwest until federal court orders in the 1960s and 1970s required them to do so. State boards of education did not see desegregation as a priority.

Many Black families saw desegregation as a means to equitable education resources and many groups moved to sue their segregated districts. Reluctant school boards sought to avoid court desegregation orders by implementing various "volunteer" options, such as magnet schools and interdistrict transfers. Massachusetts and Missouri supported busing of Black students into White suburbs on a voluntary basis. The Metropolitan Council for Educational Opportunity (METCO) program in Massachusetts exists today. While some of these programs were popular, none succeeded in avoiding court orders to desegregate districts.

Access to Education

By 1960, in contrast to 1860, in the United States, only 1.6 percent of Whites and 7.5 percent of Blacks were illiterate, unable to read or write in any language (NAAL, 2022). In 1960, 70 percent of American seventeen-year-olds graduated from high school (Goldin, 1999).

Learn More

Chapter 1, "School as We Know It," describes the impact of international competition, changing the focus of curriculum and highlighting the importance of testing. Chapter 2, "On Teachers," gives an overview of how the teaching profession addressed the need to provide improved science and math education and meet the needs of different types of students.

Chapter 3, "School Choice," explains how public schools initiated various choice options as a voluntary means of achieving desegregation. Chapter 4, "Engagement," looks at the atrophy of earlier activist groups for education as one side effect of the Red Scare.

Chapter 5, "School Governance in America," provides information about how school governance changed in response to school consolidations, expanding services, and national pressure for providing technical training and address the needs of different populations of students.

1965–1980: Equal Educational Opportunity

In his State of the Union address in 1964, President Johnson declared a War on Poverty. In the early 1960s, Michael Harrington published a book called *The Other America* (1962). He documented the increasing number of poor American citizens. This book made poverty more visible to the general public. Congress passed numerous antipoverty programs. The Economic Opportunity Act of 1964 was passed and created the Jobs Corps to improve employment for the poor, as well as the Community Actions Programs. To help the poor improve their conditions Volunteers in Service to America (VISTA) recruited volunteers to work in poor depressed areas all over the country to combat poverty.

Legislation

Civil Rights Act. The Civil Rights Act of 1964 mandated a report on major achievement gaps between White and Black students. The *Coleman Report* named after author Dr. James Coleman from John Hopkins University noted differences in education attainment and achievement by students' peer groups and family background. Desegregationists applauded this report and used it as an argument to push for the desegregation of American schools.

Opponents looked to the research of Arthur Jenson from California. Jenson argued that poor academic achievement is a result of hereditary factors that could not be mediated. His research was in direct conflict with the Title I compensatory education program for poor Black and urban children (Jenson, 1969). By the mid-1970s Jensen's work, and that of other sociobiologists claiming genetic/racial determination of intelligence, was rejected, owing to a lack of adequate controls in the foundational IQ research that had focused on twins raised separately. Other comparative IQ studies were found to be flawed or fraudulent (Rosenthal, 1977).

Elementary and Secondary Education Act. Building on the success of the NDEA, Congress in 1965 passed the first of many reauthorizations of Elementary and Secondary Education Act (ESEA). Disadvantaged children were targeted for funds with the creation of Title I of this bill, which received about 75 percent of funds for ESEA. ESEA funds were distributed across all states and used by local school districts for reading and mathematical literacy. Other funds included cultural and social programs, libraries, parent involvement activities, nutritional services, social and medical services, and innovations in teaching practices. Many districts used this money in different ways, some of which were not spent on disadvantaged students. Realizing that districts had misappropriated some funds, state departments of education grew in staff to monitor school districts compliance in implementing many federal programs that were administered by the states. Many in Congress were disappointed in the results of these federal investments. Others felt that there needed to be a much stronger federal investment to be effective.

Bilingual Education Act. The United States is a nation of immigrants. Passed on the heels of the Civil Rights Action, the Bilingual Education Act (BEA) of 1967 recognized the needs of students with limited-speaking ability. It provided school districts with federal funds to establish educational programs for these students.

Title IX. In 1972, an Education Amendment was signed into law by Richard Nixon. It prohibited sex discrimination in any educational program that received federal aid. In 1975, Gerald Ford signed the final version of Title IX. This legislation has inspired many women to participate and compete in sports.

Education for All Handicapped Act. President Ford in 1975 signed Public Law 94–142, which guaranteed a Free Appropriate Public Education (FAPE) for children with disabilities in all states and localities. It had very specific requirements regarding the delivery of these services.

Major Reforms and Initiatives

War on Poverty. To fight poverty, Congress passed several antipoverty programs that greatly increased the access to quality education. Head Start programs were established to involve parents in their children's cognitive, social, and physical developments. It was established to meet the emotional, social, health, nutritional, and educational needs of preschool children from low-income families.

Desegregation. Although *Brown v. Board of Education* was handed down in 1954, desegregation was slow in coming to schools. Federal funding, with a requirement of compliance with desegregation requirements was offered to assist in "levelling the playing field." Opponents of desegregation efforts worked to shift focus from racial integration to the use of buses to transport students to newly assigned schools. Some organized to claim a right to "neighborhood schools" (*The New York Times*, 2019).

Funding. In 1972, Christopher Jencks et al. conducted an extensive study to demonstrate that family background is related to educational outcomes (Jencks et al., 1972). Daniel Patrick Moynihan from Harvard University, who was working for Richard Nixon, suggested that direct economic aid to the poor would be more effective than compensatory programs (Urban, Wagoner, & Garther, 2019, p. 300). This idea was rejected by Nixon and never took root in American educational policy. Nixon did have the Office of Civil Rights threaten to withhold dollars from school districts that did not adopt bilingual education. Nixon advocated for more federal research in education rather than spending on federal programs to the states (Urban, Wagoner, & Garther, 2019, pp. 286–287, 300). He vetoed the Comprehensive Child Development Act of 1971, which would have given federal funds to childcare centers across the country.

U.S. Department of Education. During President Carter's campaign in 1976 he promised the NEA that he would support the establishment of a federal education department with a cabinet head to administer it. The U.S. Department of Education was established in 1978, broken out from the Department of Health, Education, and Welfare. The intent of the new department was to focus on education, establish policy, collect data, and enforce federal educational laws.

Educational Materials and Curriculum

In the 1960s and 1970s, a series of books by Jonathan Kozol, Herbert Kohl, John Holt, Paul Goodman, Peter Schrag, Ivan Illich, David Rogers, and Paulo Freire were indictments of the traditional essentialists' pedagogy and large urban bureaucracies. These authors inspired the open school movement of the 1960s and 1970s. Schrag described the inefficiencies of the Boston school system bureaucracy in his book, *Village School Downtown* (1968). Rogers criticized the New York City Board of Education in *110 Livingston Street* (1968). While these publications did not significantly change the way schools were operated in America, they did inspire a group of young adults who wanted to improve education equity. As Dan C. Lortie explained in his classic book, *Schoolteacher: A Sociological Study*, no matter how good our intentions, we are coopted by the system, and we learn as we are taught (Lortie, 1975).

Teaching Profession

As teacher unions became empowered, they clashed with reformers of the community control movement of the 1960s. Community control activism occurred in New York City, Detroit, and Oakland. It alienated liberals and some community members from teacher unions and set the stage for attacks on teacher unions in the next era (1980–present) (Altshuler, 1970; Berube & Gittel, 1969).

Access to Education

By 1980, 71 percent of American seventeen-year-olds graduated from high school (Goldin, 1999).

Learn More

Chapter 1, "School as We Know It," describes the explosion of curricular materials and instructional methods to meet the need for higher educational standards with a growing population of students. Chapter 2, "On Teachers," gives an overview of how teachers addressed the challenge to provide education to a greater number and range of student needs through more teacher training and professional development. It also addresses the impact of teacher unions on education.

Chapter 3, "School Choice," explains how alternative schools began to provide school choice to address integration and the needs of students who did not succeed in existing school settings. Chapter 4, "Engagement," details the marginalization of some parent and community groups, despite codified federal requirements for "parent involvement."

Chapter 5, "School Governance in America," provides information about how school governance responded to the federal initiatives for social, economic, and demographic changes.

1980–Present: Top-Down Education Reform

When Ronald Reagan became president in 1981 and was reelected in 1984, conservative educators were overjoyed. The policies of the Reagan administration set the tone for the federal and state policies from 1980 to the present.

Reagan increased military spending but reduced many education programs as well as taxes. He first wanted to abolish the U.S. Department of Education and reestablish school prayer. These initiatives failed. He was greatly influenced by Milton Friedman, a market economist at the University of Chicago, and Chester Finn Jr., an administrator in the U.S. Department of Education, who supported tuition tax credits for parents, charter schools, and vouchers.

Terrell Bell, who served as Reagan's first Secretary of Education, managed to sidestep many of Reagan's proposals. Bell established the National Commission on Excellence of Education, known for issuing "A Nation at Risk," a report that enumerated the challenges facing American public education. Businessmen, academics, and state and national policymakers used the report to usher in a forty-year era of national and state education reforms (National Commission on Excellence in Education, 1983).

Legislation

No Child Left Behind Elementary and Secondary School Act. No Child Left Behind. The Elementary and Secondary Education Act (ESEA), originally passed in 1965, was reauthorized as the No Child Left Behind Act (NCLB) in September 2001. The Act required states to test students in reading and mathematics in grades 3–8 with science tests in three grades. Tests were aligned with state-adopted content standards. States were required to set standards for "proficiency" and set goals to ensure "adequate yearly progress" (AYP) toward the goal of all students meeting the proficiency standard by 2014. Districts that continually failed to meet these measures received harsher penalties as reconstitution of the school or becoming a charter school. In addition, all teachers needed to become highly qualified even though they were certified in their subject area.

Race to the Top. This competitive grant funded as part of the 2009 American Recovery and Reinvestment Act was created to incent and reward innovations in K–12 education.

Every Student Succeeds Act. The December 2015 of ESEA, named Every Student Succeeds Act (ESSA) was intended to promote education equity by establishing high expectations with national standards in reading and mathematics and establishing resources or meeting and assessing achievement.

Major Reforms and Initiatives

A Nation at Risk. Education became both a national and state issue because "A Nation at Risk," released in 1983, was a media sensation. The document argued that Japan, Korea, and Germany were surpassing the United States in technology. States needed to put more rigor into the curriculum by establishing academic standards. Teacher education programs were

criticized. Teachers' salaries were a concern because they were not comparable to other professions, and there was a shortage of well-qualified math
and science teachers. The report suggested that teachers' compensation
should be linked to student achievement (National Commission on Excellence in Education, 1983).

Goals 2000. When George Bush Sr. became president in 1988, he aligned
himself with the reform agenda of the National Governors Association
(NGA) and called for a presidential summit on education held at the University of Virginia in September 1989. The outcome of this summit was
America 2000, which included six education goals to be accomplished by
the year 2000. These goals were embraced by governors including Bill
Clinton of Arkansas. Later Clinton's Secretary of Education was Richard
Riley, former governor of South Carolina. This group of governors, including Lamar Alexander (Reagan's last Secretary of Education), shared a passion for state standards and standardized testing.

When Clinton left the White House in 2000, none of Bush's America 2000
Goals or Clinton's Goals 2000 had been met, although these movements
had inspired a lot of activity. Over the course of a decade, departments of
education implemented state and national policy changes in teacher education requirements, adopted state standards, and aligned state testing. States
had also set targets of improvements in achievement for different groups of
students: special education, racial minorities, poor, and bilingual. School
funding formulas were revised based on state court decisions. State departments of education began to publicize district and school achievement
results with disaggregated student data (Urban, Wagoner, & Garther, 2019,
pp. 325–327).

State and National Standards. Beginning in the 1980s, rigorous, college
and career readiness standards were developed for every subject with the
goal of outlining the essential elements of high-quality curriculum. Some
of these efforts include the following.

State Academic Content Standards. These were developed and adopted by
states to define grade-level expectations for each content area to comply
with No Child Left Behind.

National Council of Teachers of Mathematics. National Council of Teachers of Mathematics (NCTM), in 1989, developed the first set of national
standards, adopted by some states in place of developing their own.

Other National Standards. Various national groups created standards for
reading, language arts, science, history, geography, art, physical education,
and educational technology throughout the 1990s. Some states adopted
these rather than creating their own.

Common Core Standards. Race to the Top (RTTT), a competitive federal grant, required states to convene in the development of a common set of mathematics and English language arts standards.

Testing and AYP. With the standards movement, the ESSA reauthorizations in 2000 and 2015 included guidelines for rigorous testing to measure whether students could demonstrate proficiency according to the standards. AYP goals were set by states to guide progress toward ensuring that all students meet proficiency.

School Choice. Since the 1980s, many alternatives to district-operated public schools have been developed to expand options available to students and families. In the past, other options were limited to non-publicly funded academies and parochial schools. Homeschooling that is regulated by each state is increasingly an option, depending on the state. Recent years have seen an expansion of other, publicly funded options. Depending on the state, choices can be funded through educational savings accounts, school vouchers, or tax credits. Other options include publicly funded charter schools, district-created magnet schools that offer specialized curricula, various interdistrict and intradistrict transfer programs, and a range of online, digital learning schools.

Twenty-First Century Skills. These identify and prioritize the knowledge, skills, work habits, and character traits that will be critically important to succeed in college and the workplace.

Educational Materials and Curriculum

In 1988, E. D. Hirsch Jr., from the University of Virginia, helped to revive the back-to-basics movement. In his book, *Cultural Literacy; What Every American Needs to Know*, he bashed the progressives for ignoring specific education content (Hirsh, 1988). He developed a series of texts, *Core Knowledge*, specifying what school-age children needed to know at each grade level. In his several books that followed, he advocated for excellence as well as equity, and his writings influenced educational policy in the 1980s and 1990s.

Beyond *Core Knowledge*, as a result of the development of national standards, there was a transformation in educational materials. Whereas publishers previously tailored materials to state standards, prioritizing large states that allocated funds for adopted materials, publishers produced new materials using the national standards as a foundation.

Technology also played a major role in educational materials. Whiteboard activities, multimedia experiences, educational software applications, and online curricula transformed the way lessons are presented and assessed.

Multicultural education also had a major impact on educational materials. Instead of focusing on white males and their achievements, educational materials are expected to present a balance of males and females in significant roles and a positive representation of people of color and people with disabilities, so all students see themselves reflected in school materials.

Teaching Profession

Since 1980, the teaching profession has been challenged in many ways.

A Nation at Risk. This 1983 study motivated states to examine their academic standards and goals, stimulate reforms in teacher education, and plant the seeds for teachers' evaluations to be linked to student performance (National Commission on Excellence in Education, 1983)

Teacher Education and Accreditation Standards. Setting standards for teacher education had a major impact on continuing education and professional development for teachers.

Standards. The national standards movement transformed what teachers teach in each subject in each grade.

Testing. Teachers began to be evaluated on how well their students do on standardized state and national achievement tests. They are accountable for making AYP. As a result, many teachers report a pressure to "teach to the test" and abandon their individual teaching methods.

COVID-19. When the pandemic hit in 2020, teachers were forced to adapt to online teaching and inconsistent scheduling. Massive numbers of teachers, particularly older and immune-compromised teachers left the profession when schools reopened. This caused significant staffing shortages, calling on substitutes and even the National Guard to step in.

Equality

Two movements have significantly addressed the issue of educational equity since 1980.

Multicultural Education. This initiative came out of the civil rights movement and evolved to present an accurate representation of the diverse population in the United States, including ethnic and cultural groups who have been subject to discrimination and ignored. Multicultural education has impacted educational materials, teacher education programs, school staffing, curriculum and instruction, and assessment.

Individualized Instruction. Since 1980, significant emphasis has been placed on meeting the needs of all students. Teachers are challenged to provide differentiated instruction and scaffolding for different ability levels, adapt lessons for students with different levels of English proficiency, teach to multiple intelligence strengths, and provide appropriate instruction for gifted students as well as those with learning disabilities.

Access to Education

During this period, concern focused on whether our students would be competitive in a new global economy. National and International Assessments, such as the NAEP and the Trends in International Mathematics and Science Study (TIMSS) have revealed weaknesses and strengths among different states and nations.

Liberal educators often see these assessments as an attack on progressive child-centered focus. David Berliner and Bruce Bittle wrote *The Manufactured Crisis* (1996), criticizing the report by presenting NAEP data that showed slightly improved reading and math scores. The authors also explained that Scholastic Assessment Test (SAT) scores declined with a change in the test-taking population, as a broader segment of the population was being urged to consider college. However, Urban, Wagoner, and Garther pointed out that by controlling for race and class, SAT scores were flat (Urban, Wagoner, & Garther, 2019, p. 323). These assessments show that we have a lot of work to do to compete with other countries for a bright and productive future.

Learn More

Chapter 1, "School as We Know It," describes the effect that national standards had on curricular materials, instructional methods, and assessments. Chapter 2, "On Teachers," gives an overview of how teachers responded to national standards in teaching and teacher certification.

Chapter 3, "School Choice," delves deeply into the explosion of school choices, as well as the historical setting for choices. Chapter 4, "Engagement," addresses systemic barriers to building school communities that recognize the potentials of engaging parents and others.

Chapter 5, "School Governance in America," provides information about how school governance responded, meeting national standards and student achievement.

BIBLIOGRAPHY

Altshuler, A. (1970). *Community control: The Black demand for participation in large American cities*. Hanover, NJ: Pegasus.

Battistella, E. L. (2019, October 6). *Reading, writing and readability—appreciating Rudolph Flesch*. OUPBlog. https://blog.oup.com/2019/10/reading-writing-and-readability-appreciating-rudolph-flesch/.

Berliner, D., & Bittle, B. (1996). *The manufactured crisis: Myths, fraud, and the attack on America's public schools*. New York: Basic Books.

Berube, M., & Gittel, M. (1969). *Confrontation at Ocean Hill-Brownsville: The New York school strikes of 1968*. New York: Frederick A. Praeger, Publishers.

Brown, J. (2019, November 18). *What percent of high school graduates are illiterate in the United States?* The Knowledge Burrow. https://theknowledgeburrow.com/what-percent-of-high-school-graduates-are-illiterate-in-the-united-states/#What_state_has_the_worst_literacy_rate.

Bruner, J. (1960). *The process of education.* Cambridge, MA: Harvard University Press.

Cimbala, P., & Miller, R. (1999). *The Freedmen's bureau and reconstruction (reconstructing America).* New York: Fordham University Press.

Coleman, J. S., Campbell, E. Q., Hobson, C. J., McPortland, J., Mood, A. L., Weinfeld, F. D., & York, R. L. (1966). *Equality of education opportunity.* Washington DC: U.S. Government Printing Office.

Conant, J. B. (1959). *The American high school today: A first report to interested citizens.* New York: Mc-Graw Hill.

Conant, J. B. (1961). *Slums and suburbs: A commentary on schools in metropolitan areas.* New York: McGraw-Hill.

Cremin, L. (1957). *The republic and the school: Horace Mann on the education of free man.* New York: Teachers College Press.

Cremin, L. (1961). *The transformation of the school: Progressivism in American education, 1876–1957.* New York: Alfred A. Knopf.

Cummins, C. (2006). *Understanding and implementing reading first initiatives: The changing roles of administrators.* Newark, DE: International Reading Association.

Duncan, A. (2019). *How schools work: An inside account of failure and success from one of the nation's longest-serving secretaries of education.* New York: Simon & Schuster.

Education. (2022, April 1). USA FACTS. https://usafacts.org/state-of-the-union/education/.

Education Week. (2009). *The Obama education plan: An education week guide.* San Francisco, CA: Jossey-Bass.

EDweek-Quality Counts. (2006). https://www.edweek.org/policy-politics/state-highlights-reports/2006/01.

Ellison, R. (1952). *The invisible man.* New York: Random House.

Du Pont de Nemours, P. S., & Du Pont, B. G. (1923). *National education in the United States of America.* Newark, DE: University of Delaware Press.

Finger, L. K., & Hartney, M. K. (2020, November 10). What determined if schools reopened? How many Trump voters were in a district. *The Washington Post.*

Fraser, J. W. (2000). *Between church and state: Religion and public education in a multicultural America.* New York: St. Martin's Griffin.

Goldin, C. (1999). *A brief history of education in the United States.* National Bureau of Economic Research.

Goldstein, D. (2014). *The teacher warrs: A history of America's most embattled profession.* USA: Anchor Books.

Harrington, M. (1962). *The other America.* London: Macmillan Publishing Company.

Herold, J. (1974). Sputnik in American education: A history and reappraisal. *McGill Journal of Education,* 143–164.

Hess, F. M., & Eden, M. (2017). *The Every Student Succeeds Act: What it means for schools, systems and states.* Cambridge, MA: Harvard Education Press.

Hirsh, E. J. (1988). *Cultural literacy: What every American needs to know.* New York: Vintage.

Jencks, C., Smith, M., Acland, H., Bane, M., Cohen, D., Gintis, H., . . . Michelson, S. (1972). *Inequality: A reassessment of the effect of family and schooling in America.* New York: Basic Books.

Jenson, A. R. (1969). How much can we boost IQ and scholastic achievement. *Harvard Education Review,* 39, 1–124.

Jobrack, B. (2012). *Tyranny of the textbook: An insider exposes how educational materials undermine reforms.* Lanham, MD: Rowman & Littlefield.

Kantrowitz, M. R., & Larson, M. (2003). *Framingham state college.* Mount Pleasant, SC.: Arcadia Publishing.

Katz, M. (2001). *The irony of early school reform: Educational innovation in mid-nineteenth century Massachusetts.* New York: Teachers College Press.

Kimmelman, P. (2006). *Implementing NCLB: Creating a knowledge framework to support school improvement.* Thousand Oaks, CA: Crowin Press.

Learning Point Associates. (2004). *A closer look at the five essential components of effective reading instruction: A review of scientifically based reading research for teachers.* Naperville, IL: Learning Point Associates.

Lepore, J. (2022, March 23). The parent trap. *The New Yorker.*

Lortie, D. C. (1975). *Schoolteacher: A sociological study.* Chicago, IL: University of Chicago Press.

NAAL, N. A. (2022, May 24). *120 years of literacy.* National Center for Education Statistics. https://nces.ed.gov/naal/lit_history.asp.

National Commission on Excellence in Education. (1983). *A nation at risk: The imperative for educational reform.* Washington, DC.: National Commission on Excellence in Education.

Norton, M. B. (1996). *Liberty's daughters: The revolutionary experience of American women, 1750–1800.* Cornell University Press.

Perlmann, J., & Shirley, D. (1991). When did New England women acquire literacy? *William and Mary Quarterly,* 50–67.

Putnam, R. (2020). *The upswing: How America came together a century ago and how we can do it again.* New York: Simon & Schuster.

Riesman, D., Glazer, N., & Denney, R. (1953). *The lonely crowd: A study of the changing American character.* New York: Doubleday.

Rogers, D. (1968). *110 Livingston Street: Politics and bureaucracy in the New York City School System.* New York: Random House, Inc.

Roos, D. (2019, August 13). *How the cold war space race led to U.S. students doing tons of homework.* History. https://www.history.com/news/homework-cold-war-sputnik

Rosenthal, M. D. (1977, February 8). *Sociobiology: Laying the foundation for a racist synthesis.* The Harvard Crimson. https://www.thecrimson.com/article/1977/2/8/sociobiology-laying-the-foundation-for-a/.

Schmidt, W., Blomeke, S., & Tatto, M. T. (2011). *Teacher education matters: A study of middle school mathematics teacher preparation in six countries.* New York: Teacher College Press.

Schneider, J., & Berkshire, J. (2020). *A wolf at the schoolhouse door: The dismantling of public education and the future of school.* New York and London: The New Press.

Schrag, P. (1968). *Village school downtown: Boston schools, Boston politics.* Boston, MA: Beacon Press.

Skinner, B. (1938). *The behavior of organisms: An experimental analysis.* New York: Appleton-Century.

The New York Times. (2019, July 18). *The myth that busing failed (podcast transcript).* The Daily Show. https://www.nytimes.com/2019/07/18/podcasts/the-daily/busing-school-segregation.html.

Urban, D., Wagoner, J. L., & Garther, M. (2019). *American education history, 6th Edition.* New York: Routledge.

U.S. Department of Education Office of Educational Research and Improvement. (1993). *120 years of American education: A statistical portrait.* Washington, DC: U.S. Department of Education.

Watters, A. (2015, June 20). *How sputnik launched ed-tech: The National Defense Education Act of 1958.* Hack Education. http://hackeducation.com/2015/06/20/sputnik.

Whyte, W. H. (1957). *The organization man.* London: Jonathan Cape.

Wingo, G. M. (1965). *The philosophy of American education.* Lexington, MA: D.C. Heath and Company.

Chapter 1

School as We Know It

CURRICULUM, INSTRUCTION, AND ASSESSMENT

Education involves a myriad of elements, but there are three pillars, which equate to the most stable seating of any kind, a three-legged stool. The first leg is curriculum or what is taught daily in every subject. The second is instruction, how lessons are taught. The third is assessment, the measure of what the student has learned.

Many people have had the experience of potty-training toddlers, teaching young children to tie their shoes, or teaching a teenager to drive. These experiences reveal the complexities of developing a curriculum, choosing a teaching method, and assessing the learning. In each case, it may be clear *what* needs to be taught and how to assess whether learning has occurred simply by observing whether the students use the bathroom, can tie their shoes, and are able to drive. But even in these familiar experiences, there are many different modes of instruction and different curricula that can be used.

Some instruction may be exploratory, giving students lots of safe experiences, relying on their innate desire to learn, and allowing them space for trial and error. Another type of instruction may present preliminary simulated lessons and examples before attempting to experience the real thing. Other instruction may focus on the development of discrete skills, building a repertoire that may eventually be applied to problem-solving or independent learning. Of course, a combination of many different types of instruction is likely to be applied simultaneously. Success depends on the age and ability level of the student, the patience and ability of the teacher, the content to be learned, and the difficulty of the task. There is no single right way to teach.

Teaching a child how to read, write, how to use mathematics to solve problems, and how to understand the world and scientific means of inquiry involves not only a multiyear process but also attention to the incremental age and developmentally appropriate daily lessons. It also involves ongoing assessment of what each student knows and can do to judge readiness for a next level, or appropriateness of the means of instruction. Education is complex and demands substantial effort to teach a single child, let alone an entire population.

Educators and the general public can face the future of education by understanding the lessons learned through history. This is particularly important in contextualizing the recent COVID-19 experience. History tells us that in the time of worldwide pandemic, significant innovation may occur. The 1918 flu epidemic led to the development of the field of epidemiology and public health systems. The bubonic plague stimulated the Enlightenment with classic works of art and music—as well as changing the social and economic structure of Europe.

This chapter explores the interrelationships of the three legs of the education stool: curriculum, instruction, and assessment. An understanding of the relationships among these pillars provides a necessary grounding for planning productive educational experiences for future generations. COVID-19 has provided an opportunity to reimagine school. A thorough understanding of the three pillars of education will help reinvent school so we can build a stable future.

CURRICULUM: WHAT IS TAUGHT

Curriculum is the road map that lays out what students are to learn. It is defined by scope and sequence. Scope refers to the broad overview of what is expected to be taught. Sequence provides a prescription for the order in which things are to be taught. For example, addition comes before subtraction, and both are to be mastered before attempting an understanding of multiplication, and so forth.

Most Americans are familiar with school subjects or disciplines, such as reading, English/language arts, math, science, social studies, art, health, and physical education. A consideration of why each of these subjects is important, and what is appropriate at different grade levels, as well as what is the most effective presentation of concepts is critical to charting the future. As described in the Introduction, since colonial times, the history of American education has reflected ongoing dialogue regarding these questions.

The Introduction to this book offers a general overview of the history of curriculum throughout different periods in the history of American education. Many factors over time have influenced school curricula. Some influences are philosophical, others derive from educational research, while others are a response to historical events or technological advances. Yet, over time, American education has pulled from two main traditions: essentialist and progressive. While each has had periods of ascendancy, both have always contributed to, and to be fair, at times, detracted from student achievement.

The Essentialist Tradition: Defining Skills and Content for All

Influenced by the period of industrialization and organization of factory work in the late nineteenth century, American education is often described as being factory-like, emphasizing the development of age-based grade levels and the movement of students from class to class. This organization enabled mass education with some efficiency, based on an assumption that children of similar age have similar educational needs, and efforts aimed at some mid-range of needs could succeed in reaching many. At upper-grade levels, teaching became more specialized into courses and curriculum that could be "tracked" with ability, grouping according to assumptions about students' future life and employment needs.

Basic Skills

One essentialist model of education emphasizes basic skills, concerned with teaching rudimentary facts and skills. Basic literacy, for example, involves being able to read at a middle-school level, with writing skills sufficient to understand and fill out documents. Similarly, basic mathematics skills should prepare students for everyday uses of arithmetic.

The essentialist approach got a boost in the United States following the launch of the Russian Sputnik satellite during the Cold War period of the history of American education outlined in this book's Introduction. At that time, fears of the United States falling behind in the space race led many to be concerned that U.S. students were learning less math and science than Soviet students.

Not only did Sputnik spur a new emphasis on teaching science and mathematics, particularly to a select segment of the population, it also inflamed existing concerns about the teaching of reading. Rudolph Flesch published *Why Johnny Can't Read and What You Can Do about it* (1955). The popular book became still more popular as Americans obsessed in comparisons between "Johnny" and "Ivan," representing a Russian student. Flesch was critical of the "see-say" or word memorization method of teaching found in texts such as the *Dick and Jane* reading series. His embrace of using phonics to teach reading led Houghton Mifflin to commission Theodor Geisel to write *The Cat in the Hat*. These books with their phonetically based use of rhyming words were helpful in marketing the books to parents as one that their children could read by themselves (Battistella, 2019).

Core Knowledge

Another branch of essentialism is found in movements like E. D. Hirsch Jr.'s Core Knowledge curriculum, which occurred during the Nationalized Education Reform period of American educational history after 1980. Instead of just teaching everyone how to read, write, and cipher, Hirsch defined a body of knowledge comprising content, including literature, history, geography, and science that "successful" people know.

Challenges

Essentialism, while focusing on the greatest good for most students through defining what all should know and know how to do, can be didactic. Content selection and presentation can also suffer from being morally and culturally bound (to the exclusion of marginalized groups). Further, definitions of what all students should know are often backward-looking, drawing on notions of school as we have known it.

The Progressive Tradition: Whole Child Individualized Learning

Progressive education, which came about during the movement of Education Reform and the Progressive era between 1890 and 1946, was promoted by educators like John Dewey, and embraced by the National Congress of Mothers (NCM), founded in 1897, as the precursor to the modern Parent-Teacher Association (PTA). Progressivism stressed "whole child" development, in parallel to the American Child Health Association (Roos, 2019). Theorists like Jean Piaget, Thomas Dewey, and Maria Montessori focused on individualized learning. Their constructivist theories recommended teaching methods that would encourage students to construct, or discover, knowledge through activities that applied and extended their prior knowledge. Such methods emphasized individualized development of the whole child. Daily lessons encouraged students to test and discover knowledge, rather than simply absorb a prescribed body of knowledge. In contrast to age and grade-level expectations, progressive curriculum sought to address the needs of a broad diversity of students, including newly arrived immigrants, as public education became more and more universal.

In the 1980s, the progressive movement promoted the whole language approach to reading and writing with the philosophy of immersing children in engaging books, which would generate a desire to read and write, as opposed to skill and drill phonics and spelling exercises.

Challenges

Progressivism argues for the teaching of the major constructs of the disciplines and how the discipline discovers its own knowledge. In its application, progressivism may lack rigor and core knowledge within a discipline. In allowing students space for discovery, there is always the danger of creating an "anything goes" environment.

Essentialist versus Progressive Education

The pendulum swings back and forth between essentialist and progressive movements in education. The successful 1957 Soviet launch of the Sputnik space capsule figured heavily in moving education from progressive to essentialist thinking. While criticism of American education was not new, fears of losing the space race suddenly escalated its perceived importance. The pendulum swung further toward essentialism in 1958 when President Dwight Eisenhower signed the NDEA and condemned Dewey and progressive education. Not only did the newly created NSF have an expanding role in researching and supporting curriculum in mathematics and science, but this represented a new federal role in education (Watters, 2015).

1960s and 1970s

During the Equal Education Opportunity era of the history of American Education between 1965 and 1980, in spite of the emphasis on science and math for all, the notion of some students having "unusual talent or potentialities" that should be identified and especially nurtured became desirable. Teaching to the average student was no longer enough, so some progressive individualization was seen as important. While NDEA spurred the development of "gifted" education, resulting in a tracked curriculum, it should also be noted that nondiscriminatory subtext and concern for equity served as precursor to later acts such as Individuals with Disabilities in Education Act (IDEA) and the ESEA. These acts are supportive of the broad inclusion of all students, with an emphasis on access to a common, rather than tracked, curriculum (Watters, 2015).

The swing toward progressivism occurred in 1959 when the Carnegie Foundation published James B. Conant's study *The American High School Today*. Conant suggested that 15 to 20 percent of students were "academically able" and should be provided advanced coursework in mathematics, science, and language—supportive of the NDEA provision. The bulk of students, however, should receive a general education, with an emphasis on vocational courses (Herold, 1974). The NDEA was augmented in 1963 by the Vocational Education Act (later the Carl D. Perkins Vocational and

Technical Education Act of 1984), which provided additional funding for such coursework.

President Kennedy's challenge to land on the moon inspired essentialist science and math education. Yet, throughout the 1960s and 1970s, domestic unrest and educational inequities, which could not have been foreseen by reformers of the 1950s, pushed the need to move focus back and forth from a collective vision of essential education to an individualized progressive one.

1980s, 1990s, and 2000s

In the period of Nationalized Education Reform after 1980, the whole language progressive movement influenced reading instruction. It was no longer enough just to possess the mechanical skills of reading, a love of reading and literature was important, too, with some leaders claiming that surrounding students with good literature would inspire them to learn to read. Reading research, however, stressed the importance of a foundation in phonics as essential to be able to read successfully. While the teaching of reading remains a contentious issue, sometimes referred to as the reading wars, current practice in teaching reading incorporates Flesch's recommendation for phonics. To codify this approach to reading, The National Reading Panel Report of the National Institute of Child Health and Human Development expanded this practice and defined, from research, five critical areas of reading instruction: phonemic awareness, phonics, fluency, vocabulary, and comprehension (Learning Point Associates, 2004). The report also notes that while these areas are foundational, there are many ways of teaching them, with systematic and explicit instruction being the most effective.

Present Day

COVID-19 has also had an influence in the pendulum swing between essentialism and individualized learning. During the pandemic, there were continuous disruptions to in-class education, including school closures, remote learning, and staff shortages. These disruptions inspired an effort to shift from the factory model of education to a customized, individualized approach. Expanding on the model of Individualized Education Plans (IEP) that schools create for students with special needs, some are advocating for educational navigators to chart a course, which could be responsive to changing needs, for each student (Reville & Canada, 2022).

In a nod to incorporating best practices for teaching reading, in 2022, Lucy Calkins, an educational literacy expert, who published books and balanced literacy curricula in the 1980s, revised her curriculum to more fully include phonics and the science of reading (Goldstein, 2022).

Where Does Curriculum Come From?

Teachers

Many people assume that curriculum is intuitive and derives from teacher training. Some believe that all teachers or groups of parents can easily develop a curriculum. Historically, individual teachers and superintendents decided what would be taught in their classrooms and schools. Once the subjects were determined, however, the actual curricula with daily lessons in each subject were seldom developed by these local actors. Most local schools and districts relied on published resources, choosing specific textbooks to provide daily content lessons.

School Districts and States

As school districts were centralized and consolidated, many districts and then states took on responsibility for curriculum and developed guidelines for teachers to use. Sometimes states relied on other states to develop guidelines and then edited them to suit their specific needs. Then individual school districts reviewed and identified which published texts teachers would use. After reviewing, some states approved and funded textbooks for use in the public schools in the state. The educational materials defined the scope and sequence of the curriculum. Teachers then developed lessons from the required texts and content.

Educational Materials

Developing curriculum is a full-time job, incorporating many experts in each field. To develop a curriculum, textbook publishers employ subject matter experts who have expertise not only in the subject matter but also how students learn the subject matter. The experts lay out a scope and sequence of concepts and skills for each grade level and then develop content and thorough lessons that teachers use in the classroom.

In the 1800s, people and publishers, including Noah Webster, created spelling books, geography and history textbooks, and the McGuffey readers. Publishers responded to market forces and demands and periodically updated their texts or created new editions to incorporate new information, discoveries, educational research practices, or to appeal to different types of students.

Today educational publishing companies spend years and millions of dollars developing an educational curriculum for a single core subject. They employ thousands of people, including subject matter experts, educational researchers, writers, editors, designers, artists, programmers, and page production facilities.

Because the educational materials industry is predominantly a for-profit enterprise, textbooks must compete for business. Textbook companies have catered to large states that appropriate money in specific years for textbook purchases. Large states that have legislated state approval (Texas, California, Florida) of textbooks have received particular attention. Publishers do everything they can to ensure their materials meet those state guidelines and standards. Meeting the guidelines of a large state, such as Texas, with legislated approval, can reap a financial windfall for a publisher.

Political Pressures

In 2022, some state legislatures like Florida's passed laws prohibiting the teaching of topics like critical race theory (CRT) and sexual orientation. About 41 percent of the math books that were under review for adoption were initially rejected by the state, alleging that they included references to CRT, the Common Core standards, or social-emotional learning (Education, 2022). As a for-profit industry, publishers revise their materials to meet the state guidelines and state legislation. Otherwise, they will not be able to sell in the state. This has a significant effect on curriculum.

Multiculturalism and Historic Integrity

Controversy over state-adopted curricula is not new. In 1966, California's adoption of a history text for middle school drew fire from the public. Responses to the new textbook included the following views:

- The text would agitate Black students and instill self-loathing in White students.
- Emphasis on past injustices would harm race relations.
- A "positive" side of slavery should also be included in the text.
- Black activism should not be nurtured, as it had resulted in riots and black crime.

The 1966 textbook was *Land of the Free: A History of the United States* by Black historian John Hope Franklin. It should be noted that various Black student groups also organized against similarly inclusive texts, preferring separate courses and texts on Black history (Zimmerman, 2002, pp. 107–110).

Controversy with regard to teaching American history is a continual battle. In developing the National History Standards in the 1990s, the writing team was attacked for presenting a critical instead of heroic view of American history, de-emphasizing and ignoring some Americans, like the Wright Brothers, and extolling others, like Harriet Tubman (Nash, Crabtree, & Dunn, 1997). Some state standards reaffirmed conservative approaches to teaching history, while others emphasized cultural diversity and issues of equality. Other states tried to balance traditional approaches and multiculturalism. On the one hand, there was a realization that, without understanding America's historical roots, our traditions would perish. On the other hand, there was a belief that we should teach the past without shame or blame to create a better future.

Critical Race Theory

In the 2020s, social studies curriculum has been challenged once again. To counter the Black Lives Matter movement that exploded after the George Floyd killing by police in 2020, as well as diversity and inclusion efforts in both education and business, some people on the far right latched onto a construct called CRT. This construct came out of a legal analysis in the late 1970s and early 1980s, which is a way of understanding how American racism influenced public policy in such areas as housing, criminal justice, and education. This theory relates to the work of sociologists and literary theorists who study the links between political power, social organization, and language (Sawchuk, 2021). Most educators and parents had not heard of the term, which is primarily taught in law school. The term, however, became misused as a handy shorthand by which to oppose many things, including anti-bias training, diversity, and inclusion efforts in hiring and employment along with less Eurocentric views of American history (Wallace-Wells, 2021).

There have been considerable disagreements on what CRT means and whether it is even being taught in American schools. The theory also affects teaching in the humanities, social sciences, and teacher education. The far right sees CRT linked to the Black Lives Matter protests, LGBTQI+ clubs in schools, criminal justice reform, and disciplinary policies. Extremists claim that this theory portrays Americans as inherently bad and racist, and that teaching this theory will radically alter our American way of life.

Most Americans would agree that all students should know how American government works and what is means to be a citizen. Yet there is a great disagreement over what an American patriot is. In *A Search for Common Ground* the authors from different political orientations emphasize the need for history to tell the whole story, understand the constitution in its historical context, and be inspired by American ideals. Unfortunately, some Republican state legislatures are passing bills that may inhibit teachers from doing this (Hess & Noguera, 2021).

Others argue that the solution is not to ban one ideology or another, but to teach both, making room for alternative views (Bernstein, 2022). Teaching multiple perspectives on controversial issues would encourage open inquiry and provide a better educational experience than just learning one side of an argument.

Book Banning

Throughout the United States, as in past periods of national anxiety, parents have been urging school boards, teachers, principals, and superintendents to ban books and have banned culturally sensitive curriculum and training (Plotinsky, 2022). Banned books include books by Black authors; books that deal with gender, sex, and sexuality (i.e., not violent or abusive); books on Critical Race Theory, ethnicity, and racial inequalities; and books on nontraditional family situations. Others have advocated for these types of materials as resources designed to enable teachers to understand the student's cultural backgrounds and to use curriculum materials that include positive cultural role models.

In polling educators, the Education Week Research Center found that 57 percent of teachers and 63 percent of principals agree in banning books that have sexual violence, abuse topics, white power/nationalism, and CRT. About 17 percent of teachers do not want books that discuss LGTBQI+. On the other hand, some Democratic women across the country have shown up at school board meetings to hand out banned books and provide free copies of these books to be placed in public libraries (Pendarkar, 2022).

Financial Pressures

Throughout the country, because of cost concerns, there is also a growing movement toward open-source materials, which are available to anyone free of charge. There is no guarantee, however, that these materials will meet state guidelines or reflect current research or understanding. Because college instructors have content expertise, they can evaluate open-source materials more effectively than many public school teachers who often do not have advanced degrees in content knowledge.

As online and multimedia learning expands, larger districts across the country are looking to avoid or reduce the cost of expensive textbook adoptions and transform the print classroom into digital formats. Curriculum directors are looking for publishers to provide high-quality open education resources. It is estimated that this can save districts an estimated one-third of the cost of textbook purchases. And if educational publishers offer these materials, districts can be assured that the materials have integrity. In addition to saving money, a customized digital curriculum better meets individual student needs and reflects the composition of the community. To meet the needs of these school districts, new companies are emerging to work with districts using artificial intelligence tools to scan the Internet to meet specific content needs of curriculum staff in central office.

Challenges

Teacher Uncertainty. Political and cultural pressures influence how teachers interact with students and can influence teaching practices. In some states, Republican legislators are passing bills that address what teachers can say and do in their classroom. This has added to teachers' stress and fears about job security. In the 2020s, teachers have grown more and more concerned about how to teach science and social studies that address controversial topics such as these.

Race. As a result of political controversies about CRT, educators may now be afraid to talk about racial issues in the classroom. On the one hand, Governor Glenn Youngkin of Virginia put in place a hotline to report teachers' comments and actions. On the other hand, Anthony Brown discusses the struggle of integrating Black history into our schools and the need for teachers to focus on Black people's historical perspective. Brown makes the point that we should think of teaching Black history and other cultures that relate to ideals, art, philosophy, and culture that may not only counter (White imagination) but also speak to our common humanity. As Brown suggests, we need to teach the full spectrum of humanity: beauty, sadness, joy, perseverance, and love (Brown, 2022).

Sexuality. State laws have been passed regarding the discussion and teaching of sexuality, leaving educators uncertain about what is and what is not appropriate and acceptable.

Personal Beliefs. Students often ask teachers about their own personal beliefs. Teachers are uncertain about how to respond honestly and appropriately.

Educational Materials Selection. Sometimes the for-profit model can result in poor choices for improving education. Textbooks are often chosen, not because they have better curriculum or instruction, but because they incorporate current educational fads, have better graphics, more bells and whistles, or because they don't require teachers to change what they are currently doing.

Reluctance to Change. The resistance to change is strong in American education. One definition of conservative is to be averse to change. In this sense, many parents, teachers, administrators, and government officials are resistant to change. Parents want their children to experience what they experienced in school. They feel incapable of helping their children with new ways of solving math problems or teaching reading in a way they were not taught. Experienced teachers have been reluctant to modify what they teach or how they teach it even when they have updated materials and technology. Administrators and government officials rarely want to rock the boat. Every change has unintended consequences.

The Impact of No Child Left Behind 2002

In reaction to a chaotic situation in which fifty states determined curriculum in each subject area differently, the U.S. education law known as the NCLB required that academic content standards be set by states as a condition of continuing to receive federal education dollars. The intent was to combat regional variability—sometimes referred to as the "soft bigotry of low expectations," which was coined by President George W. Bush in 2000 when launching the NCLB. The underlying philosophy was that all children can learn to defined standards if their specific learning needs are identified and met. This contrasts with the Eisenhower-era emphasis on individual excellence and seeking out those having "unusual" abilities.

While perhaps idealistic, NCLB was in keeping with the ongoing justification for the federal involvement in education, which was to ensure equity in education. The notion was that where students live should not limit or define what they learn. As an outgrowth of the Civil Rights movement, there was a realization that not only had segregated systems of education created achievement gaps, poverty levels in some states and regions would likely be an insurmountable barrier to overcoming this reality. This occurred simultaneously with the realization that a well-qualified workforce was the key to the economic vitality of all states.

Today, most schools have a scope and sequence aligned with state standards, either approved by a local board of education or set by a state department of education. State standards, as required by NCLB as a condition of receiving federal aid, set a minimum level of student achievement. This level defines what students are expected to know and be able to do at various grades.

While the standards should guide the development of scope and sequence, there has continued to be great variability across districts. In addition, within each district there is great variability of implementation. Smaller, or under-resourced, districts may provide little to no curricular guidance to teachers. Dr. William Schmidt, of the Michigan State University Center for the Study of Curriculum, has done considerable research into the extent to which an intended curriculum is actually taught in the classroom. His work supported the notion that despite defining state standards, and even locally adopting a set curriculum, standardization of what is taught was fairly elusive. He also placed blame on standards in mathematics that were overly broad, lacked depth, and were highly repetitive by comparison to those in other countries (Schmidt, Houang, & Cogin, 2002, p. 3).

EdWeek's Quality Counts offered a slightly different view in a 2006 evaluation. They reported that mathematics standards in forty-one states were "clear, specific and grounded in content at all levels." They reported, however than only ten states had similarly acceptable English language arts standards. Beyond the quality of standards, however, EdWeek reported wide variance in their content (Editorial Projects in Education Research Center, 2007).

Implementation of more rigorous standards was inconsistent. Although the general public might assume that Algebra I is the same in New York, Michigan, or Kansas, that was not the case. Fifty sets of state standards came up with fifty different sets of measures. Further, the NCLB requirement of demonstrating gap closing by raising all students to a state-defined level of "proficiency" had urged on a "race to the bottom." While states might aspire for improved educational outcomes, they also felt themselves to be in competition with other states to demonstrate percentages of students meeting their own defined levels of proficiency. Individually states were reluctant to raise proficiency standards for fear of being shown up by other states with lower standards and criticized by stakeholders. There was reason to fear loss of support from the business community and higher education. Higher education also had screening mechanisms in place. High rates of students determined to need remediation prior to college-level courses was deemed problematic.

Responding to a perceived need for guidance for states in developiing standandards, educational organizations, such as the National Council of Teachers of Mathematics (NCTM), the National Art Education Association, and the International Society for Technology in Education, employed educational researchers, academicians, teachers, and parents and practitioners to develop standards for individual subject areas in their areas of expertise. These national efforts served as exemplars for states in developing their own standards.

Common Core: Standardizing across States

To further help standardize the standards across the fifty states, in the early 2000s, the Council of Chief State School Officers (CCSSO) and the NGA, funded by the Gates Foundation, worked to produce the Common Core Standards in English Language Arts and Mathematics for adoption by the states individually. These standards were benchmarked against high standards from other countries outperforming the United States on International (TIMSS and Program for International Student Assessment [PISA]) tests.

The hope was that deeper learning and thinking in classrooms would become accessible to all. The Obama administration provided an incentive for adopting the standards by offering competitive RTTT grants. In order to be considered for this funding, states had to commit to the Common Core standards and one of the aligned assessment systems.

But the Common Core standards have been controversial as well. Every state had the option to adopt the standards and make a percentage of changes. By 2021, forty-six states had adopted them. However, five states refused to adopt the standards and five states that adopted the standards later repealed them.

CURRICULUM ISSUES TO ADDRESS FOR THE FUTURE

While we have discussed the major curricular traditions in American education, as well as several historical movements that have influenced the shaping of curriculum, we must also consider both our present conditions and how they might impact the future. What follows is a list of challenges facing public education at present. Readers should consider each of them to be a question, rather than an answer, regarding future direction.

Setting Appropriate Standards

In the U.S. Constitution, education is left to the responsibility of each state. Many parents, teachers, and policymakers believed Common Core Standards, despite having been developed by a coalition of states, overstepped the federal role. But understanding the integrity of core disciplines is essential for interdisciplinary curriculum and problem-solving. If students have neither basic skills nor knowledge and understanding of the major tenets of a discipline, they will be unprepared to use interdisciplinary methods for complex problems they will face in an unpredictable global world.

Some educators, citizens, and parents are concerned that existing standards are too broad, or not broad enough. Parents and others have concerns about whether the expectations of the standards are too rigorous, or not rigorous enough, for some students. They question the support the curriculum provides for particular students with special needs.

State and national departments of education are concerned with whether schools and districts apply state content standards with integrity so that schools demonstrate AYP toward a goal of all students being proficient.

Controversies in writing state standards, such as science or history, must be addressed and resolved in the writing process, so that teachers know what the goals of instruction are. Committees of parents, teachers, and subject matter experts can resolve these issues so they present a united front in the face of concerned parties.

Observations Regarding Curriculum

While our earlier categorization of educational theory as being either essential or progressive (or various other dichotomies) may provide a convenient organization, the reality is that our classrooms are, and should be, far more eclectic. The genius of education is not in choosing one way of teaching over the other, but in finding ways to combine strengths from both.

Not only are all three legs (curriculum, instruction, and assessment) of our education stool needed, but a good builder understands that different types of wood contribute different strengths to a piece of furniture. One type may make the piece sturdy, while another is used for flexibility. And another may have decorative qualities. Similarly, as we learn from our history, it is best to draw from multiple experiences, combining them in planning for the future.

One way that good teachers can address opposing views of culture and history is to teach across the curriculum the diversity of all cultures that are present in our country. They can, and should, share different cultural ideas: art, music, customs, and traditions. While highlighting the differences, we can demonstrate that we share a human condition. Students must examine history critically and, as good historians, understand the complexities of each era and come to their own conclusions. Good social studies teachers must address the issues in an intellectually honest way, and when asked what they believe, defend their position, while allowing students to come to their own conclusions. This is a way to assure that students have the knowledge and skills to participate in democracy.

The best curriculum is ever-evolving. It is responsive to advances in knowledge and understanding of educational research, science and technology and changes in literature and the arts, and should reflect the history, culture, and diversity of a changing population. For the best future, we can build on the work that has been done to develop elevated expectations for all American children. To do this a common set of academic standards in all subjects should be reviewed and updated on a regular basis by state panels of educators, parents, subject matter experts, and educational researchers.

INSTRUCTION: HOW LESSONS ARE TAUGHT

While curriculum defines what is to be taught, instruction is concerned with how it is to be taught. This comprises all of the activities of education, such as reading from texts, listening to lectures, projects, explorations, recounting, questioning, and using multimedia. Once standards and a curriculum are in place, there are many different methods of instruction. Frequently the methods of instruction are the complete responsibility of the teacher. Many different methods may be used effectively by educators for different subjects with different groups of students.

There are several significant instructional methods that have been used widely throughout American education.

Teacher-Centered Instruction

Teacher-centered instruction is a method in which an authority figure, such as a teacher, delivers knowledge directly to students. Positive and negative reinforcements are used in response to student demonstrations of compliance with learning goals. Teacher-centered instruction may be considered traditional. Using traditional methods schools may respond to student learning differences, using tracking or "pull-outs," to group students for instruction.

There are several types of teacher-centered instruction.

Direct Instruction

Lessons are targeted for the average student. The teacher presents the lesson and then provides a model and opportunity for students to practice.

Kinesthetic/Multiple Modalities

Teachers present lessons through physical activities or using various media to access different learning modalities.

Modeling

The major constructs of a discipline and how the discipline discovers its own knowledge are modeled by the teacher. As an example, a teacher might demonstrate how scientists provide models of the methods of inquiry to test hypotheses and advance scientific research. Students then use similar methods of inquiry to uncover knowledge in the classroom. This might include the provision of opportunities to test intuitions, make errors, and go back to try other options. Students might also model behavior of writers, researchers, and mathematicians, to prepare them to be citizens with careers.

Student-Centered Instruction

Student-centered methods sometimes refer to the teacher as a "guide on the side" as students learn from group projects and class participation. Student-centered instruction allows for meeting individual needs through personalization, individualization, and differentiation of curriculum. The goal of student-centered instruction is for students to learn different things by different means. Recent requirements, under standards, have attempted to move in a direction of students learning the same content standards, but through different means of instruction.

There are many forms of student-centered instruction.

Differentiated Instruction

Lessons and activities are individually tailored to how each student learns best. The following are some examples.

Inquiry-Based

Lessons are designed to allow students to pursue answers to questions they develop.

Experiential

Students engage in real-world applications of the curriculum.

Individual

When instruction is individualized, each student follows personalized, self-directed learning plans. They may use technology or other educational resources.

Thematic

Overriding themes, concepts, or practices organize the curriculum. For example, lessons may be organized around the Four Cs: Critical thinking, Collaboration, Communication, and Creativity. The idea is that if students are taught and encouraged to be curious, think, and communicate, they can master any subject matter.

Special Education

Often intended for gifted children or children with learning disabilities, all students need "enriched" curriculum and instruction, the kind many think gifted students need. When schools provide such enrichment broadly, low-achieving students benefit. Sadly, students assigned to "special ed," often not only miss out on such enrichment but also, rather than being given a boost back to being on track, end up falling further and further behind.

We need to be wary of differentiating curriculum (what students learn) rather than instruction (how students learn). No Child Left Behind included a requirement that students be taught by teachers who are "highly qualified" in content areas. Many teachers certified in special education sought professional development to become "highly qualified" to teach content at grade levels below that of their students. This provided insight into a disturbing differentiation of content rather than instruction.

Lesson Design

Every day in every subject area, teachers choose from among the various teaching methods to provide instruction. They may follow a lesson model such as the one shown in Table 1.1.

Teachers choose from different ways of designing lessons. Teaching methods may be combined, blended, or turned upside down. For example, in a flipped classroom, students receive "instruction" (such as a recorded lecture) at home and then complete their assignments and practice in the classroom where the teacher is available to guide them.

Teachers may start with a lesson objective, choose the activities that they think will meet that objective, and then assess students to determine if they have met the objective. In backward design, teachers start with the objective and then design the assessment before they figure out what activities are most appropriate to meet the objective.

Disruptions in Instruction

Disruptions cause change. Sometimes innovations are disruptions that dramatically change behavior. In the 1970s, by taking advantage of unmet needs in the business market, even clunky desktop computers and later laptops were accepted by consumers and overtook the mainframe computer market (Christensen, Horn, & Johnson, 2010). In one generation, having a personal cell phone upended the way people communicate within one another. COVID-19 has spurred healthcare systems to expand the use of telemedicine. Major

Table 1.1. Lesson Models for Various Teaching Methods

Step	Teacher-Centered	Student-Centered	Structured Problem-Solving
1	Activate prior knowledge	Explore	Present a problem
2	Introduce	Generate questions	Generate solutions
3	Model	Narrow questions	Discussion of solutions
4	Guided practice	Research	Summing up
5	Practice	Review and edit	Exercises
6	Assess	Assess	Extensions

drug companies are sharing intellectual property and experience to quickly develop vaccines.

In March 2020, governors across the United States announced temporary closing of all school buildings to protect the public from the spread of the coronavirus. Closing schools has been both a blessing and a curse. As a blessing, it forced educators, policymakers, and families to realize the comprehensive services that schools provide. Districts needed new ways to get food and technology resources to families that lacked these things. Some creative responses included school bus Internet hotspots, grab-and-go food and lessons, and drive-in graduation ceremonies.

On the negative side, teachers and teacher unions were also seriously concerned about the potential workplace health threats. *The Washington Post* (Finger & Hartney, 2020) reported on the multiple influences, including political, that influenced decisions about whether to reopen school buildings. Sadly, health data were often far down the list of factors correlating to such decisions.

Closing schools also exposed the lack, or inequality, of technological experiences available across the country and internationally. The world of online instruction had developed first for poorly served "markets" of students, such as "drop-out recovery" or "credit recovery" programs. But these online instruction programs lacked elegance, while their poor track record stood as little barrier in teaching students already doing poorly in regular classrooms. Until COVID-19, education had not yet wholly embraced the advances that technology could offer in the extensive use of collaboration, data sharing, and best practices from other states and countries to enhance our own systems. Many teachers had heralded the availability of computers in the classroom but could not find a way to use them beyond allowing students to play computer games as a reward. Many classroom desktop computers gathered dust as teachers conducted their lessons.

Reich makes an important point about why the cutting-edge work of MIT scientists Seymour Papert and Mitch Resnick, teaching student-focus-related languages, "Logo" and "Scratch," never became part of our traditional elementary and middle school curriculum (Reich, 2020, p. 69). The experience is that districts will only use new innovative software programs when they are integrated into traditional classroom and curriculum. There is an unwillingness to rethink teaching traditional subjects, class periods, grade structures, and testing.

With school closings and disruptions to education, the existence of computers for students with special needs led to further development in the form of programs allowing teachers to provide greater levels of individualization within a traditional classroom. The COVID-19 crisis created a high level of demand for a wide range of products and services, both general and special-ized, and enhanced innovation.

These changes were so new in the 2020s, and the educators had not yet arrived at consistent means of evaluating the many online options in terms of parent, student, and teacher satisfaction, or student learning and growth.

In response to school closings, alternative patterns of instructions emerged.

Synchronous Online Learning

As teachers moved into distance teaching for the first time, many reached for online meeting apps. They used these in an attempt to replicate the regular in-per-son classroom experience, in real-time. This is known as synchronous learning.

Asynchronous Online Learning

Teachers modified lessons to make them appropriate for online presentation. Lessons could be formatted as a video or Microsoft PowerPoint and accessed by students at any time. Classes met at fewer scheduled times, intended to bring all students together online. This also allowed time for individual student-to-student and teacher-to-student interactions.

Hybrid Learning

As schools responded to the uncertain environment, following health guide-lines, some moved into "hybrid" learning experiences. These typically involved face-to-face learning for part of the week and online, at home, experiences for the other days. This allowed for greater social distancing. In some cases, the at-home students were brought into the classroom digitally (synchronous) and in others they worked independently on assignments (asynchronous), which may have been project-based.

In these hybrid settings, the various digital programs provided an important tool. Similar to self-paced workbooks, programs provide a pattern of pretests, content presentation and testing to determine that the student is ready to move on. However, many offer additional enhancements have been added. Indi-vidual adaptations may include read-aloud features or talk-to-text. Reading levels (Lexiles) may be set to deliver content at a comfortable (or challeng-ing) level. Ongoing data analysis may track patterns of errors that a student is making and provide "just in time" interventions to correct. These data are available to teachers on an ongoing basis.

Distance Learning

Distance learning requires that students complete assigned online activities, which are overseen by a teacher. This kind of curriculum has been used in the past for credit recovery, or individualized learning within a traditional classroom. In a wholly online environment, such lessons may be enhanced using online meeting apps to allow teacher-student interaction, or small group opportunities. In addition to variations on hybrid learning, many districts are offering families a full distance-learning option. This has the advantage to families of providing consistency for the whole school year. Districts may be offering this as a means of keeping families in the district rather than opting for online charter schools.

Educational Pods

An emerging trend in the 2020s is educational pods. Parents who could afford it hired teachers to educate the children of a small group of families—either providing support to online district learning or providing an entire home-school environment. Entrepreneurs began developing services to help parents form these pods and evaluate available curricula. Some are poised to provide a complete soup to nuts product. Therefore, equity gaps between families wholly dependent on public education and others with more choices (private schools or the new pods) are likely to increase.

Educational Materials

As buildings across the country shut down, nonprofit and for-profit vendors offered free resources and pilot experiences. Their hope was that if teachers found their products useful and easy to use, districts would purchase them. Many of these materials were supplied by small educational companies who were more agile in adapting to the COVID-19 crisis than the large educational textbook companies that have dominated the field. As a result, large companies may lose market share, making way for new and innovative materials. This might be considered a massive disruption, necessary for improvement (Christensen, Horn, & Johnson, 2010). Others see this as a great opportunity for the educational establishment to rethink and reestablish the delivery of curriculum and instruction in American public schools.

Professional Development

In preparation for the school years during and following the pandemic, many districts provided teachers with intensive professional development on online curriculum and assessment resources. In addition, states focused on providing diagnostic tools for assessing the levels of incoming students and meeting their needs.

Professional Resources

During the pandemic, Educational Service Centers banded together to provide services to districts to evaluate the quality of online digital learning tools. As an example, four Ohio Educational Service Centers, under the leadership of two counties, formed an alliance to assist with this, also helping to reduce the cost of purchases by individual districts through bulk purchasing. Some groups, such as EdReports, looked at alignment of curriculum materials to state and national standards. There is not, however, a national system in place that can give educators and developers useful information to individualize curriculum and assessment to meet the needs of all children and promote human growth and development in the cognitive and socio-emotional domains. We do not know what the long-term impact of online and hybrid learning will be for different types of students. We have early evidence of the difficulties (and inequities) of online learning for impoverished students and those with special needs. Some districts continue providing hybrid experiences for these students.

Social-Emotional Learning

COVID-19 has had a tremendous impact on educators, students, and their families. Educators were fearful for the own health and safety. Unions were cast by some as villains for advocating to protect the safety of teachers as well as school children. Most teachers were poorly prepared to effectively use technology as a teaching tool prior to COVID-19. They had to pivot quickly and learn new skills. Students missed their teacher and peer interactions. They lost the opportunity to learn from and socialize with their schoolmates. As schools reopened, teachers began to see that students had suffered from social isolation. Students returning to third grade, for example, had the social skills of first graders. The development of social skills requires a social setting. With a return to regular classes, poorly developed skills have resulted in reports of fights erupting in our schools.

Many states have provided more funding for social and emotional supports for teachers and students. Federal dollars began to be used for this as well. Students have experienced the following events, which have the potential for serious emotional disturbance.

- COVID-19
- Black Lives Matter movement
- Russian Ukraine war
- Natural disasters. Students particularly in the south and far west are facing the fear of climate change with tornadoes and fires destroying their schools and community.

What Influences Instruction?

All too often teachers rely on using the teaching methods that were successful in their own learning. They model the practices of their own favorite teachers. The problem is that many of these methods are not effective with all students. Teacher education programs, new educational materials, professional development, and continuing education requirements are resources for teachers to learn about new and more effective instructional methods. Too often, however, teachers, especially teachers who have spent years developing their lesson materials, do not see a need to change.

History also influences instruction. Our old industrial model sought to reach the greatest number of students by teaching to a broad mid-range of students, perhaps offering enhancement or tutoring for students at the fringes. One option for a post-COVID-19 model will be to provide better teaching not only to those at the fringes but better meeting the needs of all those in the middle as well. This raises questions about how and when to individualize? As an example, the same content can be delivered at multiple reading levels to provide appropriate challenge to a range of students. In addition, content can be delivered through different approaches, or pathways that may stress various different applications of knowledge.

While teachers may want to change teaching methods to individualize, their ability to do so may be inhibited by a system that defines education in terms of static units. Since 1908, U.S. colleges and universities have relied on "Carnegie units" of 120–180 hours of class time (sometimes referred to as "seat time") to define a single credit high school course.

This same unit has been used to determine teacher pay and pension eligibility. While the development of online coursework allows for more individualized pacing, such courses have frequently only been in use for "credit recovery." Credit recovery allows students who have already expended the required hours of seat time, but failed to pass a course, to move at their own pace through a series of lessons designed to ensure that they have achieved "mastery" or a required level of content.

Since 2009, Ohio, for example, has had in place an option for credit flexibility to allow some students to earn course credits by demonstrating learning in ways other than seat time. Credit flexibility still requires district oversight and writing an extensive plan for demonstrating equivalent learning. This makes the option appropriate for a fairly small number of students having clear alternate means of learning, such as apprenticeships or capstone projects. An expansion of available options could allow more students to benefit.

Another instructional influence is simply the workload required to meet the needs of an entire classroom of learners. Technology may provide the means by which multiple students can meet learning standards under the guidance of a teacher who can match their needs. Digital content can easily provide various accommodations, or developmental "scaffolding," needed by some students, such as hyperlinks to word definitions, read-aloud options for text (ranging from reading of all text to voicing individual words when clicked), student highlighting, enhanced font size, or altered reading levels. Some content may offer options such as video presentations rather than text (with teacher presets to limit or allow) or minimize or enhance visual elements along with text.

FUTURE ISSUES IN INSTRUCTION

In building a vision of instruction for the future, we cannot assume psychic talents. But we can consider potential areas of concern.

Ongoing Research

While research points to a relationship between the amount of time a student engages in learning activities and learning outcomes, we know very little about how this plays out across a broad spectrum of engagement possibilities. We simply do not know how time engaged virtually compares to time engaged in a traditional classroom. In fact, researchers have even found it difficult to measure the student engagement as distinct from "seat time" in a traditional classroom. This compounds the difficulty of evaluating current experiences.

Health Concerns

In a new, and rapidly changing, environment, many parents have been thrust into thinking about what options they have for safely educating their children. Parents may be juggling new pressures of working at home, or loss of before and after school childcare, as well as loss of income that might have provided options in the past. In an era with few good options, parents are faced with trying to make good decisions to assure that students do not lose ground but are also safe. Following the current pandemic, maintaining good health is a critical issue.

COVID-19 Gap

There is emerging evidence of a "COVID gap," or learning loss, as a result of pandemic-related changes. The education system must be prepared to bring students to grade-level expectations.

Emerging Technologies

In the twenty-first century, software gives teachers the ability to get just-in-time feedback on how all students are acquiring certain knowledge and skills. They can use this feedback from devices that automatically group students based on knowledge and skill attainment. Better software not only supplies real-time explanations directly to students with incorrect answers but also provides enhanced tutoring for students who need it. While these programs may never replace a teacher, they are an important resource to allow better use of teacher time and help pinpoint students' progress.

Such time-saving tools, where available, can also provide time for student-lead teams and project-based learning. Some software programs can train teachers on how to interact with students. This can aid in learning to provide student agency, or students taking control over their own learning using computer-based adaptive tools. Some new platforms allow students to both develop and access their own interest and strengths. They allow students to explore careers and provide material about the world of work and relate careers to student's interest. These platforms provide informational text related to student interest based on the Lexile reading level of the student.

Despite the great potential of technology, issues are challenging.

Resources

The lack of resources for public schools who have socio-economically disadvantaged students make them highly vulnerable in the transformation.

Access

Many districts have faced access barriers in reaching their students when not in face-to-face settings.

Professional Development. Teachers need support to be able to use online tools.

Parent Involvement. Parents may need to expand their understanding of "teaching" to include online lessons, in addition to face-to-face teacher-led sessions. Further thought and development are warranted to determine how best to use such innovations in a post-COVID-19 world.

High-Speed Internet. Many rural and inner-city areas, or homes, lack access to high-speed Internet. The COVID-19 pandemic shone a light on these inequities and federal and state COVID-19 relief funds have enabled most districts to purchase devices for each student, Wi-Fi hot spots, and the expansion of broadband (Reich, 2020).

Childcare. Schools are newly confronted with a need to provide parents training to support their children with online learning, Parents who are service providers, whose jobs prevent working from home, need access to affordable childcare, which must now also include learning supports for online learning. State agencies having separate responsibilities for childcare and education need to develop agility and flexibility to provide just-in-time regulations to ensure student safety and human resource capabilities. This raises questions of overall capacity to meet the need: staffing, facilities, transportation, and cost.

Equity. New emerging technologies have helped affluent students far more than students already confronting opportunity and achievement gaps. In particular, many rural and urban students do not have access to devices and broadband (Reich, 2020). New technologies and ways of teaching and learning need new systems of support from states. Such systems must include professional training, software and hardware purchases and broadband expansion. Concerned parents and citizens may want to look into the state-level supports as ongoing ways of ensuring that all students have online access.

Outdated Methods. Schools and colleges are the most conservative of our social institutions. Instead of upgrading and updating instructional methods, both higher education and K–12 faculty frequently used video cameras to simply teach as they did before (Reich, 2020).

Observations Regarding Instruction

The best instruction involves ensuring that all students meet the same standards. This necessitates the use of multiple teaching strategies or pathways to address the various learning styles and needs of all children. There is a continual need to build teacher awareness of different approaches across the students in their classroom. There must be appropriate levels of challenge for all students—not watered-down curriculum or a subset of standards.

We have an opportunity to change the ecology of schools and provide extensive professional development to disrupt the way we do school and close achievement gaps. We need to reinvent schools if we want to take advantage of new emerging technologies.

Moving forward, we will need to see how the technologies coming rapidly into play in the form of distance learning can be a positive disruption to fulfill the promise of American education. New, emerging technologies can result in broader and better access to quality education for all of our students. Moving forward, emerging technologies can help close achievement gaps and support both cognitive and socio-emotional learning. Technology may also increase student agencies in their own learning and create a passion for lifelong learning.

As vendors of more technologically delivered or supported instructional supports arrive with products to sell, wise districts will give thought to how their purchasing decisions are to be made. In the past, textbooks have competed not only on their coverage and approach to content but have also sought to woo teachers by offering easy-to-plan lessons, colorful illustrations, vocabulary lists, or printed tests. These things are important to busy teachers but can also serve to outweigh instructional impact. As schools and districts move forward into more technological supports for instruction, they will need to exercise caution to keep instructional aims in the forefront of decision-making, along with the many new supports that will be available.

In addition, educators need to provide a safe, free, and protected environment so that all students can feel free to express their options and have open dialogue to learn and explore. Educators must model a civic and civil dialogue in their classrooms. Schools must become a place where civil discourse should be encouraged issues and fears discussed and to help children learn how to cope. We are moving into an era of a very unpredictable set of changes. We have a moral responsibility to support our children and help them create a sense of hope and not despair.

At the same time, all stakeholders in education need to acknowledge that teachers are human beings and should be able to talk about their own personal beliefs, making it clear that they have their beliefs and that students must make their own conclusions. Teachers must be able to show students defensible partisanship.

Furthermore, as educators and parents, and members of a community we must ensure that all students are welcomed into our public schools. People must be able to respectfully address their concerns about what is happening in our schools.

ASSESSMENT

Assessment involves all the ways to tell if instruction has resulted in students learning the curriculum. America is a nation built on a heterogeneous student population. Social mobility for poor and working-class students relies on access to educational opportunities provided to the upper classes. Assessment provides critical information about student ability levels. There are two main purposes for assessment.

Summative Assessment or Assessment of Learning

This includes quizzes, tests, exams, and standardized tests, and high-stake assessments, such as proficiency tests. These determine whether a student has learned what has been taught and can meet the standards and objectives.

Formative or Diagnostic Assessment for Learning

Formative assessment provides ongoing and point-in-time information to students and teachers. It may assess what students already know about a topic to be introduced. It may also inform a teacher if instruction is on track, so they can make adjustments. This kind of assessment can take the form of pretests, questions, quizzes, self-assessments, and peer assessments.

Assessment Creation

Different assessments may be created by different stakeholders.

Teachers

Teachers create or select most classroom assessments, particularly formative assessments that inform their own teaching. They may select both formative and summative assessments, such as chapter pretests, quizzes, and end-of-chapter test that are provided by educational publishers to accompany their instruction.

States

Each state creates assessments to evaluate students in the state.

Kindergarten. States often have entry assessments to determine preparedness for school.

State Achievement/Proficiency Tests, Grades 3–8. Standardized tests in English/language arts, mathematics, and science are administered in most states in grades 3–8 as part of the No Child Left Behind requirements for federal funding. These tests provide information for teaching to assure that students are making AYP. Test results also inform citizens about how well local schools are performing.

High School Graduation. Most states have summative standardized proficiency exams for certain courses that must be passed before a student can be awarded a high school diploma.

National Exams

Common Core Assessments. A major initiative with the publication of the Common Core Standards was to develop aligned assessments to assess student knowledge of rigorous academic content as well as critical-thinking and problem-solving skills. The U.S. Department of Education funded two state consortia to develop assessments aligned with the new Common

Core state standards: Smarter Balanced Assessment Consortium (managed by the State of Washington) and Partnerships for Assessments of Readiness for Careers and College, produced by Achieve, a nonprofit. While each consortium developed Common Core aligned assessments, their approaches were quite different. States that adopted the Common Core standards also chose between these state assessments.

From the beginning, there were controversies. Suits were filed regarding the companies that got testing contracts. In addition, the Common Core tests held teachers, schools, districts, and states accountable for meeting the Common Core standards. Teacher evaluations were frequently tied to how well their students performed on the tests. Tying assessment outcomes to state teacher evaluation systems was deemed by many to be a punitive, not capacity-building, strategy. This resulted in widespread criticism of the tests.

Furthermore, when students did not do well, many claimed the tests were too hard and needed to be revised. Others complained that the tests, which only tested reading and math, took on such heightened importance, the eclipsed focus on all other subjects and any creative projects or enrichment activities. "Teaching to the test" became a frequent accusation. Some schools reduced project-based, engaging curriculum to dedicate class time to practicing with students on anticipated test items.

Backlash against the Common Core assessments was so severe that many legislatures replaced the Common Core test requirements with state-developed tests. While the Common Core standards and assessments were to stimulate rigorous scope and sequential curricula to enhance teaching and learning, most states caved into political pressure and set lower bars.

NAEP. This assessment is administered to a sampling of students across the United States to evaluate how well students in each state are progressing in key subject areas. This not only informs the public about the state of American education, but it particularly incentivizes need for reform by highlighting gaps and opportunities for growth.

International Tests. Tests such as TIMSS and the PISA measure international scholastic performance in math, science, and reading to provide comparable data to enable countries to improve their educational outcomes.

FUTURE ISSUES IN ASSESSMENT

American education faces several assessment challenges in the future. These have to do with how students are assessed: how often, using what methods, as well as what is important to measure. But the more critical question about assessment has to do with how we apply the information garnered from assessments to guide the other two legs of our educational stool: curriculum and instruction.

Across states with Common Core assessments, there is a return to wanting more local control and a desire for less federal interference in state policy. Balancing access and equity against the professional judgment of teachers facing classrooms of actual students is not only difficult, but efforts to do so through standards and compliance may have unintended consequences. Assessment to measure what students are learning may result in narrowing what is taught to what is believed will be tested. Rather than exploring better ways to teach, we may have simply taught less and fallen back onto rote learning in a false belief that this will produce "learning" that shows up better on tests. This is reminiscent of pre-progressive thinking and risks losing a child-centric emphasis.

Abandoning challenging assessments and relying heavily on attendance and passing grades raise questions. Alarming data from the Organisation for Economic Co-operation and Development (OECD) and Progress in International Reading Literacy Study show that U.S. students score far below the peers on various assessments.

Observations Regarding Assessment

American public schools have resisted education reform movements for the past hundred years. We know, from international assessments (TIMMS, PISA, etc.), that many of our students lag behind their international peers. While the COVID-19 crisis has served to disrupt our vision of education, it will require political will (legislators, Congress, federal and state departments of education, local entities, and the teaching profession itself) to consider hard questions about our schools and address equity issues. State board of education members face the need to balance increased rigor against ensuring access to a diploma or other meaningful credential for all students.

COVID-19 has given us an opportunity, and a need, to seize this moment to understand the past and the present and restructure for the future. Rather than being feared, assessments should be seen as valuable tools to understanding our ability levels and informing the best instruction. In the same way, Russian competition highlighted by the Sputnik satellite of the 1960s presented us with a challenge. It helped to encourage investment by the federal government in innovative curriculum and instruction. The inequities highlighted by our current health crisis reveal a need to invest greater intellectual capital and resources to transform our education system. Our response to this need must be appropriate to the current time and needs of today's students.

Observations Regarding Curriculum, Instruction, and Assessment

Curriculum, instruction, and assessment are tightly interwoven. Student achievement in meeting curriculum goals based on state standards must be able to be evaluated. Quality assessments will inform whether curricular goals are appropriate and if instructional methods are effective. Without assessments, as painful as they might be, no one will be able to judge what students learned and whether the instructional methods actually worked.

Technology offers so much potential for advancing the ability to deliver curriculum, and assess student achievement, teaching methods, and teacher proficiency. The pandemic exposed not only the underbelly of inequality of access to and misuse of technology but also the need and opportunity for individualizing curriculum and instruction.

REFERENCES

Battistella, E. L. (2019, October 6). *Reading, writing and readability—appreciating Rudolph Flesch.* OUPBlog. https://blog.oup.com/2019/10/reading-writing-and-readability-appreciating-rudolph-flesch/.

Bernstein, D. (2022, April 10). Teach "1619" and "1776" U.S. history. *The Wall Street Journal.*

Brown, A. (2022, February 18). The expansiveness of black history: The discipline can counter White racism. *EdWeek* https://www.edweek.org/leadership/as-book-bans-spread-suburban-moms-who-oppose-them-are-fighting-back/2022/02.

Christensen, C. M., Horn, M., & Johnson, C. W. (2010). *Disrupting class: How disrupting innovation will change the way the world learns.* New York: McGraw-Hill.

Editorial Projects in Education Research Center. (2007, January 1). From cradle to career: Connecting American education from birth to adulthood. *EdWeek.* https://epe.brightspotcdn.com/28/b4/141122b54aa085bd448ce75436c9/17shr.us.h26.pdf.

Education, F. D. (2022, April 15). Florida rejects publishers' attempts to indoctrinate students. Florida Department of Education. www.fldoe.org.

Finger, L. K., & Hartney, M. K. (2020, November 10). What determined if schools reopened? How many Trump voters were in a district. *The Washington Post.*

Flesch, R. F. (1955). *Why Johnny can't read: What you can do about it.* New York: Harper & Brothers.

Goldstein, D. (2022, May 22). In the fight over how to teach reading, this guru makes a major retreat. *The New York Times.*

Herold, J. (1974). Sputnik in American education: A history and reappraisal. *McGill Journal of Education,* 143–164.

Hess, F., & Noguera, P. (2021). A search for common ground: Conversations about the toughest questions in K–12 education. New York: Teachers College Press.

Learning Point Associates. (2004). *A closer look at the five essential components of effective reading instruction: A review of scientifically based reading research for teachers.* Naperville, IL: Learning Point Associates.

Nash, G. B., Crabtree, C., & Dunn, R. E. (1997). *History on trial: Culture wars and the teaching of the past.* New York: Alfred A. Knopf.

Pendarkar, E. (2022, March 9). As book bans spread, suburban moms who oppose them are fighting back. *EdWeek.*

Plotinsky, M. (2022, February 2). The spread of book banning movement. *EdWeek.*

Reich, J. (2020). *Failure to disrupt: Why technology alone can't transform education.* Cambridge, MA: Harvard Education Press.

Reville, P., & Canada, G. (2022, April 12). *Reville & Canada: The time has come for truly personalized learning—with a navigator to make sure each child succeeds.* The 74 Million. https://www.the74million.org/article/reville-canada-the-time-has-come-for-truly-personalized-learning-with-a-navigator-to-make-sure-each-child-succeeds/

Roos, D. (2019, August 13). *How the cold war space race led to U.S. students doing tons of homework.* History. https://www.history.com/news/homework-cold-war-sputnik.

Sawchuk, S. (2021, May 18). What is critical race theory and why is it under attack. *EdWeek.*

Schmidt, W., Houang, R., & Cogin, L. (2002, Summer). *A coherent curriculum: The case of mathematics.* American Education. https://www.aft.org/sites/default/files/periodicals/curriculum.pdf.

Wallace-Wells, B. (2021, June 18). How a conservative activist invented the conflict over critical race theory. *The New Yorker.*

Watters, A. (2015, June 20). *How sputnik launched ed-tech: The National Defense Education Act of 1958.* Hack Education. http://hackeducation.com/2015/06/20/sputnik.

Zimmerman, J. (2002). *Whose America? Culture wars in the public schools.* Cambridge, MA: Harvard University Press.

Chapter 2

On Teachers

BUILDING A HUMAN RESOURCE SYSTEM FOR A PROFESSION

If the three legs of the education stool are curriculum, instruction, and assessment, the key to making everything work in the classroom so that students meet the standards and have a successful experience is the teacher. In 1966, a critical report on educational opportunity concluded that "the quality of teachers shows a stronger relationship [than school facilities and curricula] to pupil achievement" (Coleman, 1966). Recent research confirms this finding. Teacher quality is the most important variable in effective education (Goldhaber, 2016).

Most have a favorite and least favorite teacher in their school experience. Senior citizens can readily recall a positive or negative teacher experience that occurred more than fifty years before. Teachers are frequently surprised to learn that something they said or did changed the direction of a student's life

Teaching is a profession that shapes all other professions. In every classroom, there are future leaders, doctors, politicians, and students who will follow future career pathways no one can yet imagine. Teachers truly touch the future.

Today there are approximately 4 million teachers in the United States with 3.5 million public school and 500,000 private school teachers (USA FACTS, 2022). Because teacher quality has such a significant effect on student achievement, it is obvious that improving teacher quality is a key opportunity for a better future of schools. This chapter examines the emergence of teaching as a profession in America and the status of state certification of teachers and how this relates to both teacher preparation and ongoing professional development. This includes an examination of current studies in the recruitment and retention of educators in the United States and discussion of the role of professional development.

THE ART OF TEACHING

Because the vast majority of Americans have been to public school, many believe that they understand what it takes to be a teacher, and many believe anyone can teach, whether they have any training or not. Especially during teaching shortages, movements to recruit untrained, inexperienced teachers take hold. Some think that teachers just need to be strong disciplinarians, like military sergeants, to demand that students behave and do their work.

But teaching is a complex human act that engages students in curriculum, instruction, and assessment in a context that supports the learning environment. Teachers have different strengths. Some have in-depth content knowledge, but that is not enough. Some have great classroom management skills and discipline, but that is not enough. A teacher can understand how children learn and be able to identify effective teaching methods, but if that teacher cannot control the class, he or she is seen as a failure.

By the same token, no one teacher appeals to all students. For example, some students learn best with a highly structured, strictly disciplined teacher. Others rebel against that and learn most effectively with a teacher who provides a creative, unstructured environment. Because students represent a wide array of talents, dispositions, and knowledge, a variety of teaching styles, methods, and personalities allows for students to develop relationships with a wide variety of adults.

The following characteristics are supported by research in teacher quality:

1. Knows subject matter;
2. Possesses differentiated instructional techniques and strategies;
3. Uses state standards to guide instruction;
4. Possesses excellent classroom management skills;
5. Creates learning environments in which children feel safe and secure and eager to learn;
6. Shares and collaborates with colleagues;
7. Likes students of all backgrounds;
8. Is a curious learner; and
9. Understands motivation and how to engage students, parents, and the community (Solmon & Agam, 2007).

THE HISTORY OF EDUCATOR PREPARATION
AND CERTIFICATION

The Introduction to this book provides a broad overview of the history of American education. A closer look specifically at teacher education within that framework reveals the history of the development of teacher education.

As outlined in the Introduction, the earliest efforts at public schooling in the United States took the form of Common Schools in the early 1800s, and education requirements for teachers were initially minimal. Teachers were expected to have completed education at or above the level at which they were to teach. In addition, they were expected to be able to "manage" their students (Labaree, 2008).

As communities added higher levels of schooling, up to the high school level, recognition of the need for formal education of teachers grew. Initially this need was met through summer teaching institutes, typically offered by groups of school districts or counties.

From State Normal Schools to State Universities

In response to the growth of public schooling across the country and the resulting demand for trained teachers, summer institutes began to take on a more formal level of organization in the "normal school." The name, normal school, referred to the aim of educating teachers about the cultural norms embodied in the community. This is derived from the French *ecole normale*, dating to 1685 in France when the Brothers of the Christian Schools, a Catholic congregation of lay religious leaders set out to establish a school for the religious education of the poor. They wanted to set a pattern or establish a norm after which all other schools would be modeled.

Normal schools in the United States first trained high school graduates at teacher institutes during summers. They progressed to two-year and then four-year degrees. Normal schools served as both an avenue to higher education for women and a means by which to provide teachers as state-developed systems of public education. Initially such schools were both private and public, with public normal schools developing at local levels (Labaree, 2008). Competition with state colleges and universities for students (and tuition dollars) and desire of students for more liberal arts focus led the addition of other degree programs. Some normal schools expanded to become teacher colleges. Meanwhile state universities added education departments.

The first public normal school in the United States was established in Lexington, Massachusetts, in 1839 and soon after moved to Framingham, Massachusetts. The evolution to the current Framingham State University

(FSU) gives a good example of the development of both public and private normal schools.

Framingham Normal School first offered courses for completion in two years to train high school graduates as teachers. Their coursework included pedagogy and basic curriculum, such as reading, writing, speaking, mathematics, and geography. In the twentieth century Framingham Normal School became Framingham State College (now University), adding liberal arts majors and professional programs such as nursing. Currently, FSU is organized as a research university. FSU has state-approved teacher training programs requiring a bachelor's degree as well as master's and doctorate degrees in education.

The growth of state normal schools was rapid, from 39 in 1839 to 180 by 1910. However, even when augmented by an equivalent number of private schools, the normal schools graduated only a quarter of needed new teachers by 1898. This created tremendous pressure to maintain relevance by focusing on quantity of graduates, even if some quality had to be sacrificed (Labaree, 2008).

In recent years, U.S. teacher education programs embedded in the modern university system have become cash cows for universities, with the monies obtained from education programs being diverted to build stronger academic departments and other professional programs. State universities sacrificed the focus on high-quality teacher education programs, as their mission expanded to other professional and liberal arts programs. As a result, teacher education lost its important status within the mission of the state university and is often considered a weak academic link.

Progressive and Behaviorist Teacher Education

There is, today, great variability in quality and content within and among departments or schools of education. Some departments or schools of education stress essentialism and behaviorism, while others emphasize constructivist teaching and classroom management approaches, similar to those ideas of the progressives. This tension between philosophies has been present in teacher education in the United States throughout our history, with each having periods of ascendancy.

The Progressive era in the United States, spanning from the 1890s to 1940s, was characterized by social and political reforms, frequently led by educated women, such as teachers, social workers, and public health nurses. Progressive educators felt that instruction in state colleges for educators reflected too much of an essentialist approach, emphasizing the teaching of basic courses on how to teach reading, writing, arithmetic, and language skills such as spelling and handwriting. The progressives sought a greater emphasis on understanding the whole child. Many state colleges at the time emphasized the work of Thorndyke and psychological behaviorists while progressives were emphasizing the relationship between human growth and development as the underpinnings of education philosophy.

The Bureau of Educational Experiments, later the Bank Street School, undertook an intensive study of child development to create schools appropriate for children throughout stages of growth. Bank Street, under the leadership of Lucy Sprague Mitchell, tended away from the notion of education as being strictly "intellectual," or imparting bits of knowledge and skills. Her vision, and that of other progressives, was that education prepares students to build a better world and democratic society (Nagen & Shapiro, 1999). This approach required considerable interaction between the school and community in order that children be able to explore the uses of knowledge.

Constructivism is an educational theory that emphasizes that students understand knowledge based upon their own experiences; they construct their own knowledge. John Dewey, the progressive philosopher; Jean Piaget; and Lev Vygotsky are major theorists of this movement. Teacher training programs in this movement emphasize strategies, follow the Socratic method with small group social interactions, and emphasize problem-based learning. These strategies suggest that teachers are guides to help students construct their own knowledge, based on the unique cultural factors of the students. The constructivists argue for the implementation of real-world problem-solving, case-based learning, local role models, and self-reflection techniques, such as journaling. In general, this philosophy supports social collaboration rather than individual competition.

Behaviorist theorists explain human behavior by setting conditions and consequences in the environment. They are also concerned with the learner's prior experience in other environments. Historically, conservative teacher training programs embraced the work of B. F. Skinner, whose ideas called for both positive and negative reinforcements. Albert Bandura, a Canadian American psychologist who is the David Starr Jordan professor emeritus of social science in psychology at Stanford University, talked about the importance of teacher modeling behaviors, attitudes, and emotions. This contribution expanded behavioral and content theory. For example, students are rewarded for tutoring classmates by modeling both cognitive and social strengths of the instructor. Behaviorist pedagogy advocates direct instruction, drills, questions and answers, guided practice, reviews of material learned, and positive rewards for achievement and good behavior.

This debate between progressive and behaviorist teacher education continues today. Justin Reich in *Failure to Disrupt* (2020) talks about these two approaches, citing multiple sources in support of his assertion that we must reject an either/or approach (Kirschner, Sweller, & Clark, 2006; Mehta & Fine, 2019). Reich advocates that educators become more eclectic, choosing approaches dependent on the outcomes they seek.

A PUBLIC PROFESSION FOR PUBLIC SCHOOLS

Unlike some other professions, teaching is a public profession. Most teachers teach in public schools, funded by local, federal, and state tax dollars. As a public profession, teachers are not only exposed to public review by students and their parents, but they are also accountable to the public to meet standards of learning and prepare students for the future.

Because most Americans have been in school, many believe that they know all about what it takes to be a teacher. Popular media, including movies and TV shows about teachers, have often perpetuated stereotypes and myths of romantic, heroic, naïve, cruel, bad, or clueless teachers. ABC's *Abbott Elementary*, which premiered in 2022, created by Quinta Brunson, is one of the few situation comedies that some believe provides a truer picture of teachers (McGarvey, 2022).

Teaching in the United States is also buffeted by political and societal changes. Teachers may be lauded in one place or vilified in another for teaching certain topics in history or science. In the 1920s, some states banned the teaching of evolution. In the 2020s, some states are legislating the abolition of teaching CRT. Teaching sex education has been seen by some as a valuable part of understanding human physiology and family planning. Others see it as an invasion of family privacy.

Writing in 1963, Richard Hofstadter described a phenomenon he termed American anti-intellectualism (Hofstadter, 1963). By this, he was not describing a love of ignorance but rather those who attain a level of unquestioning certainty from their accumulation of knowledge and facts. He termed such people "experts," exemplified by business or salespeople and fundamentalist religion. He saw the role of intellectuals to question and critique (possibly from a distance) the static beliefs of such experts.

He decried the "democratic" invasion of academia by those favoring practical training over "book-learning" or too great a concern for the emotional well-being of students. At the same time, he tended to see a necessary tension between those he regarded as intellectual or possessed of habits of thinking and questioning and those convicted in the certainty of their information (Lemann, 2014). Hofstadter's tension continues to be played out across campuses and in American schools today.

Types of Teachers

In public schools, there are different types of teachers. Requirements to become a teacher vary by state. Table 2.1 shows the typical descriptions and qualifications of teachers.

Table 2.1. Teacher Types and Corresponding Qualifications

Career Type	Description	Grade Level	Typical Minimum Qualifications
Preschool Teacher	Focus on language, motor, and social skills for children younger than five years.	Pre-K	Associates degree in early childhood education or related field.
Kindergarten Teacher	Supervise, assess, and teach basic skills and development for a future of education.	K	BA in elementary or early childhood education; pass state standardized tests.
Elementary School Teacher	Teach basic subjects and prepare students for later grades.	K–6	Bachelor's degree and state licensing exams.
Middle School Teacher	Specialize and teach a single subject.	6–8	Bachelor's degree and state licensing exams.
High School Teacher specializes in one subject (Biology, Chemistry, Physics, Math, History, Government, English) or elective (physical education, art, or music)	Prepare students for life after graduation. Present understanding and experience of field.	9–12	Bachelor's degree usually in field and state licensing exams.
Music or Art Teacher	Teach history and elements and principles of music or art.	K–12	Bachelor's degree in education with a specialty in art or music; teaching certificate for specific grades.
English as a Second Language (ESL) or English Learner (EL) Teacher	Teach students to read, write, and speak in English as their second language.	K–12	Bachelor's degree and state licensing exams.
Special Education Teacher	Responsible for teaching all subjects to students with learning, mental, emotional, and/or physical disabilities.	K–12	Bachelor's degree and state licensing exams.
Gifted and Talented Teacher	Work with students who need more rigorous work.	K–12	Bachelor's degree and state licensing exams.
Physical Education Teacher	Focus on physical development and ability of students of all ages.	K–12	Bachelor's degree and state licensing exams.
Substitute Teacher	Temporary replacement for regular teachers at any grade.	K–12	Bachelor's degree.
Teaching Assistant or Teacher's Aide	Work under the guidance of a licensed teacher.	K–12	Associates degree and passage of state assessment.

Certification and Educator Preparation

Teaching in a public school in America generally requires state certification, or licensure, in addition to a bachelor's degree. The time it takes for certification as a teacher is usually four or five years, depending on the requirements of the degree-granting institution and state certification requirements. A state may require passage of a national or state exam. Most states also require field placements as well as student teaching or an internship. The minimum number of hours required for this varies from state to state. States typically publish educator certification requirements as well as the names of individuals whose licenses have been revoked for cause. As with certification requirements, revocation standards and processes vary from state to state. Teachers must renew their teaching certificates every few years with additional coursework or experience.

Where state approval is housed within the state bureaucracy, the location varies by state. In some states, it is contained within the state department of education or a department of higher education. Other states have independent standards boards to regulate certification and education programs.

State Certificates to Teach

Under the U.S. Constitution, each state has the responsibility for education in that state. Having unique requirements by states makes reciprocal certification agreements difficult. Teachers newly certified in the state where they attend college may find themselves limited to job-seeking within that state. A state facing a teacher shortage, as following the COVID-19 pandemic, may face difficulties recruiting teachers from other states where certification requirements differ. In response to this difficulty, the National Association of State Directors of Teacher Education and Certification (NASDTEC) serves as a clearinghouse of reciprocity information. The organization also encourages the adoption of common certification standards across states.

The Relationship between Certification and Teacher Preparation

In addition to setting standards for teacher certification, states also oversee teacher preparation programs within colleges and universities. Depending on the state, this authority may rest within various state-level boards or departments. This can lead to inconsistency between standards for certification and those for the educator preparation programs. As an example, in Ohio, teacher preparation standards are set by a board of regents having responsibility for higher education. Teacher certification standards, however, are set by the state board of education, which has responsibility for pre-K through twelfth grade education. This necessitates alignment between certification standards and the state's academic content standards. However, it also necessitates ongoing communication with colleges and universities, through the board of regents, to ensure that teacher preparation programs are also in alignment with state content standards.

Some states, such as Massachusetts and Ohio, have panels of teachers and administrators to review the applications of certification candidates. They recommend certification of candidates or other actions such as additional coursework or internship.

Contemporary Certification Programs

Institutions of higher education prepare teacher education students to meet certification requirements in various ways. Some colleges and universities offer a joint bachelor's and master's degree program. Some states require a master's degree in either education or the subject matter in which certification is granted.

The Council for the Accreditation of Educator Preparation (CAEP) is a national organization approved by the U.S. Department of Education to accredit teacher education programs in colleges and universities. Many states follow their accreditation standards and may require their institutions to be accredited by this association. Similar to the work of NASDTEC in certification, CAEP helps to establish both quality and commonality in teacher education programs across states.

In looking at the CAEP standards in relationship to educator preparation standards in other countries, the CAEP standards are disappointing. CAEP standards do not put strong emphasis on teacher-led action research or education collaboration. CAEP standards require evidence that prospective students score in the top 50th percentile on nationally validated assessments. Higher-performing nations require incoming students to score among the top 30 percent on national examinations.

Examples of Alternative Education Programs

While traditional routes to certification offered by state-approved college or university programs take four to five years, alternative routes to certification may take less time. Such alternative programs are frequently developed in response to either generalized teacher shortages or the need for high-quality teachers in specific areas.

Shortages can result from a variety of demographic shifts, such as the post–World War II baby boom. States can respond by lowering certification requirements or by creating new certification programs. As an example, during the Vietnam War, when there was a mandatory military draft, local draft boards granted deferments to young men in "essential occupations," which could include teaching. In 1968, when many deferments, including the 2S student deferment (granted to many undergraduate and graduate students) ended, there was a great fear that colleges and universities would lose students, and that graduates would be drafted rather than being available to teach.

Other circumstances that create new teacher training demands include public policy changes. As an example, the Education for All Handicapped Children Act (1975) required the public education of many students previously underserved (Iasevoli, 2017). The NCLB (2002) required that students be taught by "highly qualified" teachers.

Mid-Career Certification Programs

As noted above, both the post–World War II baby boom and the Vietnam era military draft impacted the supply and demand for traditionally certified teachers. In response, New York City colleges developed ten-week programs for college graduates seeking provisional teacher certification. This no doubt included young men of draft age seeking a position that would garner them a deferment. A later program, Troops to Teachers (1994–2019) was established by the U.S. Department of Education. This program provided financial assistance to returning veterans seeking to enter the teaching field.

Recently there has been growth in online teacher training programs to meet alternative state requirements for mid-career professionals. While traditional undergraduate programs generally require four years, mid-career programs provide focus on pedagogy and child development for adults who have already achieved a degree in a content area. The time it takes to get certified for a mid-career professional using these online programs can vary based on a private for-profit, a private nonprofit, or a public or private university. They may or may not require an internship. The quality of these programs varies depending on various state requirements for certification.

Teach for America and The New Teacher Project

Teach for America is a variation of the mid-career certification program. Initially supported by federal dollars, this program seeks highly capable recent graduates from non-education majors and provides intensive coursework and support while placing them immediately in teaching positions in poorly performing or poorly resourced schools. Arguments in favor of this approach suggest that it brings the best and brightest into classrooms with high numbers of low-income students. Arguments in opposition point out that these teachers lack sufficient educational background and are destined to move on after a year or two, creating instability in the schools they are intended to help.

Also initially funded by the U.S. Department of Education was The New Teacher Project (TNTP). This program also sought to attract qualified teachers into inner-city schools through provision of an urban residency program. Implementation was hindered by red tape in hiring and onboarding new teachers through complicated urban school district systems. Now rebranded as TNTP, it continues to provide teacher residency programs in urban districts throughout the United States.

IMPROVING TEACHER QUALITY

Teaching is not static. The population of students, standards, educational research, and educational materials are ever-changing. Accommodating such changes has the potential to make education more responsive to societal needs and change education for the better. Improving student achievement in the United States requires improving teacher quality. This involves not only teacher preparation but also teacher support, professional development, and continuing education. At the same time, teachers can be resistant to change, especially if they believe their methods and lesson plans are successful. Seasoned teachers have often experienced many unsupported or unsustainable educational reforms and initiatives and can be justifiably wary of change.

A 2009 report from TNTP highlighted a tendency of districts to view all teachers as being of similar quality, rating 99 percent as "satisfactory." This was particularly worrisome, considering the data showing that teacher quality was the most important in-school factor influencing student learning. This led to the inclusion of a requirement that states applying for competitive grants in the new RTTT funds commit to evaluate and improve teachers and principals using multiple measures, with an emphasis on student progress measured by statewide tests. This requirement also became a part of the No Child Left Behind reauthorization. By 2015, forty-three states required that evidence of student learning be included in teacher evaluations, although fewer (twenty-three) tied teacher tenure to performance (Aldeman, 2017).

By 2013, various groups had begun asking for flexibility in a variety of federal requirements tied to funding, particularly accountability measures relating to student growth as indicated by statewide assessments. The CCSSO requested a two-year period to allow for implementation of the new Common Core Standards. The AFT advocated for a temporary suspension of "high stakes consequences" of new Common Core assessments (McNeil & Gewertz, 2013). The timing of the teacher evaluation requirements coinciding with the implementation of new Common Core assessments led to public confusion and pushback against all reforms, frequently viewed as burdensome rather than helpful (Aldeman, 2017).

An independent assessment of teacher evaluation systems based on student growth and coupled with teacher incentives, as implemented by federal Teacher Incentive Fund (TIF) projects, reported gains in student learning. The broader RTTT and NCLB requirements, however, were less targeted than TIF projects. As one piece of a broad set of required reforms, teacher and principal evaluation ranked very low when it came to actual implementation (Aldeman, 2017).

A related development in 2016 established rules in conjunction with the federal Teacher Education Assistance for College and Higher Education (TEACH) grant program, a tuition program for students planning to teach in a high-need field in a low-income area. These rules, following multiple years of negotiation, would require that teacher preparation programs demonstrate effectiveness through the classroom impact of their graduates, using student learning data (Inside Higher Ed, 2016). The idea was that teacher-prep programs would use what they learned from the ratings to improve training. Some argued that this was federal government overreach. Others were concerned about unintended consequences as teachers avoided positions that might be too difficult to demonstrate advances in student achievement. The rules were rescinded a few months later by the Trump administration (Iasevoli, 2017).

"A Nation at Risk" and Subsequent Reports and Suggested Reforms

While many regard No Child Left Behind and RTTT as groundbreaking in terms of federal involvement in teaching, actual roots are deeper. Just as reports responding to concerns arising from Sputnik in the 1950s spurred reforms in education generally, so did later reports focus attention more specifically on teaching. In 1983, when "A Nation at Risk" was issued by the U.S. National Commission on Excellence in Education, people became aware that American schools were failing, and a major reason was the quality of its teachers. The report urged that both teacher compensation systems and teacher preparation needed to be evaluated and addressed. This report stimulated reform efforts at the federal, state, and local levels.

"A Nation at Risk" notably warned of "a rising tide of mediocrity that threatens our very future as a nation and a people." This conclusion was based, in part, on comparatively poor U.S. performance on international assessments. Of the nineteen indicators examined, American students were never in first or second place internationally but placed last compared to other industrialized nations on seven indicators. Also mentioned were high levels of functional illiteracy among both older adults and seventeen-year-olds (U.S. Department of Education, 1983).

Of interest to teacher preparation programs, the report urged both higher expectations of students ("in some metropolitan areas basic literacy has become the goal rather than the starting point") and increased graduation standards. The report cited public support for four years each of high school mathematics, English, history/civics, and science. It also noted that no state met the rigor of those standards, and that they exceeded the entrance requirements of most colleges and universities.

Overall, the conclusions of the report were upbeat in looking forward. It called out the dedication of teachers and public support for funding education, while setting an expectation that the country undertake massive improvements. This report stimulated a thirty-five-year era of reform by the U.S. Department of Education, state agencies, teacher organizations, and reform-minded academics.

Response to "A Nation at Risk"

Among the academics and authors proposing solutions were Theodore Sizer and Linda Darling-Hammond. Sizer argued that schools had come to set low standards of academic learning in exchange for compliant and well-behaved students (Sizer, 1984). Among principles stressed by the Coalition of Essential Schools, founded by Sizer, were an emphasis on depth of learning rather than broad "coverage," and student demonstration of mastery of content. Teachers were envisioned as "coaches," enabling students as worker-learners (The Coalition of Essential Schools, 2021).

Darling-Hammond described American schools as being structured to produce failure. Specifically, she cited

- poor use of time, as students move from teacher to teacher for short periods;
- non-productive staff assignments, isolating teachers from one another and requiring too many staff outside of classrooms, which impedes collective goal setting and knowledge-sharing; and
- poorly allocated resources, denying teachers resources (time and supports) needed to educate students well (National Commission on Teaching and America's Future, 1996).

Darling-Hammond's report recommended that the nation aspired to meet the following goals by 2006:

1. All children will be taught by teachers who have the knowledge, skills, and commitments to teach children well.

2. All teacher education programs will meet professional standards, or they will be closed.
3. All teachers will have access to high-quality professional development and regular time for collegial work and planning.
4. Both teachers and principals will be hired and retained based on their ability to meet professional standards of practice.
5. Teachers' salaries will be based on their knowledge and skills.
6. Quality teaching will be the central investment of schools. Most education dollars will be spent on classroom teaching (Darling-Hammond, 1997).

Meeting these goals would require standards for both students and teachers; an overhaul of teacher preparation and professional development; improvements to teacher recruitment and the assurance of qualified teachers in every classroom. Efforts should also encourage and reward teacher knowledge and skill and create schools that are organized for student and teacher success (National Commission on Teaching and America's Future, 1996).

Others offered more conservative approaches. Chester Finn Jr., for instance, president of the Thomas B. Fordham Foundation, endorsed recommendations from The Teachers We Need and How to Get More of Them, a manifesto with support from a range of educators, governors, and state school officers (Education Commission of the States, 2000). The manifesto urged moving away from certification requirements (particularly those focused on pedagogy and child growth and development). Instead, the authors advocated that preparation programs provide a large and diversely prepared pool of teachers, which could then be winnowed through empowering school principals to hire (and fire) teachers more selectively. This would necessitate moves like replacing teacher tenure with multiyear contracts and use of salary-based incentives to lure and keep the best. The document suggests that value-added algorithms be used to determine which teachers are best at producing student learning (The Thomas B. Fordham Foundation, 1999). Their approach generally supported alternative certification programs, such as Teach for America.

Reports from the Academy

Many groups were formed by deans of colleges of education and academics in the field of education to reform educator training programs. One such group was the Holmes Group, the work of Arthur Levine, president of Columbia Teachers' College (1994–2006) and president of the Woodrow Wilson National Fellowship Foundation.

Fifty deans of universities comprised the Holmes Group. Group goals included to solidify education,; to recognize the differences in teachers' knowledge, skills, and work roles; and to create standards for entry into the profession. The most interesting recommendation from the Holmes Group was the call for professional development schools. These schools were to make a better place to train prospective teachers similar to the medical profession's teaching hospitals. The schools were to have collaborative governing structures reflected in joint contracts with universities and school districts. Unfortunately, after much internal bickering, the Holmes Group disbanded.

Levine, when president of Columbia Teachers' College, issued several reports to strengthen teacher education. He noted the recalcitrance of teacher education institutions to reform themselves. When he was president of Woodrow Wilson National Fellowship Foundation, he tried to create incentives for universities to redesign science and mathematics teacher education programs. Despite the availability of funding for these programs, little innovation occurred. Before his retirement, he worked with the MIT Media Lab to start a new college of education in Cambridge, Massachusetts.

Reforms at the National and State Levels

In 1987, the National Board of Professional Teaching Standards (NBPTS) was established. The intent of creating national standards was to enable states to work together to create a national board certification of teachers. The board would define standards to improve teaching quality, thereby making teaching a more valued and honored profession. Jim Kelly, the first leader, hoped that the NBPTS would also influence teacher preparation programs by encouraging teachers to sit for certification examinations. This would lead to board standards for what teachers should know and be able to do being incorporated into master's degree programs. Kelly encouraged states to provide fiscal incentives for teachers to obtain national board certification. Many states now use board certification as their overall state certification and offer free support, conditional loans, and encouragement. This is not a reality in all states, however.

The National Commission on Teaching and America's Future was created by Governor James Hunt of North Carolina and Stanford professor Linda Darling-Hammond. In 1996, the National Commission on Teaching and America's Future issued a report that called for the overhauling of teacher education programs, strengthening licensure standards, and implementing teacher compensation programs that reward the knowledge and skills that teachers have (National Commission on Teaching and America's Future, 1996). This recommendation differed from the approach recommended by policies of the Obama administration, which required states that received RTTT or teacher education improvement grants to require evaluation of the profession based on student outcomes.

Many states during this twenty-five-year period issued their own reports to improve the profession. One author was a significant contributor to a report from Massachusetts. Then-Governor Michael Dukakis commissioned a group of stakeholders, including college and university presidents, the Massachusetts Board of Regents, and teacher associations, to make recommendations to improve the teaching profession. These recommendations included elimination of the education major and development of a statewide beginner teacher mentoring program and clinical master's degree program. While required legislation for the mentoring program passed the House of Representatives, local politics and the cost of the mentoring program prevented the needed Senate support.

TEACHER RECRUITMENT

Especially in a time of teacher shortages, a key to improving education is to recruit high-quality candidates who want a career in education. The following qualities in recruits are strong indicators that a hire will be successful.

- Positive attitude
- Strong organization skills
- Excellent communication skills and a willingness to communicate with parents
- Subject area expertise
- Respect for and appreciation of students
- Dependability
- Ability to collaborate with other teachers

Recruitment issues for schools are varied. Rural and urban districts face different needs. Needs also vary by content area. In addition, pressure for districts to hire demographically diverse faculties has created a need for education to compete with other professions for minority graduates.

Rural Districts

Rural districts are often hard-pressed to provide a wide range of course options to a small student population, particularly with limited budgets. In the past, they may have been able to get by with teachers filling out a schedule by teaching outside their area of certification. With today's emphasis on both highly qualified teachers and preparing work and college-ready graduates, this is not an option. With limited budgets, teacher salaries tend to be at the low end of the scale.

Urban Districts

Urban districts may have more generous salaries and greater flexibility in hiring to meet broad content needs but are often seen as difficult places to work. Further, while most urban districts have a range of schools from problematic to highly successful, long-established "pecking orders" may dictate that new hires go primarily to the least attractive buildings. Experienced teachers seek to move out of these buildings as openings are available elsewhere in the system (or in neighboring suburban districts).

Across all districts, there are various high-need certifications (special education, mathematics, science, world languages, and bilingual education). Despite needs, teachers having certifications in such high-need certification areas are paid on the same scale as other teachers.

Teacher Demographics

One doesn't need to spend much time in schools to recognize that 89 percent of elementary, 72 percent of middle school, and 60 percent of high school teachers are women (USA FACTS, 2022). Data from the U.S. Department of Education, National Center for Education Statistics (NCES) for 2017–2018 indicate that, while 51 percent of K–12 students are students of color, only 20 percent of teachers are teachers of color (RELNorthwest, n.d.). This mismatch, combined with the racial isolation of many schools, suggests a needed direction for teacher recruitment and retention efforts.

Teachers make many decisions that impact their students, from the selection and presentation of curriculum to judgments about student work to disciplinary actions. Research has demonstrated disparities, by race, in the ways that teachers view their Black and White students. White teachers, as a group, were less likely than Black teachers to predict that their Black students will graduate high school or earn a college degree. Such implicit bias may have a role in unequal discipline and fuel a "school to prison pipeline" for Black students (Flannery, 2015).

Despite the 1954 *Brown* decision ordering that school systems desegregate "with all deliberate speed," and multiple decisions examining systems and ordering compliance since that time, the state of education in this country remains one where racially identifiable schools are the norm rather than the exception. *De jure* segregation has given way to *de facto* segregation, resulting from segregated housing patterns. These patterns have persisted, despite fair housing laws, through economically segregated neighborhoods and the enduring results of inequitable practices in hiring and lending (Warkentien, 2015, p. 4). Nationally, 40 percent of Black and Latinx students attend schools where over 90 percent of students are nonwhite. About 20 percent of White students attend schools that are over 90 percent White (Potter & Burris, 2020).

State-Level Issues in Recruitment and Retention of Teachers

States confront multiple realities in recruiting educators.

Reciprocity

First is the lack of reciprocity agreements between and among states, as noted earlier. While state certification offices in many states have tried to address this issue, the existence of state-level certification requirements mitigates against total reciprocity.

Pensions

Educator pensions are not portable from state to state. Moving across state lines may result in the loss of accumulated service time. While teachers may be able to "buy in" to the system in moving to another state, the amount of service that can be purchased may be limited, and the cost of such purchase is high. State pension systems tend to protect dollars that educators have invested in their current system.

Incentives

A third reality is that states have frequently not been helpful to districts in filling hard-to-staff positions, based on subject matter or locality. Some states have experimented with fiscal incentives and loan forgiveness, but this has not yet become an effective national strategy. More research must be conducted to address appropriate incentives for recruitment. Many states are experiencing an increasingly diverse student body. While research has demonstrated the importance of teacher role models, states must help districts provide incentives for schools to reflect the population of the children they serve.

Previous Recruitment Efforts

Concern about recruitment of teachers is not new. In the mid-to-late 1980s, the focus on education improvements was accompanied by a fear of a coming shortage of good teachers. There were concerns that by the 1990s and continuing into the early twenty-first century, retiring teachers would produce shortages of quality school staffing. In 1986, Recruiting New Teachers (RNT), started by David Rockefeller, forecast a need for more than 2 million new teachers. This organization became a national clearinghouse for publications, conferences, public service campaigns, and technical assistance. At the same time, many states began to contract with labor economists to understand teacher shortages, using supply and demand studies.

RNT worked directly with states, such as California, to help recruit teachers for the state's growing population. Sadly, technology for tracking and forecasting on a national level was lacking. While the influence of RNT was seen in state policies that attracted new recruits to the profession, RNT lost its funding when the predicted national teacher shortage did not materialize.

In the same period, two of the previously discussed alternative certification programs (Teach for America and TNTP) emerged. These organizations recruited highly successful young college graduates for teaching positions in collaboration with large urban school systems. These programs have impacted the development of educational entrepreneurship, rather than overall systemic improvement of teacher quality. Teach for America teachers, for instance, have been instrumental in the development of the Knowledge is Power Program (KIPP) system of alternative schools, which will be discussed later.

Effective organizations in many economic sectors embrace best practices to attract and retain quality talent. Education systems may learn from considering such practices. As a first step, we need to understand how school districts currently recruit and retain staff.

A Center for American Progress (CAP) survey included more than 108 nationally representative school districts, gathering data on how new teachers are recruited. CAP reported that "school districts' recruitment strategies are hyper-local, untargeted, or non-existent." Further they found that "school district application and selection processes often emphasize static application materials—such as written applications, resumes, and proof of certification over performance-based measures" (Konoske-Graf, Partelow, & Benner, 2016).

The CAP report suggested that all school districts devote time and resources to intentional recruitment. Specific strategies include:

- development of talent pipelines;
- individual contacts with successful candidates;
- leverage of technology and personal networks;
- use of social media platforms; and
- central office predictions of teacher shortages.

Other resources include using educator recruiting websites and teacher job fairs, signing bonuses, growing your own strategies, developing compelling recruitment materials, and using data to set and reach hiring goals and develop hiring timelines (Buttner, 2020).

RETAINING QUALITY TEACHING STAFF

According to the NCES, 8 percent of teachers in the United States leave the profession annually. An additional 8 percent move to other schools. NCES, in 2019, noted that on average a school will lose three of every twenty teachers each year. According to the Brookings Institute, high levels of teacher turnover are negatively associated with student achievement. The authors cite monetary and human capital losses in replacing teachers and mention, "inequities in access to highly effective instruction across schools and districts." The authors evaluated 25,000 studies for a meta-analysis and examined three categories to explain the phenomena (Nguyen & Springer, 2019). The categories detailed are personal correlates of teachers, school correlates, and external correlates like state accountability and school improvement efforts.

Reasons Teachers Leave Teaching

There are multiple drivers of teacher turnover. A few are listed next.

Poor Working Conditions

Teachers who left teaching report that "they are fleeing the poor working conditions that make it difficult for them to teach and their students to learn." These were the key to teacher satisfaction and must be addressed in districts and schools with high turnover. Working conditions include school leadership, collegial relationships, and school culture (Simon & Johnson, 2015).

Geographical Isolation

A study of rural schools (Hamner et al., 2004) found that it was difficult to recruit and retain teachers because of geographical isolation. High school principals stressed the importance of recruiting rural residents. They also reported desperately looking for other strategies to attract teachers to their communities.

Compensation

There is some evidence that compensation affects teacher retention. A study for the NSF found that while financial compensation mattered, the effect size is very small. Science teachers were paid more than other teachers, which helped in retention. The report recommended targeting specific groups of teachers rather than increasing the subsidies for all (Hansen et al., 2004).

Reasons Teachers Do Not Leave Teaching

Research by Nguyen and Springer (2019) provide some counterexamples. Following are the reasons for teachers to remain in the field.

Satisfaction

Teachers' satisfaction was identified as a leading component of the personal correlates. Highly satisfied teachers were less likely to leave.

Traditionally Certified

The authors also found that traditionally certified teachers were less likely to leave than those certified through alternative routes.

Student Body Characteristics

Regarding school correlates, the study found that characteristics of the student body did not influence attrition. The finding that student body characteristics were not a cause of teacher turnover is also supported elsewhere. A study of six comprehensive urban schools found that teachers in urban areas do not flee their students.

Teacher Evaluation and Accountability

Researchers did not find negative consequences for teacher evaluation and accountability. Teachers who were evaluated were less likely to leave.

Professional Development

The provision of professional development was also found to have a positive impact on retention, as did merit-based pay programs.

Agility to Maintain a High-Quality Faculty

Assembling a qualified set of teachers is important for all schools and districts. So is attending to their ongoing satisfaction to maintain stability. However, another, equally important, factor is to assure a level of agility to meet changing needs.

Changing Needs

Changing needs may impact both the size and makeup of staff. Student populations may decline as neighborhoods age or increase with revitalization. As discussed earlier, the demographics of the student population imply a need for teacher demographics to respond. Changing student populations may bring students whose first language is not English, requiring specifically credentialled teachers. As the economy relies increasingly on global connections, schools have been encouraged to develop language programs, and particularly to expand beyond the traditional Romance languages. Economic needs have driven the development of Science, Technology, Engineering, and Mathematics (STEM) courses.

Social-Emotional Learning

Emphasis on "whole child" needs has led to demands that schools (or some schools) be attentive to social-emotional learning, move from punishment-based discipline to restorative practices, and incorporate teacher training on trauma-informed care. Such changes imply the need for new positions, new responsibilities for teachers, new relationships with outside organizations, or all the above.

Health Issues

The pressures of COVID-19 have included a need for more teachers to accommodate smaller socially distanced classes. At the same time, many teachers who are older or have a range of health issues are fearful of returning to school buildings. While such fears may be balanced by economic need to maintain employment (or health coverage), as the economy recovers, schools may experience a spike in teacher turnover (Barnum, 2021).

Online Education

Perhaps the most significant of immediate pressures is the need to transition to online education. This more than any other result of the pandemic has revealed broad inequities in our system of education as a whole. While families have very different levels of both online access and "devices" for access, schools and teachers have widely divergent levels of preparation for using online tools.

Keeping Current: The Professional Development/Continuing Education Conundrum

As states, through licensure, began to see teaching as a profession, akin to others, like medicine or law, there was a recognition that teachers needed to keep abreast of new information in their field. This generally took the form of a set number of credits, or credit hours, that must be obtained from an accredited institution, such as a college or university, prior to each renewal of the license. Many teachers accomplished this by taking courses over the summer, reminiscent of the summer institutes that preceded the development of normal schools.

Continuing Education Units

Over time, various professional organizations began to offer conferences, attracting speakers or presenters and granting Continuing Education Units (CEUs) through arrangement with a college or university. These conferences had multiple advantages. They were a benefit that helped to boost membership. They provided an opportunity to disseminate stances (pedagogical and otherwise) being taken by the organization. And the large gatherings were attractive to vendors wishing to gain exposure for products ranging from textbooks and curriculum packages to school buses and cafeteria equipment.

As the accumulation of CEUs was a licensing requirement, unions negotiated for various accommodations or supports (tuition reimbursement, time off, etc.) to be included in teacher contracts. Within this general framework, teachers had wide latitude in their selection of the content of their learning. Some worked toward advanced degrees, while others took a more eclectic path.

Master's Degree Requirement

As No Child Left Behind raised questions about the quality of teachers, particularly the match between a teacher's academic background and the classes they taught, states and districts felt a need for tighter control. Ohio, for instance, instituted a requirement that incoming teachers with a bachelor's degree acquire a master's degree within five years to maintain their certification. In addition, many districts were facing a timeline to ensure that existing teachers meet "highly qualified" status in the content area in which they taught. Rural districts, where a single teacher might "cover" biology, chemistry, and physics (but have a degree in just one) were particularly hard-hit in the race to upgrade credentials.

Professional Development

As pedagogical knowledge has developed over time, as seen in the teaching of reading, districts have recognized that teachers must be kept "up to speed" in areas of need as determined by testing data. There have been broad efforts to educate teachers beyond early elementary in such topics as "reading in the content area." Similar efforts have followed in the teaching of mathematics and science.

Resistance and Responses

The trends toward continuous teacher education have set up tensions between the key stakeholders: teachers and their unions, districts, and the states. Unions have sought to maintain the contractual benefit of individual choice in use of professional development time and funds. Districts have been faced with expanding the funding dedicated to development to meet district-specific needs that they have determined. States, held accountable by federal funding programs, have sought to use their credentialling ability to lay groundwork.

The attempt to upgrade the teaching profession by instituting a master's degree requirement and multiple summer institutes aimed at specific content areas (reading, mathematics, science) to assist teachers and districts in meeting highly qualified requirements with their existing staff was regarded as overly burdensome for beginner teachers (particularly those in low-paid and rural districts). It was also found to have little impact on the efficacy of teachers.

Another problem is the lack of official direction and oversight for course-taking. In response, Ohio developed the Individual Professional Development Plan. Under this requirement, each teacher meets with a local supervisory group to plan the direction of their professional development. This group affirms not only that the proper number of hours are accomplished, but also that they follow an agreed-upon plan. The state has also developed a five-tier certification system to provide guidance. The various levels of certification are intended to support a long-range career ladder for teachers to take on the roles of master teacher, master lead teacher, and so on, by garnering years of experience as well as advanced degrees or documentation based on extensive classroom observations and the like.

To manage specific needs, many districts have formalized "professional development days," which are paid days during the regular school year. These allow the district to set the learning agenda. As they are single days scattered across the year, they are somewhat limited regarding the depth of content. As such, they are not always popular. Districts have taken to scheduling them mid-week to counter the tendency to call in sick and make a three-day weekend. Unions have sometimes taken a role in urging members to attend to avoid more punitive responses to poor attendance.

The use of teaching coaches and mentors, grounded in research into how to change classroom practice, provides intensive training to a small group of teachers who then provide sessions throughout the school year, coupled with modeling of new methods in actual classrooms, observing teachers and giving feedback. While effective, this is an added expense for districts, sometimes covered by short-term grant funding.

The Role of Unions in Teacher Retention

The teaching profession has benefited from unions in many ways. The AFT and the NEA together and separately have been very powerful forces in American education. They continue to advocate for increased salaries, improved working conditions, and educational reform.

Although the public generally views unions as working-class institutions, teacher unions historically have supported the professionalization of teaching. While teacher unions primarily support educators, it is also in the public's interest to support the teaching profession. Teachers are the key to our children's viable futures in personal, social, citizenship, and career development. Al Shanker, union leader extraordinaire, supported the establishment of the National Board of Professional Teaching Standards, as well as the standards reform movement, desegregation, and charter schools. Shanker's vision for charter schools was "for creative teacher-led schools that reach children in new ways" (Kahlenberg, 2003).

While business interests tend to oppose collective bargaining, it has proven effective in advancing the professionalism of educators. The bargaining process has had a direct effect on the conditions that children experience when in school. We have seen that in high-performing nations, teaching salaries are comparable to those in other professions. This is not necessarily so throughout the United States, but collective bargaining has also directly affected teachers' working conditions, such as granting increased autonomy in classroom management and inclusion in curricular decision-making. Historically, union leadership has fought boldly to protect public education from the narrow interests of businesses favoring tax abatements, which limit available funds to support schools.

In representing a female-dominated profession, teacher unions have had a singular role. In the 1800s, during the Common School era, Horace Mann saw teaching as a women's profession because women could be paid less than men. This was a common rationale, based on the stereotype that women did not support families. At the turn of the past century, women teachers were required to leave their jobs when they married, so they would not take the job of the head of a family. Throughout the Progressive era of American education, clear barriers prevented women moving beyond the classroom to leadership and administrative positions. Efficiency and good management were believed to be better implemented by male administrators. Dana Goldstein, in her book, *The Teacher Wars: A History of America's Most Embattled Profession* (2014), describes how the progressives argued for the results of teacher evaluations to be withheld from teachers. They did not view them as a tool for teacher improvement and development.

Goldstein notes that during the Progressive era, the powerful Chicago teachers union persuaded the Illinois legislature to promote teacher tenure to free teachers from local school politics that fostered favoritism and nepotism. Strong teacher unions, led by women, helped states to enact women suffrage laws and push for the Nineteenth Amendment (Goldstein. 2014, p. 178).

Unions in some states have also established through legislative action the right of teachers to bargain collectively. One detriment of union action has been the promotion of teacher seniority over effectiveness in reduction of staff situations. Seniority-based benefits have also contributed to the pooling of experienced teachers in some schools in large districts, to the detriment of "troubled" or undesirable buildings. Contract negotiations can be bitter, and teachers' strikes can be harmful to both the perception of teaching as a profession and children who miss time in school.

Caution is prudent in regarding unions as an exclusive voice in support of schools and students, as there are times when the rights of teachers and the needs of children diverge. Progressive educators in the past and present have understood that successful teachers make a difference in children's lives; however, we see this conflict playing out today with the COVID-19 epidemic. Teacher unions have responded to teachers\ concerns for the potential impact on their own and their families' health should they return to brick-and-mortar classrooms. Meanwhile some members of the public and policymakers advocated for return to buildings based on a spectrum of need, including the concern for lost learning and parental need to return to work. Conflicts in major cities among governors, mayors, boards of education, and teacher unions have occurred. Some unions were able to negotiate for teacher vaccinations and compliance with Centers for Disease Control guidelines for masks, social distancing, and other precautions. A new president, friendly to labor, promoted, and Congress passed, federal funds to help schools to make these safety adjustments.

Since the 1980s, there has been a national assault on unions, including those representing teachers. This has co-occurred with increased global privatization of schools. Our next chapter will discuss this phenomenon in detail. Currently, international businesses are working to privatize schools and profit from the educational system. Unions provide a progressive force to work with the public to promote educational equity across the globe (Compton & Weiner, 2008).

EMPOWERING EDUCATORS: LEARNING FROM OTHER COUNTRIES

Based on international assessments conducted by the OECD, students from many other industrial nations outperform U.S. students. OECD is an international organization that works "to build better policies for better lives." Its goal is to "shape policies that foster prosperity, equality, opportunity, and well-being for all." The United States is one among the thirty-seven nations that participate in OECD. OECD publishes a wealth of detailed information on member countries, including education statistics, available online.

A recent report from the OECD suggested that countries must make teaching more financially and intellectually attractive. The report urges all countries to improve teacher opportunities continuously, particularly in the use of technology and to promote more professional development. Ludger Schuknecht, OECD deputy secretary general, in launching the report, stated, "The acceleration of technological, economic and social changes make it imperative that our education systems adapt almost in real time" (Organisation for Economic Co-operation and Development, 2019). Andreas Schleicher, OECD director for education and skills, added:

> Governments should empower their teachers and school leaders with trust and autonomy they need to innovate and instill a collaborative culture in every school. They also need to better recognize the importance and value of involving teachers in designing better practices and policies to create classrooms fit for the future.

Key findings from this report have important implications for the American teaching profession. For example, 90 percent of teachers surveyed reported that the opportunity to contribute to children's development was a major motivation to become a teacher. About 61 percent say that a steady career pathway is important.

Best Practices

It is instructive to consider best practices of the teaching profession in countries with high-performing education systems. Darling-Hammond et al.'s work presents research results compiled by a team of experts examining excellent education systems around the world (Darling-Hammond et al., 2017). This study investigated seven countries on four continents to understand how they are preparing their students to meet the twenty-first-century challenges. These countries have built systems of improvements from which we can learn. Their recommendations, if adopted, can add significant value to our certification, teacher preparation, recruitment, retention, evaluation, and professional development systems.

The National Center on Education and the Economy (NCEE) summarized the Darling-Hammond recommendations in five policy briefs. What follows is a summary of these briefs, offered to stimulate the thinking of U.S.

policymakers and the public about possibilities in making teaching a more valued and honored profession in the United States.

Recruiting Teachers in High-Performing Education Systems

The first NCEE brief looks at teacher recruitment. It makes the point that in the countries studied, teaching is "an esteemed profession." Because the profession is highly valued, educator shortages are not a challenge. For example, in all surveyed countries (Australia, Canada, Finland, China, and Singapore), recruitment of highly capable individuals is taken seriously to ensure that the brightest and most committed pursue a teaching career. In these countries, teachers are well paid and are eager to join the profession. Schools have "an abundance of candidates to choose from." During the selection process, candidates must present evidence of a commitment to children and a capacity to work well with other adults in the system. In many of these countries, compensation is comparable to pay in other professions such as doctors, lawyers, computer scientists, and accountants (National Center on Education and the Economy, 2016c).

Increasing teachers' salaries in the United States could make teaching a more attractive profession. In the 1980s, under the leadership of Gerald Tirozzi, former Connecticut commissioner of education, the state increased teachers' salaries by up to $50,000. While this policy was in place for only a few years, highly qualified applicants from throughout the country came to Connecticut to teach. Policies, practices, and resources committed at the federal level could, over time, result in teaching, as a profession, being more competitive with other professions, drawing more highly qualified personnel into the field.

Preparing Teachers in High-Performing Education Systems

The second brief, focused on preparing teachers, emphasizes that demonstration of knowledge, skills, and dispositions are the key elements to teachers' success in the countries studied. "Strong preparation programs and intensive mentoring in the early years of teaching are essential." While there is variability in the preparation and induction into the profession, "universities in these countries are not trying to prepare a large number of teachers who will enter and the leave the profession quickly. They are investing in individuals who will stay in the profession for a substantial career" (National Center on Education and the Economy, 2016b).

In these high-performing countries, admission into teacher preparation programs is limited to the top 30 percent of secondary school graduates. In general, in the United States, the top 50 percent of secondary school graduates are admitted into teaching programs. This puts a great reliance on districts to be able to discern the fittest from a very broad field of applicants. Rethinking the admission standards of teacher preparation programs would likely result in a better pool of applicants for districts to consider.

In the countries studied, teacher education programs focus on strong academic content. Undergraduates are required to major in a subject discipline. Elementary and middle-school teachers are prepared in all content areas in which they teach. The programs also distinguish between preparation for professions that have disciplinary knowledge, such as chemistry or physics, and the preparation to teach such subjects. The international programs emphasize the importance of content-specific pedagogy. Thus, a chemistry teacher, in addition to possessing the knowledge required of a chemist, must also understand how one teaches chemistry. And such understanding, or pedagogy, differs across content areas (Schulman, 1986).

Teachers who have studied in the graduate programs are encouraged to advance in different supportive roles in their schools. Roles that support teaching and learning may include master teachers, mentors, and curriculum developers. Programs emphasize that teacher education standards are the framework for professional growth and development throughout teachers' careers (National Center on Education and the Economy, 2016a).

One commonality is that the teacher education programs "are grounded in research and prepare teachers to use and conduct research." Teacher education programs in these countries have well-mentored clinical experiences. Candidates spend time in classrooms with expert mentors who model and coach them on professional practice (National Center on Education and the Economy, 2016d).

An advantage observed in the countries is that preparation and induction are part of the same system that fosters professional learning throughout a teacher's career. Unlike the United States, where there are thousands of institutions preparing teachers, a few institutions prepare teachers in Finland, where the teacher training school is an important feature. The training school budget is allocated to the university through the Ministry of Education and Culture and the school serves neighborhood students. Student teachers have their own place in the school: activities are defined to enhance student teachers and practicing teachers' reflection on practice (National Center on Education and the Economy, 2016d).

The United States could benefit from similar institutions whose purpose is to support teacher education students in making connections between theory and practice. Teacher preparation institutions in the United States should look carefully at how high-performing nations train their teachers.

Ongoing Professional Development in High-Performing Education Systems

Empowered Educators: Developing High Quality Teaching, the third NCEE brief, describes how countries put structures and opportunities in place to improve educators' knowledge and practices. All countries in the study have aligned incentives to encourage continued learning. These include recertification requirements, opportunities for professional advancement, time to collaborate with colleagues, and time to conduct and measure the results of their own research. Schools also foster peer observation and structure the school day to allow time for these activities (National Center on Education and the Economy, 2016a).

Darling-Hammond et al. point out that the evidence is clear. Rather than focusing on the characteristics of individual teachers, collaboration among educators is critical to student success ((Darling-Hammond et al., 2017). Teachers in the United States are isolated. The research tells us that the best teaching is a team sport. We must redesign our schools to make time and opportunities for collaboration.

The NCEE found that across highly effective systems, time is allotted for joint work in curriculum planning and lesson plan study. Unlike the United States, teachers are not in front of their students every day. Teachers' organizations in these countries play a greater role in offering professional development opportunities. All the countries have career ladders with defined roles and responsibilities. Professional development experts, who are teachers, have great credibility within the profession (National Center on Education and the Economy, 2016e).

School administrators and union leadership in the United States could benefit from developing processes and structures that allow teachers to observe each other's practice, study each other's lesson plans and formative assessments, and conduct action research to discover and evaluate best practices.

Evaluation and Feedback in High-Performing Education Systems

The fourth policy brief, *Empowered Educators: Teacher Appraisal and Feedback*, found that a key element in all systems was continual appraisal. The report explains that "the goals of these teacher appraisal systems tend to provide information to help teachers improve their performance, rather than identify and sanction low performers. These systems, by and large, do not expect to fire teachers." The teacher appraisal systems are linked to national systems of professional standards of practice that include educators' contributions to their schools and communities. The teacher appraisal systems are also linked to career opportunities and compensation (National Center on Education and the Economy, 2016d).

As noted earlier, under RTTT, teacher evaluation systems required that 50 percent of an evaluation be based on student learning outcomes. While this requirement was, in part, a response to findings that most prior evaluations consisted of mere checklists, culminating in a majority of teachers being rated as "satisfactory" or "outstanding" (McLaughlin, 1984), the shift in focus to the inclusion of student outcomes has been equally problematic. As a result of this change, many teachers fear professional evaluation by administrators and do not see this as a meaningful process to support their professional growth and development. To arrive at systems that support teacher growth, policymakers need to sharpen their focus on improvement, ensure that feedback is helpful, and provide ongoing support for teacher growth.

Like other states, the Ohio Teacher Evaluation System is currently moving forward from a system that relied on growth measures, purported to account for learning by a student cohort during their time with a specific teacher, to a broader range of high-quality student data. This may enable teachers to make better use of newer technologies that provide highly focused "just-in-time" student data. Accountability assessments that rely on summative, end-of-year measures are too broad and come too late in the school year to support teaching and learning improvement. The new crop of technology-assisted assessments is better suited to both content and skill development at the individual student level, as well as guiding teachers in ways to meet specific student needs.

Career Development and Leadership in High-Performing Education Systems

Empowered Educators: The Teaching Career and Leadership for the Profession, the fifth policy brief, makes very clear that teaching is not a job but a profession. In successful systems, the vision for the profession is that teachers have many embedded career opportunities. Unlike the United States, teachers do not have to abandon teaching to advance to administration. Career ladders are based on interests and capabilities. Advancing teachers may develop curriculum and assessments, mentor teachers, or provide professional development. Advances are linked to appraisal systems and aligned with the agreed-upon professional standards and compensation. Teacher leadership thrives in these systems (National Center on Education and the Economy, 2016e).

In the 1990s, state legislatures provided incentives for career ladders. Sadly, fiscal incentives disappeared at the turn of the century and so did career ladders. As Darling-Hammond et al. note, "Education is a lever for international competitiveness" (2017, p. 111). We know that when national, state, and local policies are developed, to be successful, they must fit existing policy systems, cultural norms, and professional practices. Obviously, we do not want to adopt policies, processes, or structures without deep conviction. Too often, teachers have called national and state policies "the flavor of the month" and act as if they do not exist, hoping that they will pass away, as have many before.

It is interesting that OECD studies make it very clear that policies in high-performing nations are not static but dynamic. These nations are committed to looking at data to be used for continuous improvement. This disposition is embedded in their education cultures. Lee Schulman and Darling-Hammond note that high-performing countries understand that policies provide guidelines and set conditions under which good decisions allow professionals to respond local conditions and student needs (Darling-Hammond, 2003; Schulman, 1986). This approach, which Darling-Hammond calls "professional policy," uses professional standards to hold educators accountable rather than viewing them as prescriptions for practice that can mitigate against teachers from using their professional judgment to address issues of localism and student needs (Thompson & Zeuli, 1999).

TEACHING AS HUMAN RESOURCE

The policies and practices of the teaching profession are reminiscent of the story of the cobbler: The cobbler's purpose is to make shoes for the villagers, yet the cobbler's children have no shoes. The teaching profession is about human growth and student development, but it also must be about developing the human resources necessary to accomplish this goal. As noted by the CAP, school districts must improve their human capital systems in order to attract great teachers.

> Most districts have not adapted their human capital systems to the modern market, despite the increasing importance of attracting talented teachers. Research shows that investment in human capital improves organizational performance—including team effectiveness, employee retention and innovation in both the private and public sectors. (Konoske-Graf, Partelow, & Benner, 2016)

OBSERVATIONS

A Nation Still at Risk

"A Nation at Risk" generated many reports and some policy that impacted teacher education. Resulting reforms have ranged from master's degree or board certification requirements to alternative certification programs to widen the pool of teacher candidates. A thread of concern for accountability for student learning has sought to either blame or empower teacher preparation programs, building principals or state education departments.

While there have been some improvements in teacher education since "A Nation at Risk," the problems it highlighted, as well as solutions offered by the Report of the National Commission, are largely unaddressed. The ongoing search for solutions is symptomatic of the tensions between intellectual and anti-intellectual approaches, as attributed to Hofstadter earlier, as well as Sizer's concern for depth over breadth. In addition, the ongoing search for solutions is hampered by the lack of resolution of the divergent viewpoints regarding how to respond. Is the field best served by a strong focus on content or ought pedagogy take precedence?

The Teaching Profession

Teaching, as a profession that encourages thinking and questioning, may not be as honored a profession in America today as it is in other countries and cultures. While we cannot change the present and historical anti-intellectualism of American culture, we can work to make teaching a more valued profession in the United States.

Making teaching into a profession that is both effective and respected will require rethinking the current system of teacher recruitment and retention to retirement in order to align to the principles of effective human resource systems. We can learn from the study of human resource policies in other professions. We can also learn from teacher preparation, certification, and professional development, as demonstrated by countries with more effective education systems.

To implement the needed changes, it will be necessary to influence nation, state, and local policymakers and educators around a new mental model of teaching that goes beyond a one-teacher to one-classroom set of expectations of the profession. Such visioning may include new roles and responsibilities for teachers to develop highly effective online lessons to be employed by others. It may include new systems of supervision that reward challenge and growth rather than compliance. It may include enhanced local partnerships for learning that draw on community resources.

Teacher Preparation

There are strengths and weaknesses to both behaviorist and constructivist philosophies and their accompanying pedagogies. Therefore, all educators need an understanding of both philosophies and the pedagogies associated with them. Teacher training programs should not be biased toward one approach or another. Teachers need multiple techniques to meet the individual and collective needs of their students.

It is very difficult for traditional institutions, particularly colleges and universities, to reimagine what public schools could look like if we started over again. If academics can create a new vision for pre-K–12 education that supports equity and democracy, the issues of improving educator preparation would be easier to implement. We cannot think about reforms of the profession without thinking about the redesign of our pre-K–12 system. As universities must rethink their mission, goals, structures, and processes in a new technological age, professors and elementary and secondary educators should work together. They should reinvent the lab schools so popular during the Progressive era, to reimagine a new vision of professional development schools that can serve as a model to policymakers at the national, state, and local levels.

Teacher Recruitment and Retention

The CAP suggests that if school districts are to be successful twenty-first-century organizations, they need to develop and use twenty-first-century policies, programs, and tools to recruit and retain teachers (Konoske-Graf, Partelow, & Benner, 2016). The field of human resources tells us that educators must be vigilant in understanding market changes, new emerging technologies, and communication methods, as we seek to recruit and retain the best individuals for the jobs. Companies that attract and develop strong employees by prioritizing recruitment, investing in professional growth opportunities, and building positive work cultures, tend to have greater efficiency and better outcomes. The CAP surveyed nationally representative school districts and found a lack of modernization of human resource systems. This is in spite of the research that demonstrates the importance of high-quality teachers to improve student outcomes (Konoske-Graf, Partelow, & Benner, 2016).

What can educators learn from the new developments in human resources that successful companies employ? Seven major best practices from human resources could help policymakers and districts to better nurture both employees and students.

As we consider recruitment, retention, and professional development of educators, we should keep these best practices in mind.

Best practices include:

1. communications systems: internal and external systems aligned with the organization's strategies for optimum efficiency; open communications about strategy, finances, operations, and idea sharing;

2. motivating compensation systems: fair, transparent, and performance-based;
3. security systems that provide physically and psychologically safe workplaces;
4. self-managed and effective teams that permeate the organization management structure;
5. professional development in relevant knowledge and skills, including feedback, coaching, and peer learning;
6. hiring the right people—people who add value to the organization using new and emerging digital recruitment tools that also assess ability, trainability, and commitment; and
7. creating a flat and egalitarian organization and culture—everyone deserves equal respect and helps in promoting and sharing ideas (van Vulpen, 2020).

Ongoing Change

The pressures of ongoing change suggest a need to alter the traditional means of recruitment and retention employed by schools. Comprehensive change must consider the full range of tasks from hiring, through onboarding and supervision, development, career ladders, compensation and ultimately leave-taking. To undertake such change suggests an examination of sources from outside of American education. This includes other professions in this country, as well as systems of education in other countries.

Teacher Demographics

Although implicit bias, which operates at an unconscious level, can be managed through diversity training that builds awareness and focuses on strategies for change (Flannery, 2015), it is also important to increase the presence of teachers of color in classrooms. The Learning Policy Institute has reported improved outcomes (academic performance, graduation, and college attendance rates) when students of color are taught by teachers of color. However, benefits also accrued to all students, regardless of race (Heubeck, 2020).

Many of the strategies recommended for recruiting diverse teachers mirror those recommended as good practices for recruiting teachers generally: use of data to determine and forecast needs, building relationships with various helpful institutions, building and using personal relationships in recruiting; as well as training to manage existing bias in recruiters and decision makers (RELNorthwest, n.d.). Some approaches, however, are more proactive, such as "grow your own" programs. These programs typically focus on cultivating non-licensed staff to acquire degrees and move into licensed teaching positions. These staff are frequently more racially and linguistically diverse than existing teachers and represent a rich resource. Other approaches may focus longer term by exposing high school students to benefits of a teaching career (Heubeck, 2020).

In addition, attention must be paid to the retention of teachers of color. Teachers of color, particularly males, frequently experience isolation in largely White faculty. Efforts to combat isolation and improve retention should be guided by data, have dedicated funding, and allow minority voices to set goals and agenda (Heubeck, 2020).

Applying International Lessons

Nations with high-performing education systems have a culture that highly esteems the teaching profession with strong selective standards for entry into the profession. They provide financial support for preparation and professional learning. Strong professional standards are well grounded in curriculum content and pedagogy and emphasize research-informed methodology and collaborative peer learning. These countries have strong clinical training and career pathways for teacher leadership and equity. Readers of this book may want to follow OECD as they monitor and research educational outcomes, policies, and improvements. We can make teaching a more valued and honored profession through study of empowered educators from across the world.

This chapter described our history in trying to make teaching a more valued and honored profession. We have been resistant to change. We can no longer afford to do so.

REFERENCES

Aldeman, C. (2017, January 18). *The teacher evaluation revamp, in hindsight.* Education Next. https://www.educationnext.org/the-teacher-evaluation-revamp-in-hindsight-obama-administration-reform/.

Barnum, M. (2021, April 6). Despite pandemic, there's little evidence of rising teacher turnover—yet. *Chalkbeat.*

Bohan, C. H., & Hull, J. W. (2007). Gender and the evolution of normal school education: A historical analysis of teacher education institutions. *Educational Foundations,* 3–26.

Buttner, A. (2020, January 14). *Teacher recruitment strategies: Tried and true ways to build your applicant pool.* Frontline Education. https://www.frontlineeducation.com/blog/teacher-recruitment-strategies/.

The Coalition of Essential Schools. (2021, March 6). *Common principles.* Essential Schools. http://essentialschools.org/.

Coleman, J. (1966). *Equality of educational opportunity.* Washington, DC: U.S. Department of Health, Education and Welfare.

Compton, M., & Weiner, L. E. (2008). *The global assault on teaching, teachers, and their unions: Stories for resistance.* New York: Palgrave Macmillan.

Crook, T. R., Todd, S. Y., Combs, J. G., Woehr, D. J., & Ketchen, Jr., D. J. (2011). Does human capital matter? A meta-analysis of the relationship between human capital and firm performance. *Journal of Applied Psychology*, 443–456.

Darling-Hammond, L. (1997). *Doing what matters most: Investing in quality teaching.* New York: National Commission on Teaching and America's Future.

Darling-Hammond, L. (2003). *No dream denied: A pledge to America's children.* New York: National Commission on Teaching and America's Future.

Darling-Hammond, L., Burns, D., Campbell, C., Goodwin, A. L., Hammerness, K., Low, E.-L., . . . Zeichner, K. (2017). *Empowered educators: How high-performing systems shape teaching quality around the world.* San Francisco, CA: Jossey-Bass.

Education Commission of the States. (2000). Two paths to quality teaching and America's future. *Spring Steering Committee Meeting of the Education Commission of the States.* Cheyenne, Wyoming: ECS.

Flannery, M. (2015, September 9). *When implicit bias shapes teacher expectations.* neaToday. https://www.nea.org/advocating-for-change/new-from-nea/when-implicit-bias-shapes-teacher-expectations.

Goldhaber, D. (2016). In schools, teacher quality matters most: Today's research reinforces Coleman's findings. *Education Next*, 16(2), 56–62.

Goldstein, D. (2014). *The teacher wars: A history of America's most embattled profession.* USA: First Anchor Books. New York.

Hamner, P. C., Hughes, G., McClure, C., Reeves, C., & Salgado, D. (2004). *Rural teacher recruitment and retention practices: A review of the research literature, national survey of rural superintendents, and case studies of programs in Virginia.* Charleston, WV: Appalachia Educational Laboratory at Edvantia.

Hansen, M. L., Lien, D. S., Cavalluzzo, L. C., & Wenger, J. W. (2004). *Relative pay and teacher retention: An empirical analysis in a large urban district.* Alexandria, VA: The CNA Corporation.

Heubeck, E. (2020, June 30). *Recruiting and retaining teachers of color: Why it matters, ways to do it.* EducationWeek. https://www.edweek.org/leadership/recruiting-and-retaining-teachers-of-color-why-it-matters-ways-to-do-it/2020/06.

Hofstadter, R. (1963). *Anti-intellectualism in American Life.* Vintage.

Iasevoli, B. (2017, March 28). *Trump signs bill scrapping teacher-prep rules.* Education Week. https://www.edweek.org/teaching-learning/trump-signs-bill-scrapping-teacher-prep-rules/2017/03.

Inside Higher Ed. (2016, October 13). *New accountability for teacher prep.* Inside Higher Ed. https://www.insidehighered.com/news/2016/10/13/obama-administration-releases-final-rules-teacher-preparation-programs.

Kahlenberg, R. D. (2003). *Tough liberal: Albert Shanker and the battles over schools, unions, race, and democracy.* New York: Columbia University Press.

Kirschner, P., Sweller, J., & Clark, R. (2006). Why minimum guidance during instruction does not work: An analysis of the failure of constructivists, discovery, problem-based, experiential and inquiry-based teaching. *Educational Psychologist*, 75–86.

Konoske-Graf, A., Partelow, L., & Benner, M. (2016, December 22). *To attract great teachers, school districts must improve their human capital system.* Center for American Progress. https://www.americanprogress.org/issues/education-k-12/reports/2016/12/22/295574/to-attract-great-teachers-school-districts-must-improve-their-human-capital-systems/.

Labaree, D. F. (2008). An uneasy relationship: the history of teacher education in the university. In M. Cochran-Smith, S. Feiman-Nemser, & J. McIntyre (eds), *Handbook of research on teacher education* (pp. 290–306). New York: Routledge.

Lemann, R. (2014, September/October). The Tea Party is timeless. *Columbia Journalism Review.* Retrieved August 10, 2022, from https://archives.cjr.org/second_read/richard_hofstadter_tea_party.php.

McGarvey, E. (2022, April 12). Abbott elementary finally does right by America's most wrongly portrayed profession. *Slate.*

McLaughlin, M. W. (1984). Teacher evaluation and school improvement. *Teachers College Record*, 193–207.

McNeil, M., & Gewertz, C. (2013, June 11). *States seek flexibility during common-test transition.* EdWeek. https://www.edweek.org/policy-politics/states-seek-flexibility-during-common-test-transition/2013/06.

Mehta, J., & Fine, S. (2019). *In search of deeper meaning.* Cambridge, MA: Harvard University Press.

Nagen, N., & Shapiro, E. (1999). *The developmental-interaction approach to education: Retrospect and prospect.* Occasional Paper Series. https://educate.bankstreet.edu/cgi/viewcontent.cgi?article=1250&context=occasional-paper-series.

National Center on Education and the Economy. (2016a). *Empowered educators: Developing high quality teaching.* NCEE-Empowered Educators. http://ncee.org/wp-content/uploads/2017/02/ProfLearningPolicyBrief.pdf.

National Center on Education and the Economy. (2016b). *Empowered educators: Preparing profession-ready teachers.* NCEE-Empowered Educators. http://ncee.org/wp-content/uploads/2017/02/PreparationPolicyBrief.pdf.

National Center on Education and the Economy. (2016c). *Empowered educators: Recruiting and selecting excellent teachers.* NCEE-Empowered Educators. http://ncee.org/wp-content/uploads/2017/02/RecruitmentPolicyBrief.pdf.

National Center on Education and the Economy. (2016d). *Empowered educators: Teacher appraisal and feedback.* NCEE-Empowered Educators. http://nccc.org/wp-content/uploads/2017/02/AppraisalPolicyBrief.pdf.

National Center on Education and the Economy. (2016e). *Empowered educators: The teaching career and leadership for the profession.* NCEE-Empowered Educators. http://ncee.org/wp-content/uploads/2017/02/CareerLaddersPolicyBrief.pdf.

National Commission on Teaching and America's Future. (1996). *What matters most: Teaching for America's future.* ERIC. https://files.eric.ed.gov/fulltext/ED395931.pdf.

Nguyen, T., & Springer, M. (2019, December 4). *Reviewing the evidence on teacher attrition and retention.* Brown Center Chalkboard. https://www.brookings.edu/blog/brown-center-chalkboard/2019/12/04/reviewing-the-evidence-on-teacher-attrition-and-retention/.

Organisation for Economic Co-operation and Development. (2019). *TALIS 2018 results (Volume I): Teachers and school leaders as lifelong learners.* Paris: OECD Publishing.

Potter, H., & Burris, M. (2020, December 2). *Here is what school integration in America looks like today.* The Century Foundation. https://tcf.org/content/report/school-integration-america-looks-like-today/?agreed=1.

Reich, J. (2020). *Failure to disrupt: Why technology alone can't transform education.* Cambridge, MA and London: Harvard University Press.

RELNorthwest. (n.d.). *9 Strategies for recruiting, hiring and retaining diverse teachers.* https://ies.ed.gov/ncee/edlabs/regions/northwest/pdf/teacher-attrition.pdf.

Schulman, L. S. (1986). Those who understand: Knowledge growth in teaching. *Educational Researcher*, 15(2), 4–14.

Simon, N., & Johnson, S. M. (2015). Teacher turnover in high-poverty schools: What we know and can do. *Teachers College Record*, 117(3), 1–36.

Sizer, T. R. (1984). *Horace's compromise: The dilemma of the American high school.* Boston, MA and New York: Houghton Mifflin.

Solmon, L., & Agam, K. F. (2007). *How stakeholders can support teacher quality.* Information Age Publishing.

The Thomas B. Fordham Foundation. (1999, April 20). *The teachers we need and how to get more of them.* Thomas B. Fordham Institute. https://fordhaminstitute.org/national/research/teachers-we-need-and-how-get-more-them.

Thompson, C. L., & Zeuli, J. S. (1999). The frame and the tapestry: Standards-based reform and professional development. In L. Darling-Hammond, & G. Sykes (eds), *Teaching as the learning profession: Handbook of policy and practice* (pp. 341–375). San Francisco, CA: Jossey-Bass.

U.S. Department of Education. (1983). *A nation at risk.* Archived Information. https://www2.ed.gov/pubs/NatAtRisk/risk.html.

USA FACTS. (2022, May 23). *Who are the nation's 4 million teachers?* USA FACTS. https://usafacts.org/articles/who-are-the-nations-4m-teachers/.

van Vulpen, E. (2020). *Seven human resource best practices: A mini-guide to HRM.* AIHR Digital. https://www.digitalhrtech.com/human-resource-best-practices/.

Warkentien, S. (2015). *Stable or changing? Racial/ethnic compositions in American public schools, 2000–2015.* Teacher's College Record. https://www.tcrecord.org/Content.asp?ContentId=22776.

What matters most: Teaching for America's future. (1996). teachingquality.org. https://www.teachingquality.org/wp-content/uploads/2018/04/What_Matters_Most.pdf.

Chapter 3

School Choice

SCHOOL CHOICE

Most children in the United States, about 95 percent, according to pre-pandemic data, attend a school in a public K-12 district. Students in these districts are assigned to schools according to their place of residence (USA Facts, 2022). These schools are supported with income, property, and sales tax dollars, depending on how each state allocates school funding. Many parents choose a home based on information from state report cards or other sources so their children can attend a "good" school (Council of Chief State School Officers, 2022).

School choice describes a range of K–12 options, beyond the local public school district that are available to families. Throughout the history of American education, as outlined in this book's Introduction, many parents have chosen from private religious schools, prep schools, or academies to provide their children with specific types of education. In 2015, 5.8 million students were enrolled in Catholic, conservative Christian, other religious, or nonsectarian schools. Traditionally, parents must pay tuition to attend private schools (Wang, Rathburn, & Musu, 2019).

In 2022, in thirty-two states, parents have the option within the public school system to enroll their children in charter schools, magnet schools, or provide homeschooling. School choice is intended to allow public education funds to be used to support alternative learning environments.

The NCLB, the federal bipartisan reauthorization of ESEA enacted in 2001, specified two roles for parents. One role, that of a stakeholder having a voice in school improvement and accountability, continued an expectation that was a part of Title I funding beginning in the 1970s. However, NCLB added an additional parental role, that of a consumer of education. In this role, the parents were encouraged to access a range of educational choices on behalf of their children.

Such choices, initially focused on the families of students in poorly performing schools, included afterschool tutoring programs—at public expense—or the option of transfer to another school within the same district that had a better track record. The belief underlying the public support for this parent as consumer role was faith that a marketplace of education options would provide immediate relief to students in poorly performing schools and would also, through competition, result in an overall improvement across schools.

Since that time, opportunities for choice in public education have expanded, along with some blurring of lines between "public education" in a traditional sense and public funding for education that was once considered to be "private." There are many reasons why policymakers, educators, the business community, and parents advocate for school choice.

School choice has become a political football. Some families believe that the best educational opportunities for their children are those outside of the traditional district and desire public assistance in paying tuition. Some argue that such support would benefit low-income families, who are unable to afford tuition. Others argue that dedicating some public dollars to schools outside of districts creates a beneficial competition that will result in improvement of district schools. Others believe that private and alternative schools are always better than public schools.

A counterargument claims that school choice takes money from the public school system, thereby undermining the quality of public education. Such undermining is particularly problematic if the alternative schools have a religious affiliation or are not held accountable for the quality of education or equitable access by students. Some people argue that school choice also takes the best students out of the public school system, leaving districts in the position of being a last resort for those families having the greatest (and most expensive) level of need, such as those with students having a disability or those with language barriers and other challenges.

This chapter will explore the historical roots of public and private education, how school attendance zones historically limited choice, and concerns for racial and economic equity. This will provide a basis by which to examine multiple developments under the umbrella of "school choice," including recent support for for-profit education options.

It is important to bear in mind some critical questions as we examine the recent expansion of choice. First is whether increased choice has provided meaningful options, particularly to those otherwise poorly served through district schools. If the alternative to a poorly performing district school is merely a list of other poorly performing options, is the choice truly meaningful? Further, as we look across the broad expanse of public education (which now includes multiple non-district options), has choice brought about systemic improvement? And who (or what) have we sacrificed on the altar of individual choice?

HISTORICAL ROOTS OF PUBLIC AND PRIVATE EDUCATION

While Americans are accustomed to the notion of public education systems and the expectation that such schools are available to all, our public systems evolved from more diverse offerings. As outlined in the Introduction to this book, the earliest roots of American education were both diverse and reliant on private support. Choice in education began as a function of what a family could afford and what might be available across a changing landscape as schools opened and closed. Tracing this history is vital to understanding why the public school system is the way it is today and realizing the possibilities and limitations of "school choice."

American Foundations: Religious and Private Schools

In reviewing this book's Introduction of the history of American education, it is clear that American public education, as generally understood today to be a state function with responsibilities to all students, did not spring fully formed from any single vision. Rather, it evolved from various theories about what education should include and who it should serve. Families, churches, and employers, not formal educational institutions, provided the first broad sources of literacy.

The earliest American institutions that can be categorized as "schools" would by today's understanding be considered to be largely "private." Even the various rural schools, having close community ties and open to all (White) students, generally operated on a tuition basis with accountability to a board comprised primarily of parents. Urban areas prior to the mid-1800s featured a wide range of options including academies and seminaries, church-run schools, boarding schools, and Latin grammar schools. Funding for these institutions was derived from a variety of sources, including philanthropic grants, public tax dollars, and student tuition. In some communities, religious schools provided the backbone of "public" education and received public funding (Ravitch, 2001, pp. 6–7).

Common Schools and the Move to Universal Public Education

The notion of systems of "common schools," widely attributed to the efforts of Horace Mann during the Common School era between 1830 and 1865, grew out of public concern for both an educated electorate and for dissemination of common values. The movement gained acceptance from a broad desire that children learn, in an academic sense, but also attracted those with moral concerns. In particular, some advocates were mistrustful of "values" immigrant children might learn from their uneducated parents, while others saw Catholic education as a particular threat (Ravitch, 2001, pp. 9–10).

In Columbus, Ohio, the emerging public school system, in the mid-1840s, grew around the inclusion of "a free public school where the Protestant Bible was taught" and instruction was in the German language, using German methods of instruction. German Catholic families were incorporated into the Catholic parochial system (Uhas-Sauer, 2019).

By the early twentieth century, anti-Catholic sentiment led to attempts to position the public systems as the only acceptable option for education. Several states enacted legislation to outlaw nonpublic (primarily Catholic) schools. The Supreme Court ruled in 1925 (*Pierce v. Society of Sisters of Holy Names of Jesus and Mary*) that such attempts exceeded states' reasonable power to regulate education by forcing children "to accept instruction from public school teachers only." Later legal challenges resulted in the Court in 1963 (*Abington School District v. Schempp*), striking down state laws requiring such practices as prayer and Bible reading which had come to be accepted as common "non-denominational" (but Protestant) practices across public schools in many states (Ravitch, 2001, pp. 11–12).

The Choice to Opt Out: A Legacy of Private Education

The earlier rulings both endorsed a role for religious education and drew a clear line of separation between public and parochial education. Thus, as public and universal education developed, a parallel set of options also developed—providing a choice for those of means or access to private scholarship funds.

A range of private school choice options continue across the United States today, including those having a religious background as well as high-priced and elite "prep schools." The percentage of students attending private schools rose to a high of 12.8 percent in 1959 (Peterson, 2001a, p. 262). By 2017, the number had fallen to 10.1 percent, a slight decline from the previous year (National Center for Education Statistics, 2021).

According to survey data from the U.S. Department of Education, private schools are slightly more likely to be located in suburbs than cities or rural areas. Average school size is reported as 142 students; however, 46 percent of private schools enrolled fewer than fifty students. About 69 percent of private school students are White, with 10 percent Hispanic, 9 percent Black and 6 percent Asian (Institute of Education Sciences, 2017).

Data collected by the National Catholic Educational Association noted an influx of students from public schools into Catholic Schools during the COVID-19 pandemic. They noted that high numbers of families were Catholic (68 percent) and White (66 percent) and reported household income greater than $100,000. The association articulated a concern that this presented a departure from their original mission of serving immigrant and other marginalized families (National Catholic Educational Association, 2021, p. 1).

Many private schools operate at a low cost and charge a modest tuition, with some studies reporting a per-pupil cost to be roughly half of the cost of public schools. Studies of the quality of education provided vary, with some indication that Catholic schools may provide an education at least equivalent to public schools, with a particular advantage for low-income students (Peterson, 2001a, pp. 263–264).

A small segment of American private education consists of highly selective and high-priced elite schools, having reputations for the number of their students accepted into the prestigious halls of the ivy leagues. While fewer than 2 percent of American students attend these independent schools, their graduates comprise 24 percent of Yale's class of 2024; 25 percent of Princeton's and 29 percent at Brown and Dartmouth. Indicators are that students at these schools receive a superior education (based on advanced coursework and preparation for college success). Students and their families experience (or bring with them) a pressure to succeed, particularly in terms of elite college acceptance. Families also encounter pressure to contribute to various fundraising efforts (Flanagan, 2021).

While tuition at such schools may surpass $50,000 annually, most reserve some space for promising low-income and minority students. As reported anonymously through an Instagram campaign, many students reported that their elite education was accompanied by experiences of racial stereotyping and an expectation of "sacrificing Blackness" in exchange for the experience (Flanagan, 2021).

The Evolution of Public School Districts and School Attendance Zones

Within the realm of what most would recognize as "public" education, that is publicly funded, having public oversight and responsibility to and for all students generally, "choice" of schools is largely a function of where a family lives. States are typically subdivided into districts. Districts are subdivided into attendance zones. The school "choice" afforded (and limited) by each family's ability to choose where they live has resulted in a contentious sense of entitlement whenever redrawing boundaries is considered. This was epitomized when Ohio's former governor John Kasich, faced with voters unhappy with a possible school district annexation, articulated, "I am arguing for all the people who worked all their lives to send their kids to the school they want to send them to" (Jacobs, 1998, p. 144).

It is important to be aware that school districts evolved differently in Southern and Northern states. In the largely agrarian South, where populations were geographically scattered, districts tended to be countywide. In the more industrialized North, as recounted by Nikole Hannah-Jones, Northern counties frequently comprise multiple population centers, and districts align with cities, towns, and, eventually, suburbs (*The New York Times*, 2019). Such districts evolved over time. As an example, while Congress, via the Land Ordinance of 1785, made land grants with the stipulation that every township include parcels set aside for schools, the Ohio legislature failed to ensure that this happened. It was not until the 1850 Constitutional Convention that the General Assembly was directed to "secure a thorough and efficient system of common schools throughout the state." Even so, development of school "systems" was haphazard with both public and private entities contributing for many years (Uhas-Sauer, 2019).

In the United States, local school boards set attendance zones for the public schools in their district. A school attendance zone is an outline of an area where students are assigned to attend a particular public school. School zones were generally established so that students could attend schools closest to their homes. However, there were exceptions. As an example, the Columbus Board of Education was created by the Ohio legislature in 1845. Among the initial rules the Board passed was a specification that all children were to attend the school closest to their home. But boys over the age of ten were to attend the nearest "male school," to ensure that they be taught by male teachers. In addition, by 1855, the Columbus school district included four schools for African American students and three German schools (Uhas-Sauer, 2019).

*Setting Parameters on Choice: Southern Segregation
and Northern Redlining*

This book's Introduction, with its outline of the history of American education, relates the reality of racial segregation from the colonial era in the seventeenth century to the present. Despite the 1896 Supreme Court ruling in *Plessy v. Ferguson*, both sanctioning segregation of schools and other public accommodation, and setting a bar of equal facilities, districts across the South blatantly maintained schools for Blacks and Whites that were separate and unequal. In 1917, education expenditures for Black students in the South averaged only $0.29 for every dollar spent on White students. By 1950, this had increased to only $0.75 (Schneider & Berkshire, 2020, pp. 26–27). Under these Jim Crow conditions, Black families and communities found themselves "doubly taxed" as they attempted, through contributions of time and money, to bring their poorly resourced public schools up to the level of those available for White children (Ramsey, 2017).

Segregation in the North was subtler. In Northern states, school boards tended to achieve segregation unofficially through gerrymandering attendance zones. Typical of Northern states, in 1881, Columbus's Black population had outgrown the single school then educating African American children, which was built in 1871. In addition, the Black population at that time included pockets across the city, rather than being centrally located in a single area, so that multiple new Black schools would be required across the city to maintain segregation. Hence, for a time, schools were racially mixed. By 1909, however, a new junior high school was constructed, and later expanded, as an all-Black school. By 1922, through manipulating attendance zones, the district had established four Black elementary schools and concentrated Black students in a single high school (Jacobs, 1998, pp. 12–14).

Furthermore, Cleveland, Ohio, received several waves of Southern Black families moving north in search of industrial jobs throughout the early twentieth century. As the Black population grew, housing options available to them were limited to certain neighborhoods. By 1950, Black families lived in only thirty-nine of the city's 206 census tracts, comprising 75 percent of the population in those tracts. This resulted in overcrowding of the schools in the mostly Black Glenville neighborhood. Resistant to redrawing attendance zones to allow the use of available space in neighboring White neighborhoods, the School Board denied kindergarten to 1,500 Glenville students in 1956. By 1962, the Board implemented a system of busing Black children to White schools where they were taught in separate classrooms. A proposal to build three new schools that would keep the Black students in "their own" neighborhoods (with over 12,000 available spaces in existing schools throughout the district) led to 1964 protests by the Congress of Racial Equality and others. Several lawsuits against the Board followed, but it was not until 1976 that a court finding of intentional racial segregation resulted in a desegregation plan, which was implemented in 1979 (Kaeser, 2020, pp. 33–34, 50–53).

The use of gerrymandered attendance zones within districts is only one piece of the picture of *de facto* segregation. The end of Reconstruction in 1877 ushered in a pattern of both legal and extra-legal efforts at maintaining racial separation and protection of opportunities for Whites. Multiple racial zoning laws sought to prevent race mixing in neighborhoods. The Supreme Court decision in *Buchanan*, 1917, overturned a Louisville, Kentucky, Racial Zoning Ordinance, which had prevented Blacks from purchasing property in White areas. The court found that the Ordinance interfered with the rights of business to sell to whomever they pleased. The ruling, however, did not prevent decades of variations on the Louisville Ordinance, bent on testing other means of maintaining racially separate neighborhoods. Such zoning was considered by many to be a necessity to limit racial conflict (Rothstein, 2017, pp. 44–46).

Federal policy under President Harding supported the use of such zoning through provision of pamphlets and model policies. These policies not only supported racially separate housing, but they also advocated the use of zoning to create areas (for Whites) limited to single family dwellings. Areas permitting Black residency were allowed to include rooming houses and industrial development. Over time, this encouraged economic and environmental decline of the nonwhite areas (Rothstein, 2017, pp. 47–50).

Federal policy further entrenched and developed segregation of communities through efforts to support home ownership. Government interest in home ownership was an initial response to fears emanating from the 1917 Russian Revolution. Home ownership, it was believed, would encourage citizen participation in capitalism. Among guidance provided was that families buy homes in "restricted residential districts," to ensure family safety and security. The "restrictions," although not stated, may be presumed to fall along racial and ethnic lines (Rothstein, 2017, pp. 59–61).

Such encouragement toward (segregated) home ownership received a tremendous boost under the New Deal, when government guarantee of mortgage loans not only served to rescue homeowners at risk of losing homes due to the Depression but also provided a boost to the construction industry. While the federally guaranteed loans benefited homeowners through extended terms and the ability to accrue equity, they also offered protection to lenders through the use of risk categories. Federal Housing Administration (FHA) guidelines in 1934 established racially based color coding that deemed solidly White neighborhoods as "green" or lowest risk, and Black or racially mixed neighborhoods, or those adjacent, as "red" or having unacceptable risk for home loans.

The same system, also known as red lining, was adopted following World War II by the Veteran's Administration (VA), in guaranteeing home loans for returning veterans. By 1950, half of all home loans were guaranteed by the FHA or VA (Rothstein, 2017, p. 69).

Such federal policy reached much further than individuals buying homes in racially segregated neighborhoods. Mass production builders, following the example of Levittown, Pennsylvania, leveraged federal dollars to build entire suburbs. These suburbs, under FHA and VA redlining, were built exclusively for White residents (Rothstein, 2017, p. 69). The suburbs then typically also became discrete school districts for White families.

School "choice" within the public systems of the North was limited by the rigidity of housing segregation, largely untouched until the passage of the federal Fair Housing Act of 1968, and was slow to change thereafter. Resistance to racially integrated neighborhoods (and therefore schools) remained deeply entrenched. Advocates of fair and open housing quickly learned that making discrimination in housing illegal did not end discrimination. At a 1965 fair housing rally in Cleveland, participants were directed to existing barriers including White prejudice, Black fears and a cynical housing industry (Kaeser, 2020, p. 91–93).

Brown v. Topeka Board of Education *1954 and Desegregation Plans*

The Cold War era of American educational history brought a recognition that the United States must be competitive and therefore all students must have access to quality education. In 1954, *Brown vs. The Board of Education* in Topeka, Kansas, declared racially segregated schools to be inherently unequal and, therefore, unconstitutional (Jacobs, 1998, p. xi). The court affirmed the ability of school districts to set attendance zones but also prohibited districts from using race as the basis. Districts were ordered to desegregate "with all deliberate speed."

Brown was met with substantial resistance, particularly in the South. Northern communities tended to see themselves as unaffected as segregation of schools was not codified in law, but rather aligned with racially segregated housing patterns. One Southern example is of interest not only owing to the extremity of action but also because of the introduction of vouchers as a tool of segregation. As recounted by Nikole Hannah-Jones, in 1959, Prince Edward County in Virginia simply closed their public schools for five years. During this time, there was no public education for Black children, while White families received publicly funded vouchers to attend private academies. This continued until the Supreme Court ruled in 1964 that the board of supervisors had to reopen and desegregate its public schools or face federal enforcement (*The New York Times*, 2019).

Challenges to Segregated Attendance Zones and Neighborhood Schools

While districts across the South were challenged under *Brown* for *de jure* segregation, Northern states labored under the belief that they were immune. Northern districts and attendance zones simply followed neighborhood and housing patterns. This, however, masked racially motivated distributions of resources. In New York City, for instance, population shifts resulted in partially empty schools in White neighborhoods while schools in Black neighborhoods faced overcrowding, exacerbated by inequities in funding. In response to 1964 activism by Black and Puerto Rican parents and students, a limited transportation-supported program of desegregation involving thirty White and thirty Black and Puerto Rican schools was initiated. Backlash was severe, leading to cries that students be granted a "right" to be educated in "neighborhood schools," rather than being bused elsewhere (*The New York Times*, 2019).

The anti-busing argument was addressed by the Supreme Court in 1971 in *Swann v. Mecklenberg County*. Nikole Hannah-Jones recounts the decision as follows: "All things being equal, with no history of discrimination, it might be desirable to assign pupils to schools nearest their homes. But all things are not equal in a system that has been deliberately constructed and maintained to enforce racial segregation" (*The New York Times*, 2019).

Across Southern states, from 1964 forward, the *Brown* decision, implemented using the tool of transporting students, managed to move from only 2 percent of Black students attending desegregated schools to nearly full desegregation a decade later. The South became the most integrated region in the country (*The New York Times*, 2019).

A different pattern emerged in the North. In the early 1960s, for example, Columbus, Ohio, had Black schools and White schools. A Black administrator in the system observed that the school board viewed the district as having "Black schools" and "Columbus schools." Dr. Watson Walker, the first Black school board member elected in the twentieth century, raised issues of inattention to the Black schools. At one point, Dr. Walker focused the board on the lack of lights on the East High School football field. East, the district's Black high school, was the only school lacking lights on its field. An underlying reason was a belief that if the White teams came to East to play night games they would be attacked (Jacobs, 1998, pp. 18–19).

Such incremental improvements as lights for the football field were the norm in a city with a small but established Black middle class. Despite segregation, there was a sense of community pride in the schools allotted to Blacks. As Black teachers could only teach in the Black schools, these positions tended to be very competitive, resulting in highly qualified staff (Jacobs, 1998, p. 17). The 1968–1969 school year saw East High School's first Black principal. The East High School Tigers took state championships in both basketball and baseball that year (Haygood, 2018, p. 5). Meanwhile, however, multiple studies and organizations began to call for an end to the segregated reality, with attention to differences in student achievement data. Multiple desegregation mechanisms were presented. While the school board in 1964 adopted a resolution opposing segregation, it also endorsed "neighborhood schools" and rejected transportation as a solution (Jacobs, 1998, pp. 20–21). The White majority on the school board succeeded in recasting the issue of desegregation as one of buses and neighborhood schools. Virginia Prentiss, who was elected to the board in 1972, stated: "There will be no busing strictly for racial balance if I can help it" (Haygood, 2018, p. 371).

In 1973, a Columbus coalition filed a desegregation suit. Litigation continued for twelve years. The suit challenged a continuing policy of locating school buildings in ways that maintained segregated attendance zones. The Board was committed to fight the suit, and meanwhile launched various changes they hoped would avoid an order to desegregate that would involve transportation of students. Their attempts were typical of those in many districts. The Columbus Plan, a voluntary transfer plan, drew few participants as the Board drew the line at providing transportation. In response to a civil rights suit, the district integrated teaching staff in 1973. In 1975, the district established "alternative" schools (also known as magnet schools) with special curricula and students drawn from across the city. However, by September 1979, Columbus was court-ordered to implement a desegregation plan, inclusive of providing bus transportation for students (Jacobs, 1998, p. 65).

Columbus was not alone in their attempts to offer desegregation solutions, stressing family options over revised school assignments. Boston and St. Louis offered Black students the option of attending suburban schools. Magnet schools within and across districts were developed, which will be discussed later. The number of such programs doubled from 1981 to 1992, with the number of students tripling (Peterson, 2001a, p. 255).

However, even when districts were taken to task and required to formulate desegregation plans that placed the onus on the school board, rather than family "choice," districts in the North faced a barrier that was not largely present in the South. Where school districts in the agrarian South had developed at the county level, in the North they tended to be organized around metropolitan areas. And as suburbs grew in rings around these districts, they tended to develop as discrete school districts. As urban districts were confronted with court orders to desegregate their schools, they were also confronted with "white flight" of parents out of their districts.

In Detroit, the NAACP backed a case based on housing segregation that made suburban school districts a part of the Detroit desegregation plan. That plan was struck down by the Supreme Court in *Milliken v. Bradley.* The ruling specified that integration across district lines could not be ordered in the absence of a finding that all of the suburban districts had discriminated against Black Students (*The New York Times*, 2019).

A secondary impact of *Milliken* was to focus developers on home-building in suburban areas, while chilling such development within cities. In the mid-1980s, a Columbus Development Department administrator summarized the situation:

> You've got three types of population: you've got people that are in the Columbus school district and have no choice; you have people who choose to be in the Columbus school district; and then you have people who have chosen not to be in the Columbus school district. (Jacobs, 1998, p. 161)

In Columbus, as other areas, developers invested outside of urban districts, using suburban school districts as a selling point to those having the resources to make a choice (Jacobs, 1998, p. 66). Such development tended to create an enriched suburban tax base, at the expense of urban districts. Property tax inequities will also be a topic for discussion in Chapter 5, on Governance and Finance. The impact on family choice was uneven, favoring those at higher-income levels—disproportionately White.

School districts across the United States reflect the culmination of years and years of history despite the efforts to integrate and desegregate schools. In 2019, sixty-five years after *Brown v. Board of Education*, with the increase in the Latino population in the United States, and the pushback during the 1980s on the Civil Rights legislations of the 1960s, there have been no expansions of federal desegregation laws and segregated schools in cities, suburbs, and even small towns is rampant (Frankenberg et al., 2019). This report found that, on an average, White, Black, and Latino students attend schools in which about 50 percent of students are of the same color or race.

THE CASE FOR STRONG PUBLIC SCHOOL SYSTEMS

Public education in the United States, as in other countries, rests on a belief that a well-educated citizenry has public benefits in terms of civic engagement, as well as more practical outputs like a broad spectrum of educated workers (Schneider & Berkshire, 2020, p. 5). The belief in education as a common good is truly a foundational belief associated with self-government. This belief is reflected in the Northwest Ordinances of 1785 and 1787 requirement of a set aside of real estate in each township for public schools to be supported by public resources (Black, 2018).

As we will see in the following explorations of expanding education options, our vision, and definition, how public education has lately been shifting. In the words of Florida governor Ron DeSantis, echoed by former U.S. secretary of education Betsy DeVos, "If the taxpayer is paying for the education, it's public education" (Schneider & Berkshire, 2020, p. 207). Strong systems of public education are differently defined, and aspire to a number of advantages to individuals, communities, and the larger society

Cost Economies and Challenges of District-based Systems

Funding schools through taxpayer dollars is much more cost-effective and equitable than individual tuition. This is true despite the reality that much remains aspirational in terms of achieving true equity in funding of districts. While the complex picture of federal, state, and local contributions to payment for education makes a variety of adjustments based on a district's "ability to pay," inequities in property value and local income are difficult to overcome (Education Commission of the States, 2013). As traditionally structured, the "consumer" who pays for public education is the local community, which also has a major role in overseeing (through an elected board) the education process (Schneider & Berkshire, 2020, p. 6).

Equal Opportunity

School districts provide the opportunity for education to every child in the United States. Children cannot be turned away because of income level, gender, religion, disability, or race. In this way traditional public education strives, and is obligated, to offer the population an equal playing field.

Quality Control and Accountability

The current district-based systems, coupled with state oversight, provide multiple mechanisms for overseeing quality. States support districts with teacher credentialling systems, as well as setting standards for academics and operations. In addition, elected boards of education provide local accountability.

ARGUMENTS FOR MARKET-BASED EDUCATION SYSTEMS

Economic, market-based principles provide insight into the underlying philosophy of the school choice movement. There is a "free market" belief that if parents are given multiple choices in the schools that their children attend, the resulting competition will lead to better education. Parents will vote with their feet, bad schools will disappear, and good schools will appear, grow, and develop. Parents will select schools that meet their children's needs, and federal, state, district, and educational bureaucracies will lose control over what some consider a public-school monopoly.

Those advocating market-based solutions see families as consumer units desiring freedom to operate in a system as if consuming a market good. The market is efficient they hold, while the public schools are bureaucratic and wasteful. This belief is in direct conflict with the notion that public education has a broader public benefit, with a public governance responsibility. Market-based advocates see markets as a form of "natural democracy." The common good will ultimately be best served through the aggregation of individual choices (Schneider & Berkshire, 2020, pp. 15–17).

A market-based approach to education is characterized by several basic beliefs that distinguish it from those underlying a traditional approach to public education.

Personal Benefit versus Public Good

Those who advocate market-based approaches see the benefits of education accruing primarily to the individual student, or their family, as opposed to society as a whole.

Schools Should Be Controlled by a Free Market, Not Government

Increasingly in recent years, public education has been re-classed by some as a system of "government schools," seen as potential arms of overreach and indoctrination. Further, very real problems within schools have contributed to a sense of urgency to look beyond formerly trusted institutions for solutions (Lowe, 1995, p. 194). The notion of a competitive marketplace to produce solutions to enduring issues of equity and access to quality education has lately also appealed to others beyond free-market ideologues. This new, broader, embrace does not deny that a certain core segment still rejects the very notion of public education as counter to ideals of a free-market capitalist society. Ohio senator Andrew Brenner, chair of the Primary and Secondary Education Committee of the Ohio Senate, advocated in a blog the divestment of all buildings, equipment, and real estate that comprise the public school system. Similarly, Arizona representative Paul Mosely introduced legislation to repeal the state's compulsory education law (Schneider & Berkshire, 2020, pp. 9–11).

Consumers of Education, Not All Citizens, Should Pay for Education

It is difficult to find overt and wholehearted support for the notion that consumers, that is parents and families, become the sole pay source for K–12 education. Yet there is evidence of a sliding scale of tolerance for differential contributions to education that favor those of greater means. What marketplace proponents have done, beginning with Milton Friedman in 1955, is to advocate for systems, such as vouchers, to funnel government funding through parents, as consumers. Such systems are based on the notion of a competitive marketplace that would result in greater efficiencies with better outcomes for individuals (Peterson, 2001a, p. 251).

Union Inefficiencies and Bureaucracy Prohibit Improvement

The publication of "A Nation at Risk" in 1983 ushered in the era of Nationalized Education Reform. Discussed at length in the Introduction and chapters 1 and 2 in a discussion of curriculum and teacher certification, the publication occurred at the apex of teacher union organization in the United States. This raised a question of why teachers, through their unions, were unable to solve education's problems. Further, they were blamed for preventing needed reform (Smith, 2011). Union supporters contend that such arguments fail to account for the similarity of problems faced by those states, particularly in the south, having no union presence. They also point to other industrialized countries having both unionized educators and high levels of student success (Peterson, 1995).

Supporters of Free-Market Education

Since the 1980s, with widespread dissatisfaction with America's schools, support for market-based school choice to improve the American education system has been growing. This movement has been championed by several prominent forces. Some have pushed school vouchers to relieve people who want to send their child to private schools from paying tuition. Others have focused on developing alternatives to promote competition among schools as an effort to improve the quality of education. Still others have advocated for charter schools and other alternatives to provide school choice for low-income communities to break the cycle of poverty.

Milton Freidman and Market-Based Education

The market-based theory of education was initially popularized by the work of the Milton Friedman, an economist at the University of Chicago. He advocated for the development of government vouchers that parents could use for educational institutions of their choice. His belief was that vouchers and other school choice mechanisms, through enhancing individual freedom, would provide better school quality with greater cost efficiency (Friedman, 1955). Andrew Coulson of the Cato Institute, supported Friedman, adding that state-run schools cannot be justified in a free society and that education is best delivered through the private sector (Schneider & Berkshire, 2020, p. 17).

The 1980 election of President Ronald Reagan ushered in an era of conservatism, and Friedman became a close advisor to Reagan. Reagan's election brought about a renewed interest in, and acceptance of, the potential for market forces, and competition, to foster positive change. Chester Finn Jr., assistant secretary for Research and Innovation in Education, advocated for school vouchers, but couldn't arouse public support (Schneider & Berkshire, 2020, p. 19). But it wasn't until the publication of "A Nation at Risk," which focused attention on school performance, that the public perceived a sense of urgency regarding school improvement (Smith, 2011).

The Reagan administration, with support from organizations like the American Legislative Exchange Council (ALEC), responded to "A Nation at Risk" with multiple, unsuccessful, attempts at legislating opportunities for school choice. To counter objections to the notion of government support going to support private education for well-off families, some proposals focused on moving Title I dollars for low-income families from public schools to private services (Schneider & Berkshire, 2020, pp. 20–22).

Friedman's ideas, however, did not receive much attention from policymakers for two reasons. First, the general public and policymakers remembered the failure of the market in the Great Depression. And second, vouchers were associated with Southern states, which had used them to avoid court-ordered desegregation.

Chubb and Moe Focus on Teacher Unions

In the 1980s, Terry Moe, an economist and political scientist, partnered with John Chubb in the Political Science Department at Stanford University. Moe's earlier work was concerned with the organizational foundation of public interest groups. He observed the growth of teacher unions from the 1960s to their apex in the 1980s. Moe came to see teacher unions as powerful barriers to school reform (Smith, 2011).

Chubb and Moe maintained their working relationship following a move to Brookings Institute. At Brookings they continued work they had begun at Stanford, comparing private and public education. They concluded that differences in student achievement in private versus public schools could be attributed to greater autonomy and effective organization in the private arena (Peterson, 2001a, p. 252). The causes of poor performance, they determined, are in the institutions themselves and their reluctance to change. They recommended a completely new public education system that was based on parent-student choice and school competition.

The two together published *Politics, Markets and America's Schools* in 1990. That same year, the nation's first school voucher program began in Milwaukee, Wisconsin. A year later Minnesota adopted the first charter school legislation. In an interview in 2011, Moe forecast the end of teacher unions, crediting two factors: the growth of school choice and advances in education technology diminishing the role of teachers in education (Smith, 2011).

Chester E. Finn Jr.

Chester E. Finn Jr., mentioned earlier, is known to many as president emeritus at the Thomas B. Fordham Institute, and senior fellow at the Hoover Institution (Finn & Manno, 2015). In 1983, while at Vanderbilt University, he partnered with Denis P. Doyle of the American Enterprise Institute to author a paper on "Educational Quality and Family Choice: Toward a Statewide Public School Voucher Plan." Finn and Doyle posited that a recent California Supreme Court decision requiring statewide equalization of school funding was poised to make local control of school districts obsolete. They suggested that, as assuring adequate funding was a primary function of local boards, they would now lack for a purpose. They also suggested that student residency would no longer need to determine their school assignment (Finn & Manno, 2015, pp. 4–6).

Finn and Doyle provided a thorough vision of what a statewide voucher system might look like. They assumed that funding, through the voucher, would follow the student, to whatever school their family may select (provided the student met the criteria that each school might impose). The voucher amounts would be variable, allowing for weighting to account for various student needs—which might include disability, family need, and the like. Their firm belief in the capability of such a system to result in higher quality rested in equally firm beliefs that large local school systems are hampered by bureaucracy and that "competition need not produce charlatans, deceptive advertising or chronic instability." The resulting system they envisioned would feature "the opportunity to create more educational diversity without sacrificing equality" (Finn & Doyle, 1983, pp. 8–9).

In the 1990s, the Clinton administration ushered in an important pivot to the school choice movement. While the notion of vouchers for private schools had failed to garner widespread public support, providing parents, particularly low-income parents, a greater choice of schools was growing in popularity. Clinton addressed the Democratic Leadership Council in 1991, comparing the desire for school choice to the availability of cable TV stations (Schneider & Berkshire, 2020, p. 22). As president, Clinton worked toward the implementation of support for public charter schools, pointing to the establishment of over 2,000 charters during the administration (The White House, 2001).

Betsey DeVos

Betsey DeVos, education secretary under President Donald Trump has a substantial record of educational policy activism. She and her husband, both from wealthy families, have fully embraced the notion of market principles as a tool for educational improvement.

> Having grown up in families that are in the business world, we both believe that competition and choices make everyone better, and that ultimately if the system that prevails in the United States today had more competition, if there were other

choices for people to make freely that all of the schools would become better as a result and that excellence would be sought in every setting (Graves, n.d.).

DeVos, both directly and through substantial contributions to several political action committees, has driven legislation supportive of both charter schools and voucher systems in Michigan and other states. Of particular interest to the DeVos family has been the use of vouchers for religious schools (Klein & Prothero, 2016).

DeVos, and her various lobbying groups, such as the American Federation for Children, have advocated for for-profit providers of "school choice." However, her rhetoric, such as the proclamation that "it shouldn't matter where a student learns as long as they are actually learning," has also appealed to progressive voices seeking reform (Schneider & Berkshire, 2020, p. 97). Her philosophy of education frequently suggests a firm belief that competition and a market-based approach are absolutely necessary to change and improvement. "Education is a closed system. It's a monopoly. A dead end" (Richards, 2017).

SCHOOL CHOICES

The push for school choice beyond local public schools initiated the development of alternatives to public schools beyond religious-affiliated private schools and private academies, both of which are privately funded. Charter schools, magnet schools, and increased homeschooling efforts offer varieties of school choice.

Charter Schools

Charter schools are public schools funded by public monies but operated independently of the system of local districts. The nature of charter schools is to encourage innovation and a broad diversity of options. They are tuition-free and generally open to all students. They must follow laws pertaining to health, safety, and civil rights. Depending on the state, they may be exempt from some state regulations, such as, in Ohio, teacher evaluations.

Charter schools have authorizers, which can be school district boards, educational service agencies, institutions of higher education, nonprofit organizations, or state departments of education. The schools have boards of trustees that oversee education, finances, and management as well as compliance with federal, state, and local laws.

There are several types of charter schools, such as those run by large national management companies, small local networks of charter schools, or single-site schools. Management companies can be nonprofit or for-profit.

Some companies simply provide back-office business services, such as payroll, accounting, and purchasing. Other companies manage every aspect of the school, including hiring and firing educators, professional development, curriculum, and instruction. There have been conflicts between management organizations and their boards. Only about 12 percent of charter schools are unionized (Goldstein, 2014, p. 223).

Some charter schools have a "brick and mortar" physical presence for face-to-face instruction. Others are solely online. Such e-schools vary in structure. Some have regularly scheduled online classes or calendared assignment expectations. Others allow students to progress at their own pace. Charter schools often have small class sizes and high academic standards and innovative approaches to education. Because charter schools have more flexibility, noncertified teachers can be hired.

What follows is an exploration of the development of charter schools. Examples will include both for-profit and not-for-profit management organizations and their impact on student learning. No individual example should be regarded as exemplary of the whole field. While some charters can provide insight as failed experiments, others have survived and grown. All can be instructive about what does and doesn't work.

1980s—1990s: The Rise of Charter Schools

Al Shanker, a one-time national leader of the AFT, is often credited with coining the term "charter schools" to refer to a research and design effort to stimulate innovation in public schools. In fact, Shanker was bringing forward an idea introduced in the 1970s by Ray Budde, who taught educational administration at the University of Massachusetts. His "Education by Charter," got little notice initially. Following "A Nation at Risk," Budde published his paper—which was ultimately noticed, and endorsed, by Shanker (Kolderie, 2005).

The concept that Shanker endorsed called for schools to be authorized by districts and run by teachers. He believed that this organization would allow needed space for teachers to innovate without being hampered by central office administrators. Budd and Shanker both envisioned charter schools that would operate within districts and collective bargaining arrangements (Peterson, 2010b).

Education reformers Joe Nathan and Ted Kolderie picked up the concept, working to sell the idea to Minnesota governor Rudy Perpich and the Minnesota Legislature. Legislation was signed into law in 1991. Among the Minnesota adaptations was the authorization by statewide agents, inclusive of entrepreneurs. Shanker did not endorse this version (Peterson, 2010b). Budde was also critical of the Minnesota version of his ideas, which has evolved over time, and been emulated across states in various forms. He did ultimately come to endorse the need for state laws to transfer authority from central offices to schools and teachers (Kolderie, 2005).

Other variations on the Budde/Shanker vision include a Baltimore effort, which in 1993 contracted with a private, for-profit enterprise (Education Alternatives, Inc.) to operate nine district schools selected based on their record of poor performance. The company provided new equipment and professional development; however, student achievement did not improve. Further, collaboration with the teacher's union was damaged when the company fired union paraprofessionals. There were financial disagreements with the district. The company's contract was cancelled. Shanker concluded that such privatization efforts were incompatible with public education (Ravitch, 2013, p. 157).

For-Profit Charter School Networks

White Hat Management

At one point, White Hat was Ohio's largest operator of charter schools and the third-largest nationally (Schneider & Berkshire, 2020, p. 80). White Hat Ventures operated as a business endeavor, which its founder, David L, Brennan, admitted in 2002 was "slightly profitable" (Reid, 2002).

Despite Brennan's "no-frills" approach (typically online instruction provided in rented office buildings, overseen by "classroom managers" and administrators paid much less than their public-school counterparts), he managed to collect more per-pupil than 85 percent of public schools in Ohio. The schools, however, consistently ranked among the worst in the state (Schneider & Berkshire, 2020, p. 80).

When author Susan Zelman became State Superintendent of Public Instruction in Ohio, she visited a White Hat elementary school in the Cleveland area. In conversations with Mr. Brennan, Zelman naively suggested how to improve the school by purchasing evidence-based curriculum materials, addressing the issue of teacher turnover with higher salaries, and using a combination of direct instruction and project-based learning.

Zelman began to understand that Mr. Brennan was more interested in making money than the quality of education that he was providing. During the 1999–2000 Ohio political campaign cycle, Brennan was the top individual political contributor, with contributions to nearly every Republican Ohio Legislator (Reid, 2002).

While the schools had local boards and a contractual relationship with White Hat to provide services, there were multiple questions about how dollars were being allocated. A number of the local boards moved to separate and manage their schools individually. Lawsuits sought to allocate assets such as furniture and computers. By 2018, White Hat had only one online school and ten dropout recovery centers using computer coursework to earn diplomas. White Hat eventually sold its businesses to other for-profit management companies (Schneider & Berkshire, 2020, p. 80).

Edison Schools

Another highly disappointing example of a for-profit charter network is the Edison School Network, founded by Chris Whittle, an American media mogul who became an education executive. He initially recruited Benno Schmidt, former Yale president, and John Chubb as his chief academic officer. Edison Schools was a public company from 1999 to 2003. Its stock was traded on NASDAQ. An Security and Exchange Commission (SEC) investigation into accounting practices in 2002 resulted in a 95 percent decline in stock value (Schneider & Berkshire, 2020, pp. 80–86).

Edison Schools' academic failure may be attributed to high student-teacher ratios and a lack of quality curriculum and instruction. Their instructional model relied heavily on computer-delivered instruction. Meanwhile their business model called for high numbers of students and keeping costs low. The niche that they exploited was that of "drop-out recovery" schools. This offered the advantage of a student population that districts were happy to cede, as well as very little oversight from states or partnering districts. Eventually contracts were lost as entities challenged payments for enrolled students with poor attendance (Belsha, 2019).

Today, this private company has changed focus and is establishing wholly private tuition-supported schools in the world's leading cities. It envisions a highly integrated luxury (and high-priced) global learning community of boarding, online, and day schools. They are part of a growing trend to establish private schools by unsuccessful charter school developers (Schneider & Berkshire, 2020, p. 98).

Electronic Classroom of Tomorrow

The Electronic Classroom of Tomorrow (ECOT) appealed to parents for many reasons: it provided students with computers, a tool for the future. Older students could combine school with work to supplement family income. Students who were bullied or had other social difficulties in regular classrooms could focus on academics.

ECOT was started by entrepreneur Bill Lager in 2000 and was closed by the Ohio Department of Education in 2018 because of fraudulent data on the number of students attending the school. This charter school was sponsored by an Ohio Education Service Center. A management company, also owned by Lager,

ALTAIR Learning Management, operated as a for-profit company. As an online school, students were required to receive twenty-five hours of education per week. The work consisted of online teaching sessions and independent work.

At its height, ECOT graduated 2,500 students per year. However, many students dropped out before graduation. In 2014, its graduation rate was 39 percent. ECOT, as many other privately managed charter schools, had high student-teacher ratios as well as high student-counselor ratios. In traditional schools, 80 percent of revenue goes to salaries. In ECOT, 50 percent went for salaries (Bischoff, 2021).

In 2016, an Ohio Department of Education audit discovered that ECOT had overstated the number of students that it served. A repayment of $80 million was demanded. This led to a debate regarding how student participation was counted. The Department held that enrollment was an insufficient indicator, charging that many students failed to maintain a required level of participation. The state required ECOT to provided five hours of learning opportunities daily; however, online logs showed an average online use of just a single hour per day (Tebben, 2021).

This highlighted a key difference between online and traditional brick-and-mortar schools. Traditional schools have always been required to provide a specified number of hours (seat time), with an assumption that a student in a classroom was learning, or had the option, at any rate, to learn. Poor attendance (truancy) can trigger investigation into families and a potential charge of "educational neglect," or provision of various social services aimed at supporting attendance. ECOT attempted to argue that online logs were not reflective of the whole of student engagement, and that much learning was occurring when students were offline and engaged in reading, writing, and other activities. While the brick-and-mortar seat time assumptions may not be truly reflective of engagement, or learning, the online experience was far more conducive to undetected lack of engagement or truancy.

ECOT's sponsor, at the urging of the Department of Education, closed the school. Multiple cases regarding repayment were presented before the Ohio Supreme Court prior to a final ruling empowering the Department of Education to collect $65 million. In addition, the Ohio Secretary of State responded to a federal grand jury subpoena for records of campaign contributions made by Lager and other company representatives. A state auditor's report raising allegations of fraud was also provided to federal authorities (Bischoff, 2021).

Nonprofit Charter School Networks

KIPP Public Charter Schools

KIPP Public Charter Schools are a nonprofit network of college preparatory schools from preschool to high school. The schools were founded in 1994 by

Mike Feinberg and Dave Levin, two former Teach for America Corps teachers. This network has 255 schools across the country and over 112,000 students. It is the largest network of public charter schools in the country. More than 95 percent of students are African American or Latino. Over 88 percent are eligible for free or reduced lunch. Students are accepted, regardless of their previous academic records. About 12 percent receive special education, and 18 percent are English language learners (KIPP Foundation, 2021). KIPP operates as a nonprofit, with considerable foundation support, in addition to public dollars.

All students are admitted through lotteries. After being selected by the lottery, KIPP staff meet with parents and students in their homes, and parents sign an agreement setting down their expectations to support their children to succeed and go on to higher education. KIPP has extended school days, Saturday classes (usually twice per month), and three more school weeks than most traditional schools.

According to their website, KIPP has 50 percent more time in school than traditional schools in its region. KIPP offers extensive extracurricular activities, such as sports, performing arts, and visual arts that under-resourced families cannot usually afford. KIPP promotes team and family celebrations and sponsors college visits, career nights, and job shadowing. KIPP encourages all students to take a least one college-level advanced placement course by their senior years.

Data from the 2017–2018 school year showed that KIPP's national college completion rate for its alumni is 35 percent. This statistic is three times the national average for students from low-income families who graduate from four-year colleges. Another 5 percent of KIPP alumni earn an associate's degree (Mathematica, 2022).

Beneath the hood of apparent success in providing enriched experiences and improved outcomes for low-income students are ideology and pedagogy that some have questioned. KIPP has come under fire for using a highly "scripted" approach, including a set of student behavioral expectations known as SLANT, short for "sit up, listen, ask questions, nod, and track the speaker." The genesis for this practice is a belief by the founders that while middle-class students learn and instinctively apply certain methods for school success, low-income students must be explicitly taught these behaviors (Pondiscio, 2021).

In *Scripting the Moves*, Joanne W. Golann suggests that SLANT only approximates the social capital of middle-class students and therefore serves to set unhelpful limits for the KIPP students. She points out that not only do many working-class students arrive with a no-excuses commitment to problem-solving (as expected of KIPP students), but they also need another piece of middle-class social capital, which is an ability to negotiate and bend rules to their individual benefit (Pondiscio, 2021).

Individual Charter Schools

There are many examples of individual charter schools, often arising from a group of educators advocating a particular vision. These smaller efforts represent something closer to Shanker's vision of schools operated by teachers rather than central offices. Some, as they prove successful, expand to include more grades or satellite locations. Others relish their individuality and prefer to remain small. Provided here is an example of one with a solid history.

The Graham School

The Graham School is an example of a single-charter high school located in Columbus, Ohio. It attracts families who live in the school district but who do not want to send their children to Columbus City Schools. The school, which emphasizes experiential learning, has operated for twenty years (Walker, 2022).

According to the school's website, it offers students a "balance of classroom and experiential learning opportunities." Partnered with EL Education (formerly known as Expeditionary Learning), teachers follow a school reform model that emphasizes academic growth by active learning, character development, and teamwork. The approach grew out of a partnership between Harvard Graduate School of Education and Outward Bound (The Graham School, 2022).

Graham's mission is to help urban students in central Ohio to become lifelong learners and informed citizens through "real world experiences and rigorous academics." Successful Graham students are prepared to succeed in college, the workplace, and other endeavors. Its motto is "Encounter the World and Engage the Mind." Classroom work is both traditional and nontraditional. Students take college-level courses while in high school through partnerships with higher education institutions and career technical education. To graduate, students must meet all graduation requirements of the State of Ohio in addition to what is called a "walk-about," a semester-long experiential program. For the 2018–2019 school year, the reported four-year graduation rate was 81 percent (The Graham School, 2022; Walker, 2022).

The school has a core practice called Crew, a practice that brings together students, teachers, and families in separate groups. The name comes from the notion that the groups are the crew for student learning, not just passengers on a ship. Its purpose is to support the students' academic and social-emotional growth. It started with students and teachers but expanded to include families. During the 2020–2021 school year, the school offered five evening family Crew sessions and a family Crew workshop. The school is also involved in the Ohio Collaborative for Educating Remotely and Transforming Schools

Initiatives, a partnership to learn from students, parents, and educators (The Graham School, 2022).

While there are many solid elements evident in the school's curriculum, pedagogy, community connections, and parental involvement, their recent data, as reported via Ohio State Report cards are disappointing. Their academic ratings for the 2017–2018 and 2018–2019 school years are "D" and "F," respectively. It is possible that this reflects recent changes in the Ohio rating system, as going back to the 2014–2015 school year, their Performance Index score was "C." One positive in the data is some indications of gap closing and improvement for the lowest-scoring 20 percent of students. Given COVID-19 conditions, Ohio did not report grades for the 2019–2020 and 2020–2021 school years (Ohio Department of Education, 2021).

As the target population for The Graham School is students in the Columbus School District, it seems reasonable to compare indicators to district high schools. Three high schools having assigned neighborhood populations, West High School, East High School, and Northland High School are roughly equivalent in terms of academic achievement and graduation. Columbus Alternative High School, however, a magnet school with a long history, had a 2018–2019 achievement grade of "C" and a four-year graduation rate of 97.7 percent. Another Columbus magnet, Fort Hayes Arts and Academic High School reported a four-year graduation rate of 92.8 percent, but an achievement grade of F, matching that of Graham (Ohio Department of Education, 2021).

OTHER CHOICE VARIATIONS

Several other choice options must be noted across the American education landscape. They are presented here together, not because of any natural affinity but because together they comprise a small but relatively unstudied sector. While, on the one hand, homeschool activists have tended to resist providing data and being researched, study in the realm of magnet schools, open enrollment, and transfers has tended toward impact on school demographics, with limited research into academic outcomes.

Magnet Schools

Magnet schools started in the 1960s and 1970s as a way to desegregate public schools. They rely on public funding and follow the same laws and regulations as other public schools. They often have a focus, such as arts, math, or science to attract students outside school neighborhood boundaries. Because they offer specialized programs, they tend to challenge students more and the level of academic achievement is often greater than in neighborhood schools. Because interest is high, many magnet schools use a lottery system for admission.

Alternative Schools

Alternative schools began in the 1970s to meet the needs of students who may have educational, behavioral, or medical needs that cannot be met by a local school. Alternative schools were established to provide access to a free and safe education for all students.

Vocational Schools

Vocational public schools are typically secondary schools that teach job or technical skills that prepare students for specific jobs, in contrast to academic high schools that prepare students for college.

Open Enrollment and Transfers

Open Enrollment and Transfers allow students to enroll in a public school that is not the one a student is assigned to on the basis of residence. These options, one response to the threat of school desegregation orders, sought voluntary means of changing enrollment patterns. They have also been used to provide school choice for students who are being bullied. Perhaps the earliest was a 1966 Massachusetts program that allowed minority students from Boston to transfer to suburban schools. This was expanded in 1991 to allow for interdistrict choice without regard to ethnicity. By 1995, this involved the participation of 300 districts and nearly 7,000 students (Peterson, 2001a, p. 257).

Minnesota, by 1985, allowed school boards to accept students beyond their own district, provided the racial integration was not adversely affected (Peterson, 2001a, p. 257). Similar transfer programs were also instituted in Milwaukee and Rochester, New York. By 2008, nearly half of U.S. districts had some mechanism for transfers in or out of district (Garn & Cobb, 2008).

No Child Left Behind provided a boost to intradistrict transfers, which already had some limited presence in the form of specialized magnet schools. NCLB required districts to provide families with students in some poorly performing schools the option of transfer to a school in the same district with a better record and available space (Garn & Cobb, 2008).

Much of the limited research on these interdistrict, as well as intradistrict, and specialized magnet schools, has focused on their demographic impact, rather than academic outcomes. A review of presentations at the American Educational Research Association annual conference from 1998 to 2006 found only one with a focus on the impact of transfers. A review of nine comparative studies in 2008 found a slight positive academic impact for students who accessed transfers (Miron, Evergreen, & Urschel, 2008, p. 18).

Another topic of research interest, however, is whether such transfer options have an accountability impact on schools that are vulnerable, under the various regulations, to students having transfer options. One comparison, following an East Harlem expansion of magnet schools, found improved test scores in both the magnet and traditional schools competing for students (Howell & Peterson, 2002). One difficulty, of course, in attributing impacts is that schools operate in a highly complex environment. Concurrent with any single change that interests us are many others, particularly in the realm of bringing about school improvement. Changes to standards and curriculum may be equally responsible for such improvements.

Homeschooling

While the choice to educate one's children within the family and home represents a tiny percentage of American families, there is evidence of growing interest. From 1970, when the population of homeschool students was less than 15,000 students, the numbers grew to 1.773 million in 2012 (Horn, 2021) and then exploded during the pandemic (Eggleston & Fields, 2021).

This growth reflects, in part, changes in the legal status of homeschooling. As a result of both legislation and litigation, the practice moved from being illegal in most states through the 1970s and 1980s to being legal in some form in all states by 1993. Advocates included both those arguing on the basis of religious freedom and others claiming a parental right to determine their child's education. The full range of advocates included both religious fundamentalists and neoliberals focused on child-centered approaches (Averett, 2021, pp. 19–20).

Homeschooling, as a movement, is correctly perceived as being originally religiously motivated, dominated by Evangelical Christians. This was the case well into the 1990s. However, as more families have chosen to homeschool, their reasons have grown more diverse. Other reasons that families choose to homeschool now include concerns for school environment, curricular preferences, and apprehensions regarding the education of children having unique needs (Averett, 2021, pp. 26–27). In addition, families who homeschool cite such qualitative benefits as time spent with their children, personalization of education, and improved mental health. They also appreciate the opportunity to determine how controversial topics are approached (Horn, 2021).

Homeschooling Outcomes

While homeschooling does have strong advocates within participating families, it remains difficult to evaluate academic outcomes or long-term impacts, owing to a lack of consistent regulation and reporting across states, including participation in various testing requirements. At best, many studies that show superior results for homeschooled students must be treated as having potential selection bias (Averett, 2021, p. 24). However, it is equally difficult to establish that homeschooled students, as a group, suffer any great harm (Horn, 2021).

There are concerns, however, that poorly regulated homeschooling may give cover to child abuse and neglect. The Coalition for Responsible Home Education offers a listing of studies in multiple states that raise concerns. From Illinois in 2011 came concerns of "non-purposeful homeschooling," or students with a history of truancy being reported as transferring to non-existent homeschooling. A 2014 study of child abuse found that nearly half of child torture victims studied had been removed from school to be homeschooled. Other studies reiterated the coincidence of homeschooling among families having abuse reports, and particularly the overlap with truancy. A school in Indiana, however, found that requiring that an academic plan accompany requests for homeschool transfers resulted in a severe decline in transfer requests (Coalition for Responsible Home Education, 2021).

Future Directions for Homeschooling

The advent of COVID-19, and a year of limited in-person schooling, has brought new interest in education models, including partial, if not full, homeschooling. A study by Bellwether Education Partners showed upticks in homeschooling across all demographic groups from spring to fall of 2020. This included a change from 3.3 to 16.1 percent of Black families and 6.2 to 12.1 percent of Hispanic families (Spurrier, Squire, & Rotherham, 2021). Data from the Ohio Department of Education saw a 25 percent increase in homeschooling from fall 2019 to fall 2020. A nonprofit support group for Ohio homeschool parents reports a growth of 200 percent (Shaw, 2021).

This new interest in homeschooling, coupled with ongoing uncertainties regarding COVID-19 and variants, may be spawning new variations to the form. Michael Q. McShane has written about a future including hybrid homeschool. McShane's model incorporates a mix of traditional building-based schooling with a regular schedule of home-based and parent-taught subjects. Such models build on the benefits of enhanced family time, as well as providing transparency (and parental input) in curriculum, McShane also suggests that such models provide an opportunity for schools to move from Carnegie Unit (or credit requirements based on "seat time") to mastery-based programs that allow for greater individualization of pacing (Horn, 2021).

One very recent wrinkle in homeschool practice has been that of the "pandemic pod." This covers a range of experiences from those that share family supervision duties while schools provide remote learning to the actual hiring of teachers or tutors to provide in-person lessons to a small circle of families. As is often the case, those families with greatest need (those reliant on lower-paid in-person work) and potential benefit are among those least likely to be able to access such options. Other considerations include whether students will be adequately prepared to reenter regular school at some point should they desire (particularly at the high school level) and whether the pods provide isolation from needed social experiences (Samuels & Prothero, 2020).

While still a drop in the education bucket, at even 10 percent of families, it is clear that there are lessons to be learned from homeschooling. As with each of the other choice options examined, examples range from excellent to poor. And as with the other options, there may be critical innovations that offer benefit to various niche groups of students.

SCHOOL VOUCHER PROGRAMS

While Milton Friedman failed to realize his vision of statewide voucher systems supplanting local school districts in the 1980s, multiple states have enacted programs that provide tuition vouchers to families meeting various criteria. These programs offer real-world test case evidence of whether voucher programs could actually work. Pioneered in Wisconsin, Ohio, and Florida in the early 1990s, such programs have grown in public and legislative support and garnered a small, albeit mixed, body of research into the capacity of such programs to impact student achievement, racial integration, parent satisfaction, and positive or negative effects on the larger public school system.

Milwaukee Parental Choice Program

The Milwaukee Parental Choice Program (MPCP) brought together school reform advocate Howard Fuller, Wisconsin Democratic state representative Annette "Polly" Williams, and Republican then-governor Tommy Thompson. Fuller and Williams were dismayed by the poor academic performance of Black students in Milwaukee schools, despite multiple reform efforts. Williams and Fuller blamed a White-dominated power structure in the Milwaukee schools. Fuller went so far as present a proposal to the legislature to create an autonomous, Black-led district that would separate from Milwaukee schools. Support from Black leaders backing parental choice energized the governor, already interested in vouchers, and garnered considerable support from conservative foundations and think tanks (Richards, 2017).

At inception in 1990, the program served only 300 children, allowing families to choose from seven private schools. The vouchers, worth about $2,500, could not be used in religious schools, and the schools were required to maintain a student population of over half non-voucher recipients. Pressure from stakeholders, including families, politicians, and foundations led to a legislation in 1995 allowing inclusion of religious schools. While the program passed muster in both state and federal courts, other concerns emerged. These included the lack of state controls that aimed at eliminating schools that performed poorly academically or mechanisms to detect financial fraud (Richards, 2017)

By 2000, MPCP had grown to 12,000 students. Voucher amounts approached $5,000. Over 100 schools participated (Peterson, 2001a, pp. 266–269).

Recognition, over time, of a need for both oversight and transparency led, in 2011, to a requirement that schools accepting students with vouchers participate in the state testing system (Richards, 2017). This, combined with Milwaukee's participation in the NAEP beginning in 2009, has allowed for some longitudinal research to assess the academic impact of MPCP (Carnoy, 2017).

Competitive impacts on the system as a whole have failed to materialize. Approximately one-fourth of Milwaukee students attend private schools using vouchers. Another fourth of students attend assigned district schools, while the remainder access other forms of school choice (charters, magnets, etc.). Yet NAEP scores in math and reading during 2009, 2011, and 2013 not only showed little improvement, but Milwaukee also fares poorly in comparison to other U.S. metropolitan areas. An additional study compared results matching public and private school student achievement using the Wisconsin state tests. The first three years of the study revealed no differences between district and private schools which had agreed to participate. A fourth-year comparison, thought to be impacted by a new state requirement that all MCPS private schools participate in the state testing program, did show better performance by the private school students. Researchers suggest that the new testing requirement led to curricular reforms to better focus on tested areas (Carnoy, 2017).

Despite requirements for assessment participation and score reporting, with enhanced scrutiny of fiscal soundness, there remain concerns regarding lack of transparency in other areas with potential to skew student outcome data. Grade promotion records, in years in which they were required by the state, raise questions about accuracy. In some schools a diminishing population in upper grades suggests that less successful students, in schools that appear quite successful, simply dropout or go elsewhere. Discipline policies, inconsistently available, also suggest that in some cases poorly performing students could be suspended or expelled with little behavioral provocation (Richards, 2017).

A 2017 interview brought together Howard Fuller, one of the architects of the MPCP, and Wendell Harris, who led opposition to the program. The interview brought out some enduring differences regarding the possibilities of parental choice, as well as some areas of agreement. They both spoke with feeling of the desperation of low-income Black families for safe spaces where their children can be educated. They also agreed that vouchers are now deeply entrenched. Harris stated, "That battle is lost. What we have to do now is try and make this thing the best it can be to support our children." Fuller suggested that academic performance should be augmented by other metrics in evaluating the success of vouchers (Sanchez, 2017).

A recent study from Milwaukee looked at long range (at ages between twenty-five and twenty-eight) conviction for criminal activity and paternity suits in a population exposed to private schooling through MPCP vouchers. While the male students with the private school exposure in the eighth and ninth grades demonstrated a lower incidence of convictions and suits, the study illustrates the difficulty of such research. The population studied was not randomly assigned. While the researchers used a matched pairs methodology to speculate the impact of the private school exposure (compared to similarly situated students in public schools), there is always the danger of overlooking some inherent trait (family supports or other protective elements, for instance) that accounts for the outcome (DeAngelis & Wolf, 2020). Yet the value of such outcomes, beyond academics, should not be dismissed. In the words of Wendell Harris, "In our community, a lot of people believe that if they can get their kids into a safe place so they can pray every day, they may be able to save their child's life. Education is secondary."

Cleveland Scholarship Program and EdChoice

The Cleveland Scholarship and Tutoring program was created by legislative action in 1995. Conceived as a pilot program, it relied on a voucher system to provide K–12 students, living in the boundaries of the Cleveland Metropolitan School District, the opportunity to attend a private school selected from an approved list furnished by the Ohio Department of Education. Students were required to be accepted by a school prior to applying for the voucher. Low-income students were given priority. If the voucher amount was less than tuition, parents above 200 percent of the poverty level were expected to pay the difference (Poiner, 2017, pp. 2–3).

Cleveland area opponents of the program sued then-superintendent of public education in Ohio, Susan Zelman, one of this book's authors. The suit charged that public dollars paying tuition to private religious schools were a violation of the Establishment Clause of the Constitution. The plaintiff, Simmons-Harris, prevailed in district court and the court of appeals. However, a Supreme Court ruling held that, while the vouchers used state money, the choice of school was made freely by families. Religious affiliation of schools was neither a requirement nor a barrier to state approval, and hence the state was not in violation (Poiner, 2017, p. 12).

An additional voucher program, EdChoice, was established as a pilot in 2005. Eligibility is determined by multiple criteria, but essentially targets low-income families assigned to low-performing schools in parts of the state other than Cleveland. Families may remain eligible even if their assigned school demonstrates improvement or their income level rises. Students must be accepted by a private school prior to their application to EdChoice (Poiner, 2017, pp. 5–6).

As with the Milwaukee voucher program, evaluation of outcomes tends to be nuanced. An analysis funded by the Thomas B. Fordham Institute suggested that the program attracts "relatively high-scoring and comparatively advantaged eligible students," which may account for a slight edge when compared to those eligible students who remain in their assigned public school. Analysts also observed that those students coming from higher-performing, albeit still eligible, assigned schools, did worse than their peers who did not transfer to a private school (Figlio & Karbownik, 2016, p. 39).

An additional concern with the voucher plans has to do with loss of state funding to the students' district of residence, and the impact on public education as a public good. As voucher eligibility has become broader, districts other than just the urbans have begun to be impacted. In addition, voucher amounts per student have been increasing. In response to the 2022 Ohio budget, which raised the tuition cap as well as providing a tax credit for families who send children to private schools, a coalition of seventy-five public school districts is organizing a lawsuit. They argue that the expanding voucher system interferes with the state's Constitutional obligation to fund a "thorough and adequate system" of public schools (Deng, 2021).

Florida Opportunity, McKay, and Hope Scholarships

Florida was in the vanguard of states implementing school voucher programs beginning in 1999 with "opportunity scholarships" targeting students from "failing" schools. Growth of the program was controlled by a shifting definition of what constituted a "failing" school. As the state as a whole experienced some academic improvement, based on the test scores that determined school failure, the bar was raised, resulting in a constant flow of voucher-eligible students rather than growth (Peterson, 2001a, pp. 266–267).

The opportunity program remained fairly small, serving only 720 students by 2006, when it was struck down by the Florida Supreme Court. The court ruled that public support for private schools, placing them in competition with the public system, violated the Florida Constitution (Ravitch, 2013, p. 211). At that point the state revised the program to allow students in poorly performing schools to transfer to another public school (Florida Department of Education, 2021b).

The court ruling, however, did not apply to a much larger Florida voucher program. The McKay Scholarship program allowed 24,000 students with disabilities to attend private schools in 2012. This happened despite an investigation by the *Miami New Times* reporting in 2011 that schools receiving voucher students were poorly monitored, some lacking accreditation. There was little concern for appropriate curricula, and issues with corporal punishment violations were also found (Ravitch, 2013, pp. 211–212).

The McKay Scholarships were augmented by the Hope Scholarship in 2018. Eligibility was available to students who report an experience of bullying in their public school. Some schools in the program, however, have come under fire for racially discriminatory practices (Klein, 2018b). Others reportedly either reject students who are gay or require that they participate in harmful conversion therapy (Klein, 2018a).

Florida is currently working to consolidate and expand McKay, Hope and other family choice options (including a range of tuition tax credits) under the umbrella of the Family Empowerment Scholarship (Florida Department of Education, 2021a).

EVALUATING THE IMPACT OF CHOICE OPTIONS ON PUBLIC EDUCATION

The United States now has multiple decades of commitment to and experience of enhanced choice in education. It seems reasonable, then, to ask whether various options "work" or achieve any educational benefit. While there are distinctions between the various types of options: vouchers, charter, transfers, and the like, and reason to examine them individually, it is also important to consider, in the aggregate, whether the market-based approach overall has had the positive impact envisioned by Milton Friedman, Chester Finn, and others.

Voucher School Research

Expectations for the impact of school voucher programs have always been high. Finn's 1983 California vision of a broad and exclusively choice-based system foresaw overcoming bureaucracy to arrive at a decentralized system of higher quality education (Finn & Doyle, 1983). This vision has been articulated many times over, particularly arguing that children in poorly performing schools ought to be supported in accessing education in already existing and "better" schools. Since that time, we have the advantage of multiple implementation models across many states with a wealth of research into impacts.

In terms of a primary aim of improved student academic achievement, multiple studies in various locations have shown disappointing results. There may be some indication that voucher schools achieve small improvement in graduation and college enrollment rates. These results, however, may result from push-out strategies to move poorly performing students out. Further, during the time that such research has taken place, graduation rates have risen across the board—including traditional public schools (Carnoy, 2017, p. 1). Other research has found that while voucher recipients may show a greater propensity to attend college, this impact did not appear for students from extremely low-income households or whose mothers had not attended college (Cheng & Peterson, 2021, p. 2).

Several Ohio studies have examined the impact of vouchers on schools with voucher-eligible students. The results tend toward negative results for voucher-eligible students who use vouchers (with some exceptions) but also suggest positive results for students remaining at voucher-eligible assigned schools (Figlio & Karbownik, 2016, p. 2). This could indicate that Ohio's EdChoice program, which offers voucher eligibility based on performance of a student's assigned school, creates a competitive atmosphere that spurs improvement in district schools. However, longer-term studies in Milwaukee, which found an initial improvement in district schools that might be attributed to competition from vouchers, also saw the impact fade over time (Carnoy, 2017, p. 7).

Additional concerns about the impact of vouchers include disincentives to enter teaching, as private schools have greater freedom to hire and fire and maintain a younger stable of teachers at a lower cost. Dramatic movement away from district schools has the potential to discourage young people from entering the teaching profession. Further, reliance on the promise of simply moving students from one system to another detracts from examining teaching practice and developing means of supporting methods that work (Carnoy, 2017, pp. 9–10).

Impressions on the Impact of Vouchers

Vouchers to date have failed in two respects. First, they have not, as Friedman proposed, taken the place of geographically determined and locally controlled school districts. Second, they have failed to provide an effective and sustainable challenge to spur improvement to districts, even as students, and state dollars to provide for them, left seeking greener pastures.

Further concerns have followed the development and growth of voucher plans. First is a lingering sense of public unease, despite the path laid out in *Zelman*, with public dollars going to religious schools. This unease has grown in states like Florida where religious schools have adopted policies that overtly reject LGBTQI+ students or families or offer curricula that stand in opposition to state science standards. Less extreme is the suspicion of public dollars being used, via the exploitation of low-income families, to save financially struggling Catholic or Christian schools (Sanchez, 2017).

Following close behind are broad concerns about overall quality of the schools. In Milwaukee, the long experience of vouchers has provided only mixed results from reliance on a market model. While some voucher schools, as some district schools, appear to be excellent, there are also persistently poor performers. As programs mature, there are increased calls for state regulation to bolster the role of choice in ensuring high-quality "product" across the board.

While there is little indication of vouchers going away—Ohio and Florida are currently expanding their programs—they have had to contend with competitors in addition to local school districts. Many have looked to charter schools as a more easily regulated and secular option to offer choice.

Charter School Research

Several reputable studies have suggested negligible results of charter schools at the macro level. That is, across the broad spectrum of charter schools, the aggregate results compare neither favorably, nor unfavorably, to the aggregate results of traditional district public schools (Di Carlo, 2011).

Some have raised concerns that charter schools foster school segregation. Diane Ravitch noted a concurrence between successful federal efforts at school desegregation and a narrowing of academic achievement gaps between Black students as a group and White students as a group. This contrasted with a finding in Minneapolis/St. Paul that linked the proliferation of charter schools with both increased segregation and poor performance by Black students (Ravitch, 2013, p. 293).

These big picture results do not, however, deny various nuanced results. Students who stay in a charter for multiple years achieve better than those who change. Students who had lower scores in district schools tend to improve in their charter school. And in some locations, charters outperform the district schools, while in other locations the district schools lead (Di Carlo, 2011).

The State of Ohio, responding to several charter school failures, implemented new regulations in 2015, intended to change systemic incentives and protections for bad actors. These regulations aimed to hold school sponsors and the Department of Education accountable for quality and fiscal responsibility of charter schools in the state. Also required were enhanced transparency for management company spending and authority of governing boards (Churchill & Aldis, 2015).

A study of Ohio brick-and-mortar charter school results from 2016 to 2019 did find several areas of improvement concurrent with the implementation of these regulations. Students enrolled in grades 4–8, attending charter schools for five years, showed greater improvement in mathematics and English language arts achievement than their peers in traditional public schools. There were also improvements noted in the areas of attendance and disciplinary incidents—resulting in more learning time. The study noted that the largest effect was in schools contracting with nonprofit entities for management, although schools with either for-profit or in-house management also demonstrated positive effects. The largest benefit was found for Black and low-income students in urban areas (Lavertu, 2020, pp. 5–7).

One recent national study of interest takes both a systemic view, the impact of charter schools on districts, and a longitudinal approach, examining data from 1995 to 2016. The study also incorporates both achievement and graduation data. The findings suggest significant improvement across the system when charter schools reach a level of 10 percent of all students. Such improvements maintain, but do not improve, at higher levels of charter saturation. Researchers noted the closing of low-performing district schools as one likely causal mechanism for improvement beyond the charters themselves (Harris & Feng, 2022).

Despite recent understandings, the overall ambiguity of the comparative achievement data, across time and systems, suggests caution in broad policy applications. One temptation is to set aside the question of whether charter schools offer categorical improvement over district schooling, and instead to begin to tease out what works well (and what does not) in both arenas and begin to apply it more broadly (Di Carlo, 2011). Mark Berends, in discussing results of a study by the Center for Research on Educational Opportunity, also remarked on the need to look more closely at the specific content of successful schools of choice, rather than trends from the movement as a whole. This suggests a possible return to the Shanker vision of charter schools as a testing ground for education methods (2021).

Another response, recently suggested by some charter supporters, is to examine whether schools of choice offer some other benefit than that of improved academic learning. In a recent dialogue with Robert Pondiscio, Greg Forster suggested that school choice options interrupt a systemic flaw in public education that tends away from a cultivation of a diversity of curricular and pedagogical approaches.

Allowing for parental choice, Forster argues, overcomes "culture-war politics" that result from attempts to create a single best path for all students. Pondiscio responds that Forster's ideal "would not promote viewpoint diversity; it would marginalize it. There would be room for divergent views, but in separate schools and classrooms" (Pondiscio & Forster, 2021).

Student Achievement and Education Improvement

The dream of school choice programs as described in this chapter is to give parents high-quality options on where to enroll their children. According to market-based theorists, the competition engendered by parents having freedom to choose will lead to support for the best and a withering (or spur to improvement) of the insufficient. The intended result is an overall improvement in education for all students.

John Chubb, the market-based theorist, wrote:

> Schools would reflect the interests of the parents as opposed to groups favored by the political process—because parents in a marketplace are empowered to 'vote with their feet.' This change would in effect restore some of the 'local control' that schools have lost over recent years. Schools free from the powerful interests of groups wedded to the systems' status quo would be able to change important elements of the system to enhance school performance. (Chubb, 2001, pp. 40–41)

Chubb acknowledged that markets could fail, parents could make poor decisions, and students could do poorly despite choice. He acknowledged that high-quality schools might be few and far between resulting in lotteries for entrance. There might be false advertising of school results and nonperforming students forced to leave. He did encourage governments to intervene to make markets more equitable and efficient. In summary, he advocated for a "mixed system of democracy and markets," in which government would play a role in setting standards and providing funding.

Writing in 2015, Chester Finn and Bruno V. Manno reflected on the mixed academic performance of charter schools, nationally. While still hopeful of continued improvement, they noted fundamental errors:

> We didn't pay enough attention to authorizing and governance. We focused on quantity rather than quality. We assumed that a barely regulated marketplace would provide more quality control than it has done. We didn't demand enough funding—or facilities. We didn't insist on sufficient autonomy—nailed into

place, not just promised. We wanted the infusions of capital and entrepreneurialism that accompany the profit motive, but we didn't take seriously enough the risk of profiteering. (Finn & Manno, 2015)

While it is tempting to follow Finn and Manno's lead in considering ways to tweak the vision of choice to arrive at better choice options, perhaps we might better be served by considering some of the invisible forces that also set parameters on what is possible. As an example, competitive markets have never provided well for people with low income, whether in housing, health care, or access to affordable goods and services. Children from low-income families generally arrive at school having more obstacles and fewer educational enhancements than others. Having a greater number of school options does not alter this (Ravitch, 2013, pp. 94–95). If anything, the "barely regulated marketplace" in some cases simply provided an invitation to unscrupulous "providers" who are willing to collect tuition, make excuses, and then leave town.

The Nation as a Whole

As disappointing as the research into various individual choice options is, of greater concern is that, during the decades of acceptance and growth of choice, various measures indicate stagnation or decline of student learning across the United States. The NAEP, administered periodically to a sampling of U.S. students, shows growth by comparison to 1990s achievement, but decline in mathematics and reading in the most recent decade (U.S. Department of Education, Institute of Education Sciences, National Center for Education Statistics, and National Assessment of Educational Progress, 2020). Further, as related by Peggy G. Carr, associate commissioner of the NCES, "over the long term in reading, the lowest-performing students—those readers who struggle the most—have made no progress from the first NAEP administration almost 30 years ago" (Barshay, 2019a). Perhaps it is clearer to state that as a nation, we have made no progress in our ability to educate the readers who struggle most.

NAEP also tracks long-term trends using a separate assessment that has remained constant since 2004. Measures in both reading and mathematics at ages nine and thirteen have declined since 2012. This includes declines for both ages and subjects for students in the lowest-scoring tenth percentile. Compared to 1971, reading scores improved for all percentiles except the lowest decile. Mathematics scores show a similar improvement when compared to 1978 but decline for thirteen-year-olds and no significant change for nine-year-olds since 2012 (National Assessment of Educational Progress, 2021, pp. 1, 4).

International Comparisons

Rankings based on the 2018 PISA place U.S. student achievement at mid-range, or average, in comparison to other countries in reading, and below average in math. Further, U.S. scores have remained stable since 2000, the year of the first PISA tests (Barshay, 2019b).

Eric Hanushek et al., noting that the United States trails most industrialized nations in the mathematics achievement of fifteen-year-olds on PISA, point to the long-term impact of poorly developed human capital on the nation's economic competitiveness. While acknowledging a reluctance on the part of many to accept comparisons to Finland, Hong Kong, and Korea, as being very different from the United States, they also suggest that we could look to Canada as a similar country, also doing far better (Hanushek, Peterson, & Woessmann, 2013, p. 9).

Marc S. Tucker, founder and CEO emeritus of the NCEE urges the United States to examine and learn from those countries currently outperforming us. But he also cautions that the future may not look like the past that has created successful economies and education systems. He notes a need to support improved curriculum with long-range commitment and strategies to ensure that teachers are able to deliver such content. He also suggests a need to develop lifelong learning connections to an enhanced vocational education stream in order to ensure that workers can keep pace with an increasingly mechanized economy (Tucker, 2021).

OBSERVATIONS

The United States has engaged in several decades of implementing "choice," broadly understood. As states have moved to provide more options for families, it is pertinent to take a high-level overview of the status of education when the country is viewed as a whole. Have these changes resulted in measurable improvement in our national education outcomes?

The current level of choice provides many options, but not all are of equal, or high, quality. As parents face this landscape of choice, they also have a new and greater responsibility to evaluate and make good choices. The same desperation that made vouchers and NCLB transfers attractive (some kids are in bad situations right now and deserve better) is a very real and present one for parents, realizing how short the window of childhood is, and how limited is our time to "get it right." Parents do not have the luxury of reformers to consider long-term strategies and big picture concerns. Parents are faced with the current landscape and what it offers to each of their children as individuals.

While nothing can responsibly be concluded from the co-occurrence of flat or declining NAEP scores and a growth in choice options, neither can these scores bolster the notion that a free-market approach leads to broad improvement.

The even larger question to deal with is the failure of choice to bring about broad systemic changes. The various choice options were implemented concurrent with a national focus on enhanced academic content standards and curriculum. What was lacking was a long-term commitment, as seen in countries that have made progress in implementing improved curriculum, to transforming the teaching force to one with capacity to deliver that curriculum across the board (Tucker, 2021, p. 8). The choice options were hiring teachers trained identically to those hired by the traditional public schools, and frequently even those having less experience and education.

We have, in the decades of implementing choice, regarded choice as a tool for improving education, as if competition alone could bring about systemic change. While it may be politically useful to offer such simple solutions, in the end they only serve to avoid meaningful development. Choice failed to improve the economic and racial segregation of our schools—a key driver of inequitable outcomes. More importantly, while some students may have benefited, many others had poor experiences, and the American system of education, viewed as a whole, has failed to improve in our ability to teach children.

REFERENCES

Averett, K. H. (2021). *The homeschool choice: Parents and the privatization of education.* New York: New York University Press.

Barshay, J. (2019a, October 30). *U.S. education achievement slides backwards.* Hechinger Report. https://hechingerreport.org/u-s-education-achievement-slides-backwards/.

Barshay, J. (2019b, December 16). *What 2018 PISA international rankings tell us about U.S. schools.* Hechinger Report. https://hechingerreport.org/what-2018-pisa-international-rankings-tell-us-about-u-s-schools/.

Belsha, K. (2019, September 23). *This company ran schools for dropouts across the country: Chicago is the latest district to cut ties.* Chalkbeat. https://www.chalkbeat.org/2019/9/23/21109347/this-company-ran-schools-for-dropouts-across-the-country-chicago-is-the-latest-district-to-cut-ties.

Bischoff, L. A. (2021, September 7). Two decades of ECOT political giving detailed in info sent to federal investigators. *The Columbus Dispatch.*

Black, D. (2018, December 11). *Fight for federal right to education takes a new turn.* Education Law Prof Blog. https://lawprofessors.typepad.com/education_law/2018/12/fight-for-federal-right-to-education-takes-a-new-turn.html.

Carnoy, M. (2017). *School vouchers are not a proven strategy for improving student achievement.* Washington, DC: Economic Policy Institute.

Carr, M. (2011). The impact of Ohio's EdChoice on traditional public school performance. *Cato Journal*, 257–284.

Cheng, A., & Peterson, P. E. (2021, June 19). School choice and "the truly disadvantaged." *Education Next*, pp. 1–13.

Chubb, J. E. (2001). The system. In T. E. Moe, *A primer on America's schools* (pp. 15–42). Stanford, CA: Hoover Institution Press.

Churchill, A., & Aldis, C. L. (2015, October 14). *Flypaper: Charter reform in Ohio*. The Fordham Institute. https://fordhaminstitute.org/national/commentary/charter-reform-ohio.

Coalition for Responsible Home Education. (2021). *Studies of abuse and neglect*. CRHE. https://responsiblehomeschooling.org/research/studies-of-abuse-neglect/.

Council of Chief State School Officers. (2022, April 23). *Communicating performance: A best resource for developing state report cards*. CCSSO. https://ccsso.org/resource-library/communicating-performance-best-practices-resource-developing-state-report-cards.

DeAngelis, C. A., & Wolf, P. J. (2020). Private school choice and character: More evidence from Milwaukee. *The Journal of Private Enterprise*, 13–48.

Deng, G. (2021, August 2). Ohio public schools to file lawsuit over school vouchers "very shortly" amid voucher expansion in state budget. *The Columbus Dispatch*.

Di Carlo, M. (2011, November 14). *The evidence on charter schools*. Albert Shanker Institute. Shanker Blog: https://www.shankerinstitute.org/blog/evidence-charter-schools.

Education Commission of the States. (2013, August). *Who pays the tab for K–12 education*. The Progress of Education Reform. http://www.ecs.org/clearinghouse/01/08/47/10847.pdf.

Eggleston, C., & Fields, J. (2021, March 22). *Census Bureau's household pulse survey shows significant increase in homeschooling rates in fall 2020*. census.gov. https://www.census.gov/library/stories/2021/03/homeschooling-on-the-rise-during-covid-19-pandemic.html.

Figlio, D., & Karbownik, K. (2016). *Evaluation of Ohio's EdChoice scholarship program: Selection, competition and performance effects*. Thomas B. Fordham Institute.

Finn, C. E., & Doyle, D. P. (1983). *Educational quality and family choice: Toward a statewide public school voucher plan*. Washington, DC: National Institute of Education.

Finn, C. E., & Manno, B. V. (2015, August 27). *Charter schools: Taking stock*. Education Next. https://www.educationnext.org/charter-schools-taking-stock/.

Flanagan, C. (2021, April). *Private schools have become truly obscene*. The Atlantic. https://www.theatlantic.com/magazine/archive/2021/06/the-commons/618719/.

Florida Department of Education. (2021a). *Family empowerment scholarship*. Florida Department of Education. https://www.fldoe.org/schools/school-choice/k-12-scholarship-programs/fes/.

Florida Department of Education. (2021b). *Opportunity scholarship program*. Florida Department of Education. https://www.fldoe.org/schools/school-choice/k-12-scholarship-programs/osp/.

Frankenberg, E., Ee, J., Ayscue, J. B., & Orfield, G. (2019). *Harming our common future: America's segregated schools 65 years after Brown*. Los Angeles, CA: The Civil Rights Project and CECR Center for Education and Civil Rights.

Friedman, M. (1955). The role of government in education. In R. A. Solo, *Economics and the public interest*. New Brunswick, NJ: Rutgers University Press.

Garn, G., & Cobb, C. (2008). *School choice and accountability*. Boulder, CA: Education and the Public Interest Center.

Goldstein, D. (2014). *The teacher wars: A history of America's most embattled profession*. New York: Anchor Books.

Graves, L. (n.d.). *5 Reasons Billionaire GOP donor and public school privatizer Betsy DeVos should not be secretary of education*. The Center for Popular Democracy. https://www.populardemocracy.org/news-and-publications/5-reasons-billionaire-gop-donor-and-public-school-privatizer-betsy-devos.

Hanushek, E. A., Peterson, P. E., & Woessmann, L. (2013). *Endangering prosperity*. Washington, DC: The Brookings Institution.

Harris, D. N., & Feng, C. (2022, April 18). *The bigger picture of charter school results*. EdNext. https://www.educationnext.org/bigger-picture-charter-school-results-national-analysis-system-level-effects-test-scores-graduation-rates/.

Haygood, W. (2018). *Tigerland*. New York: Alfred A. Knopf.

Horn, M. B. (2021, July 29). A robust and timely discussion of a new kind of homeschooling. *Education Next*.

Howell, W. G., & Peterson, P. E. (2002). *The education gap: Vouchers and urban schools*. Washington, DC: Brookings Institution Press.

Institute of Education Sciences. (2017). *Characteristics of private schools in the United States: Results from the 2015–2016 private school universe survey*. National Center for Education Statistics.

Jacobs, G. S. (1998). *Getting around Brown: Desegregation, development and the Columbus Public Schools*. Columbus: Ohio State University Press.

Kaeser, S. (2020). *Resisting segregation*. Cleveland, OH: Cleveland Landmarks Foundation.

KIPP Foundation. (2021, November 13). *Results*. KIPP: Public Schools. https://www.kipp.org/results/national/#question-1:-who-are-our-students.

Klein, A., & Prothero, A. (2016, December 8). Trump's Ed. Sec. pick Betsy DeVos and school choice in Michigan: A timeline. *EducationWeek*.

Klein, R. (2018a, August 9). *Exclusive: Florida wants to help bullied kids—unless they're gay*. Huffington Post. https://www.huffpost.com/entry/florida-anti-bullying-gay-students_n_5b69d2b2e4b0de86f4a5edcf.

Klein, R. (2018b, October 10). *NAACP legal defense fund asks Florida to end racist hair policies at schools*. Huffington Post. https://www.huffpost.com/entry/florida-hair-policy-naacp_n_5bbe26fbe4b0876edaa4afce?yh=.

Kolderie, T. (2005, June). *Ray Budde and the origins of the "charter concept"*. Education evolving. https://www.educationevolving.org/pdf/Ray-Budde-Origins-Of-Chartering.pdf.

Lavertu, S. (2020, October). *The impact of Ohio charter schools on student impact, 2016–2019*. Thomas Fordham Institute. https://fordhaminstitute.org/sites/default/files/publication/pdfs/impact-ohio-charter-schools-student-outcomes-web-version.pdf.

Lowe, R. (1995). The perils of school vouchers. In D. Levine, R. Lowe, B. Peterson, & R. Tenorio, *Rethinking schools* (pp. 191–204). New York: The New Press.

Mathematica. (2022). *KIPP: Preparing youth for college*. Mathematica. https://math ematica.org/projects/kipp-preparing-youth-for-college.

Miron, G., Evergreen, S., & Urschel, J. (2008). *The impact of school choice reforms on student achievement*. Boulder, CO: Education and the Public Interest Center.

National Assessment of Educational Progress. (2021, October 30). *NAEP long-term trend assessment results: Reading and mathematics*. The Nation's Report Card. https://www.nationsreportcard.gov/ltt/?age=9.

National Catholic Educational Association. (2021, June 19). *New students in Catholic schools*. NCEA. https://www.ncea.org/NCEA/Who_We_Are/About_Catholic_Schools/NCEA/Who_We_Are/About_Catholic_Schools/Catholic_School_Data/Catholic_School_Data.aspx?hkey=86ec3eb1-b329-4e98-9f0e-f271dc6b8d50.

National Center for Education Statistics. (2021, June 19). *The condition of education 2021 at a glance*. Institute for Education Statistics. https://nces.ed.gov/programs/coe/ataglance.

Ohio Department of Education. (2021, October 30). *Report card resources*. Ohio Department of Education. https://education.ohio.gov/Topics/Data/Report-Card-Resources.

Peterson, B. (1995). Which side are you on? The role of teacher unions in school reform. In D. Levine, R. Lowe, B. Peterson, & R. Tenorio, *Rethinking schools* (pp. 253–263). New York: The New Press.

Peterson, P. E. (2001a). Choice in American education. In T. M. Moe, *A primer on America's schools* (pp. 249–283). Stanford, CA: Hoover Institution Press.

Peterson, P. E. (2010b, July 21). *No, Al Shanker did not invent the charter school*. Education Next. https://www.educationnext.org/no-al-shanker-did-not-invent-the-charter-school/.

Poiner, J. (2017). *Ohio's voucher programs: An overview*. Thomas B. Fordham Institute.

Pondiscio, R. (2021, August 19). *Flypaper: A thoughtful but dated criticism of "no excuses" charter schools*. Thomas B. Fordham Institute. https://fordhaminstitute.org/national/commentary/thoughtful-dated-criticism-no-excuses-charter-schools.

Pondiscio, R., & Forster, G. (2021, September 8). *School choice and viewpoint diversity: Competing visions. A dialogue between Greg Forster and Robert Pondiscio*. Hetrodox. the blog: https://heterodoxacademy.org/blog/school-choice-and-viewpoint-diversity-competing-visions-a-dialogue-between-greg-forster-and-robert-pondiscio-part-1/.

Ramsey, S. (2017, February). *The troubled history of American education after the Brown decision*. The American Historian. https://www.oah.org/tah/issues/2017/february/the-troubled-history-of-american-education-after-the-brown-decision/.

Ravitch, D. (2001). American traditions of education. In T. M. Moe, *A primer on America's schools* (pp. 1–14). Stanford, CA: Hoover Institution Press.

Ravitch, D. (2013). *Reign of error: The hoax of the privatization movement and the danger to American's public schools*. New York: Alfred A. Knopf.

Reid, K. S. (2002, May 22). *Millionaire industrialist touts "White Hat" firm to build charter model*. EdWeek. https://www.edweek.org/policy-politics/millionaire-industrialist-touts-white-hat-firm-to-build-charter-model/2002/05.

Richards, E. (2017, January 12). Milwaukee's voucher verdict. *The American Prospect*.

Rothstein, R. (2017). *The color of law: The forgotten history of how our government segregated America*. New York: Liveright Publishing Corporation.

Samuels, C. A., & Prothero, A. (2020, July 29). *Could the "pandemic pod" be a lifeline for parents or a threat to equity?* EdWeek. https://www.edweek.org/leadership/could-the-pandemic-pod-be-a-lifeline-for-parents-or-a-threat-to-equity/2020/07.

Sanchez, C. (2017, May 16). *Lessons on race and vouchers from Milwaukee*. nprEd. https://www.npr.org/sections/ed/2017/05/16/523612949/lessons-on-race-and-vouchers-from-milwaukee.

Schneider, J., & Berkshire, J. (2020). *A wolf at the schoolhouse door: The dismantling of public education and the future of school*. New York and London: The New Press.

Shaw, M. (2021, August 16). *Data: More Ohio families are opting for traditional homeschooling for new school year*. News5 Cleveland. https://www.news5cleveland.com/news/getting-back-to-school/data-more-ohio-families-are-opting-for-traditional-homeschooling-for-new-school-year.

Smith, E. E. (2011, April 15). *Profile in school reform: Terry Moe*. Hoover Institution. https://www.hoover.org/research/profile-school-reform-terry-moe.

Spurrier, A., Squire, J., & Rotherham, A. J. (2021). *The overlooked*. Bellwether Education Partners.

Tebben, S. (2021, October). *ECOT loses latest court challenge, must repay state*. Ohio Capital Journal. https://ohiocapitaljournal.com/2021/10/06/ecot-loses-latest-court-challenge-must-repay-state/.

The Graham School. (2022). Retrieved from The Graham School. https://www.thegrahamfamilyofschools.org/default.aspx.

The New York Times. (2019, July 18). *The myth that busing failed (podcast transcript)*. The Daily Show. https://www.nytimes.com/2019/07/18/podcasts/the-daily/busing-school-segregation.html.

The White House. (2001). *The Clinton presidency: Expanding education opportunity*. The Clinton-Gore Administration: A Record of Progress. https://clintonwhitehouse5.archives.gov/WH/Accomplishments/eightyears-05.html.

Tucker, M. S. (2021, October 21). *The world's best-performing education systems*. NCEE Global Perspectives. https://ncee.org/quick-read/rethinking-education-systems-for-tomorrow-a-conversation-with-marc-tucker/.

Uhas-Sauer, D. (2019). *A history of Columbus schools, 1806–1912*. Teaching Columbus. https://www.teachingcolumbus.org/a-history-of-columbus-schools-1812-1912.html.

U.S. Department of Education, Institute of Education Sciences, National Center for Education Statistics, and National Assessment of Educational Progress. (2020, March 3). *Results from the 2019 mathematics and reading assessments*. The Nation's Report Card. https://www.nationsreportcard.gov/mathematics/supportive_files/2019_infographic.pdf.

USA Facts. (2022, April 24). *K–12 education*. USA Facts. https://usafacts.org/data/topics/people-society/education/?utm_source=bing&utm_medium=cpc&utm_campaign=ND-Education-Childcare&msclkid=c8a7e6cd2a7a1f4c6f5f84a816998a07.

Walker, M. (2022, March 9). *Graham School in Columbus offers high school seniors a chance to "Walkabout" careers*. The Columbus Dispatch. https://www.dis patch.com/story/news/education/2022/03/09/graham-school-clintonville-lets-graduating-seniors-explore-careers/6788461001/.

Wang, K., Rathburn, A., & Musu, L. (2019). *School choice in the United States: 2019*. Washington, DC: U.S. Department of Education; IES National Center for Education Statistics.

Chapter 4

Engagement

SCHOOLS, PARENTS, AND COMMUNITY

Throughout American history, education has been a top priority among the nation's key issues. In some years, education is the number one priority for both Republicans and Democrats, and it is always within the top ten priorities for the government and nation to address (Pew Research Center, 2019). Education is so important because it has been seen not only as the path for personal growth and economic success but also as community safety and well-being, and global stability.

The U.S. 2021 off-year elections took place amid an environment of education activism directed at local and state school boards. The governor's race in Virginia is thought by some to have swung on education issues.

In recent years, school boards across the country have faced unhappy, and often angry, parents confronting a range of issues. COVID-19 mitigation measures, discomfort with teaching various topics in American history, and the inclusion of LGBTQI+ students have eclipsed some accustomed battlegrounds: evolution, sex education, and prayer in school.

A common thread uniting the voices was anger that "nobody is listening to us." This raises a question of what roles are appropriate for parents, as well as other community stakeholders, to play in a range of decisions. Ought parents be granted individual opt-in/opt-out powers at the level of curriculum for their own child? Is this level of diversity sustainable (or wise)? Alternatively, are there effective mechanisms for building consensus and ownership across a diversity of needs and beliefs?

What should be the role of others outside of schools and beyond local communities? Is it possible for states, or the federal government, to regulate quality while allowing a range of approaches to curriculum and pedagogy?

And importantly, who are the silent players lurking in the background? What are the sources of "dark money" fueling education-specific races such as school boards and what is their vision? Is it possible to unite with commerce without being swallowed whole? How much privatization can be sustained in a public arena?

In this chapter, we will be exploring these themes from the perspective of what is, what have we experienced in the past, and what might be possible in the future.

BEGINNING WITH PARENTS

A consideration of how and where schools are situated within a community appropriately begins with the relationship between schools and the parents of students. Not only are parents the adults who live in the community beyond the schoolhouse doors (not always true of teachers and administrators), but they also provide an important connection to the students within. Bronfenbrenner's ecological theory highlights the importance of a positive relationship between the system of the home and the other systems, such as school, that children encounter as they grow, develop, and explore the world. Where relationships are absent, or antagonistic, children "experience disequilibrium and conflicting emotions, which will likely lead to negative development" (Psychology Notes Headquarters, 2019).

James P. Comer, who applied social and behavioral science to the improvement of student behavior and academic achievement in an urban school setting, offers a succinct description:

> If parents feel excluded, of little value and hopeless, they will be likely to transmit these attitudes to their children. Such attitudes have behavioral consequences that are the opposite of what is necessary for good school learning, or the achievement of long-range goals. (Comer, 1993)

Schools, if they are to be healthy learning communities, cannot afford to overlook the importance of cultivating mutually respectful relationships with parents. Trending over time, such relationships in American public education have varied.

Far too frequently, parent or family involvement is envisioned by educators, or the public, as being limited to concerns for one's own children. Schools call on parents to monitor homework, sign permission slips, participate in conferences with teachers, and attend school programs and sports events. Parents may be called upon for various "volunteer" activities, such as fundraising, chaperoning, or assisting a teacher. Parental interest is assumed to be limited by concerns for their own child's learning, or interactions with teachers or other students.

Multiple models of parental involvement, however, such as Epstein's, discussed later, also include higher-level, and broader, concerns regarding leadership and decision-making, and the connection between a school and the larger community. These higher-level involvements are frequently unrecognized, unsupported, and sometimes unwelcome.

A recent review of the literature probed this divide between the activities of "professionally-driven" relationships and "family-allied" partnerships. In the first, educators frequently see parents as problems and expect them to defer to professionals. Engagement is a low priority. Relationships that regard parents as valued partners, while effective, are rare. Among multiple barriers cited are poor teacher training and fears of conflicts with parents. Expansion of communication, supported by technology, may assist in altering the landscape (Van Der Wal, 2020, pp. 8–13).

A case study of an online parent group associated with a large urban school district revealed frequent discussions related to school reform and social justice issues. Various parents demonstrated a willingness to support views with data about the district and student achievement (when it was available), as well as researching possible solutions to district problems (Sorensen, 2013, p. 106). Similar parent concerns and activity have been seen at various times across the history of American public education.

A Brief History of the PTA

As public education systems developed in the United States, they were urged on by groups of parents, largely mothers. The PTA has become the symbol of parental involvement; however, the PTA has grown, developed, and sometimes atrophied, over time and other groups and models have also emerged.

During the Progressive era of American education between 1890 and 1946, outlined in this book's Introduction, the first NCM met in Washington, DC in 1897 at an event generally recognized as the birth of the modern PTA. The racially diverse, progressive, and maternalist organization, which adopted the name of National Congress of Parents and Teachers in 1924, grew out of a progressive tradition of women's clubs and coalesced around a commitment to school creation and reform (Woyshner, 2003, pp. 521–523).

While the NCM stated a vision of transcendent and unifying aims across lines of race, religion, and class, the social realities of Black and White mothers pulled in different directions. While White mothers' groups tended toward advocating for improvements within school systems, Black mothers, particularly in the South, were faced with creating and supporting schools for their children where none existed. In addition, Black mothers' groups felt a need to focus on teaching their children to behave in ways that would counteract harmful stereotypes within a racist society (Woyshner, 2003, p. 532). While White family's home education might focus on civic responsibility, Black families felt an additional need to prepare their children to work for changes to society as a whole (Ladd-Taylor, 1995, pp. 60–61).

While the White and Black groups generally operated individually at the local level, their cumulative influence was substantial. By 1908, the Department of National Women's Organizations was formed within the NEA to represent the NCM and several other organizations on behalf of a membership of 900,000 women. The membership of NEA at that time was roughly 500 male education administrators (Woyshner, 2003, p. 529).

The various local groups proved highly effective at enacting reforms through advocating for legislation and fundraising. They can be credited with such improvements as kindergartens, school playgrounds, lunch programs, libraries, health clinics and domestic science, and manual training programs (Woyshner, 2003, p. 530). Groups affiliated with the National Association of Colored Women also sought political power to advocate against lynching, police brutality, and Jim Crow laws (Ladd-Taylor, 1995, p. 62).

By the decade of the 1920s, the national leadership of the NCM divided between moderates seeking to broaden local membership, with a primary focus on the home and school environment, and progressive leaders looking to broader social issues such as women's pensions, child labor, juvenile courts, and the prevention of war. This last led to the identification of the NCM as a socialist organization reviled by many during the Red Scare. In response, the organization adopted the new name to focus more directly on school issues and set about to establish a PTA in every school (Ladd-Taylor, 1995, p. 64).

From the 1920s to the 1930s male education administrators worked to change the role of the PTA from "meddling" to more cooperative endeavors. While the mothers' clubs that coalesced at the first Mother's Congress sought to educate themselves on child-rearing and education, and to take on leadership roles based on their knowledge, the male administrators viewed them as nonprofessionals, out of touch with educational developments. They worked to recast the women as homework helpers, aiding teachers, and limiting their fundraising to school-approved activities (Woyshner, 2003, p. 530).

In the Cold War era of the history of American Education, by the 1960s, suburban PTA membership had largely devolved into a time-filling social endeavor, as observed by Betty Friedan in interviews with women of the post-1950 college generation. The women she encountered shrank from taking on intellectually challenging roles, which, she suggested, might reveal to them a discontent with their lives as "home-makers" (Friedan, 1997, pp. 347–348).

Federally Required Parent and Community Involvement

When the federal government initiated a broad program of funding support for disadvantaged children in 1965 during the era of Equal Education Opportunity outlined in this book's Introduction, a role for parents and communities was included in the requirements. As Title I funds have been reauthorized through decades, expectations and regulations have altered, but the expectation of parental involvement, while also changing, has remained a constant.

The ESEA of 1965

The 1965 ESEA, consistent with other federally funded community development programs at the time, put an emphasis on local involvement through a requirement for parent advisory councils. The intent of the councils was to ensure that dollars were being spent appropriately on needs of economically disadvantaged students (Congressional Research Service, 2009, p. 2).

Implementation of the advisory councils varied widely. A 1978 study cited confusion about the role of the councils. Training for participants was inconsistent as was the level of involvement in areas such as planning and evaluation of programs (Congressional Research Service, 2009, p. 7).

The emphasis on parents providing policy oversight by 1988 and 1994 reauthorizations had morphed into a focus on individual parent involvement in the education of their own children. This mirrors the transformation of relationship of the 1920s and 1930s as the PTA was urged away from focus on systemic improvements to homework help and school-defined fundraising.

While the ESEA reauthorizations remained respectful of potential contributions of parents, including a definition of involvement that stressed "regular, two-way and meaningful communication involving student academic learning and school activities," the thrust was clearly on parents supporting their own children as "full partners," with decision-making limited to that sphere. The law adopted the framework developed by Joyce Epstein, which delineated six categories of involvement:

1. Parenting in the home environment
2. Two-way communication with the school
3. Volunteer activities at the school
4. Support for learning at home
5. Decision-making and leadership in schools
6. Community collaboration (Congressional Research Service, 2009, pp. 2–3)

Comer notes resistance on the part of teachers and administrators, particularly in schools serving low-income or minority populations, to the last two categories. He suggests this is a reluctance on the part of educators to share power. Professionals, frustrated by students whose behavior interferes with academic achievement, find it counterintuitive to partner with parents they suspect are the cause of students' poor performance. Such parents may also prove resistant to invitations to be involved, having experienced earlier instances of rejected efforts or blame (Comer, 1993, p. 127).

The 1994 ESEA reauthorization, known as the Improving America's Schools Act, added a requirement for schools to develop parent involvement policies. In addition, schools were required to co-create, with parents, school-parent compacts, to spell out mutual expectations (Congressional Research Service, 2009, p. 8). A Google search for school-parent compacts locates millions of templates and "boilerplate" examples, suggesting how easily a demonstration of compliance might wholly sidestep the intended parental dialogue. An envisioned mutual exploration can easily become a statement by educators of what they expect of themselves and what they expect of parents.

Individuals with Disabilities in Education Act

When the IDEA was adopted by Congress in 1975 to require and ensure that students with disabilities have access to a free and appropriate public education, requirements for parental involvement over the years took on the form of an enumeration of specific rights. As a result of the legislation, parents are entitled to various notices regarding their child's progress, and to participate in planning and evaluation of specialized education services. As the various procedural safeguards can be overwhelming and technical in nature, some states may provide assistance via parent mentors or assistance centers.

Despite such guarantees, the relationship between the school and parent may become contentious as parents navigate their perception of their child's need and the district's determination of appropriate services. Some parents hire private advocates to assist them through the process of writing and enforcing their child's IEP, required under the law. This struggle is evident in this example from parent testimony given to the Ohio State Board of Education.

> At every IEP meeting for our oldest child, we felt like we were the only people at the table who understood Dyslexia. We struggled to get assistive technology . . . she did not need or qualify for these necessary tools even though she was entering third grade reading at a 1st-grade level. School administrators told us that we needed to get outside tutoring for her if we really wanted progress (Moy, 2022).

Compliance oversight of the requirements for FAPE for students with disabilities is often limited to checking on paper trails. The existence of IEPs for every student may be established by authorities. The appropriate content of the IEP is left to the judgment of parents and teachers together, leading to wide variation.

IDEA is only partially funded by federal dollars, an ongoing point of contention. Special services required for the support and inclusion of students with disabilities are often seen as draining funds from nondisabled students. Parent advocates for gifted students often feel slighted that their students have fewer codified rights to appropriate education. Such conflicts may pose a barrier to building cohesive parent groups.

No Child Left Behind

The bipartisan NCLB, the 2001 reauthorization of ESEA, was notable for creating two specific roles for parents. One was to provide parents with information on school improvement plans, with opportunities to give input. The other was to allow for within-district parental choice of school options if their child was assigned to a school falling below certain academic criteria. Parents could opt to receive supplemental tutoring, or students could transfer to a better performing school in the district, based on availability (Congressional Research Service, 2009, pp. 9–10).

The Parent Trigger—a School Reform Strategy

One silver bullet offered in the realm of school-parent relationships, is that of the parent trigger. The strategy first emerged in California where loss of revenues combined with poor overall school performance to lead the state to pursue federal RTTT dollars directed at spurring innovation and improvement. Among advocates for reform was the Los Angeles Parent Union, funded by Green Dot Charter Schools. Philanthropic and political support for the concept was broad. In essence, the "trigger," as codified, allowed parents of children in certain identified poorly performing schools to "take over" school management via petition. A successful "take over" would result in either replacement of all school staff or transforming the school to a charter operation (Rogers et al., 2015).

The strategy proved popular for a time, leading to legislative proposals in states across the country, and adoption in a handful. Criticisms of the mechanism, from various advocacy groups and researchers, have included the lack of meaningful parent involvement or reform inclusive of structural issues (such as funding) larger than a single building. In California a single large nonprofit, Parent Revolution (also funded by Green Dot) was responsible for carrying out massive signature-gathering campaigns that aimed at conversion of four schools to charters—leading to challenges and charges of parent manipulation (Rogers et al., 2015).

As a vehicle for school improvement, the parent trigger suffers from many of the weaknesses of other market-based school choice schemes discussed in chapter 3. In addition, the use of petitions as a vehicle to launch change fails to bring about meaningful empowerment of parents in bringing substantive school improvement (Rogers et al., 2015).

SIDELINING PARENTS: ISSUES OF POWER AND INCLUSION

As parents may be concerned about schools, school staff may be concerned about parents. Educators complain that they cannot get parents to be "involved" in ways they prefer. On the one hand, teachers bemoan lack of participation in annual parent-teacher conferences or support for schools. By the same token, teachers also complain of parent "involvement" in non-preferred ways ("helicopter," or "snowplow" parents). Simultaneously representatives of various viewpoints, all claiming to speak for parents, clamor for time to address school boards. At best, representatives of many viewpoints operate at cross purposes in our joint task of educating children. We see divisions between parents and educators, as well as between and among parents holding different views.

Professional Distancing

Mauricio Miller, whose Family Independence Initiative is based on peer sharing within immigrant communities, suggests that professional roles can serve as a relational barrier to sharing knowledge. His example derives from prior experience of directing an agency charged with supporting clients in areas such as employment. Although staff members participated in various personal networks, which they shared with friends and others seeking jobs, or relocating, they felt constrained from drawing on these personal resources to assist clients. The staff of over hundred workers felt that using such personal social resources, despite their potential value in helping clients, would be unprofessional (Miller, 2017, p. 76).

Dyrness, in a study of Hispanic parent advocates in Oakland, California, cites "controlling images" that educators may hold of parents as a mechanism by which to allow involvement by certain parents, while holding others at a distance. Black mothers may be subtly sorted into good servant "mammies" or aggressive "matriarchs." Other characterizations may classify parents as either "good" or "angry" (Dyrness, 2011, pp. 111–113). In recent years we have heard of "helicopter" or "snowplow" parents, terms that are not laudatory or conducive to building school-home relationships.

A series of focus groups conducted over two years with urban teachers revealed a majority of teacher statements regarding involvement with families that related to power and authority. While articulating concern for partnerships and working together, there was also clarity that teachers are to be "in charge" in the relationship. There was a concern that teachers both define engagement and communicate the parameters to parents. "I would think family engagement, the family, we tell them that it means coming up to the school, showing up at events when you're invited, Open House, parent-teacher conferences, literacy night." Not only is every example teacher-defined ("when you're invited"), but the relationship exists only within the school building and in events created by the school for parents. In one discussion of professional boundaries, home visits were defined, passionately, as beyond the scope of teaching (Durand & Secakusuma, 2019).

Parents as Projects, Objects, Problems

Educators frequently harbor deficit-based views of students based on socio-economic, cultural, or linguistic differences. Seeing the parents as deficient, they may structure family opportunities to exclude any "power-sharing" or mutual relationships. A reliance on traditional forms of involvement tends to overlook families' involvement in their students' education as well as overlooking potential contributions to the life of the school (Cooper, 2009, pp. 380–381).

A survey of teachers at an "urban fringe" high school had no difficulty in identifying a group who blamed students for poor performance on tests. Among these, a group was identified that also felt that parents were at fault for their student's underachievement. Further, these teachers indicated that they did not want more interaction with these parents (Thompson, Warren, & Carter, 2004).

Lott provides a litany of instances, drawn from research studies, of teachers articulating negative beliefs about low-income parents, some in shockingly transparent rejection. From one interview: "these people lead such chaotic lives and none of these women are married, so the boys have no role models." Another described their students as, "all the bad low-skilled kids . . . [who] come from broken homes. . . . They are either hillbillies or blacks from the poor section." One parent reported being told, "You people better do something about your kids." When the predominant view toward a group of parents is that they are substandard, the only school role they are offered (if they are welcomed at all) is that of "[compliant] consent giver" (Lott, 2001, pp. 247–251).

A "multi-year, multi-method study of Black students in three demographically distinct school districts participating in an interdistrict school choice system in the Midwest" revealed a strong tendency for teachers to envision Black students generally as living outside the district, impoverished, and coming from dysfunctional and unsupportive homes. They, and their families, regardless of actual residence and socioeconomic status, were seen as outsiders and the cause of poor academic achievement.

> Like a lot of my Black youth either live with the grandma or live with only one parent . . . and so it's hard to be, to have parent contact when you can't reach the parents, or the kid doesn't live with the parent, or they only have grandma. That's hard, that's been a challenge . . . probably 50% of the [achievement] problem right there I would say. There is no parental support. (O'Connor et al., 2019)

Comer notes that meaningful parental participation is even more important in low-income than middle- and upper-income schools. With middle- and upper-income parents, there is a greater likelihood of educators sharing values and experiences than with lower-income parents. He also suggests that lower-income parents are more likely to be negatively impacted by exclusion from meaningful involvement—feeling helpless and incompetent. Middle- and upper-class parents have more social layers of protection from such impacts (Comer, 1993, p. 126).

Invisibility

Freng, Freng, and Moore referenced Epstein's fifth and sixth parental roles in a qualitative study of American Indian education. These roles include decision-making and leadership in schools and community collaboration. In the examination of the experience of American Indian young adults, they drew a distinction between educational experiences, which they deemed to be "assimilationist," and those along a spectrum of "Native" education ("quasi" to "true"). Where the influence of Native culture was absent (and evidence of meaningful family/community/school interaction limited), or sporadic (isolated events, etc.), students reported a feeling of being torn "between assimilationist goals of the public schools and the struggles for cultural continuity in their communities" (Freng, Freng, & Moore, 2006). Students felt they were being offered a choice between their native culture and being educated.

The failure of educators to seek or appreciate the importance of Epstein's fifth and sixth dimensions, tending to focus instead on more traditional school-based (and school-defined) contributions, leads not only to an atrophy of meaningful avenues of involvement but also to the invisibility of the positive and supportive efforts of culturally marginalized groups. Put more succinctly, there is a need for more "home involvement" by educators, rather than more "school involvement" by parents. Such community outreach can lead to recognition of parental strengths and enhanced trust between parents and educators (Auerbach, 2007).

In Ohio, as COVID-19 shut down school buildings, many educators were drawn into their communities on missions to ensure that school lunches continued to be available, and that Internet connectivity was possible. On visits across the Appalachian region, superintendents reported a new level of teacher awareness of both the struggles and the strengths of parents and families (Zelman, 2021).

Chelsea Public Schools, near Boston, implemented "trust visits" as a response to school building closings during the COVID-19 pandemic. Teachers were trained in protocols for these visits that were conducted on front porches, driveways, or other outdoor locations in the communities. One such protocol, called the Hopes and Dreams Protocol, began with asking families about their hopes and dreams for their student(s). As schools moved back into regular school building mode, they have been able to build on these relationships, as well as to continue regular "check ins" to be aware of stresses or potential crises that students or families may be experiencing (Zalaznik, 2022).

TODAY'S BATTLE FOR THE SOUL OF EDUCATION

Today we are met, to paraphrase Lincoln, on a great battlefield for the soul of American public education. Today's battlefield may well determine the future, if not the very existence, of universal public education.

Ideological battles over the content of education are not new. The Scopes trial in the 1920s provided a focal point for fundamentalist and evangelical Christians wishing to ban the teaching of evolution. The battles of these religion wars, focused as well on school prayer and Bible reading, "intelligent design," or the teaching of various sex education content, have been ongoing with greater and lesser periods of focus and fervor (Zimmerman, 2021).

The teaching of American history also has a history, with various voices advocating for inclusion. Early efforts advocated to expand accounts to ensure that the heroes of ethnic groups were represented in historical events, such as the American Revolution (Zimmerman, 2021). By the 1960s, with demands for Black studies at the university level, there was a new focus on deeper changes to curricula (Berkshire, 2021).

Within a deeply divided national political context, today's battles seem more acute than those of the past. Within an environment championing "choice" that is subdividing school funding along a continuum of public school districts, publicly funded charter (or alternative or community) schools, and voucher-supported private schools, one wonders if "the center" can hold. Is the "public" in public education being threatened by these divisions? And to what extent is the public being manipulated by other interests?

Astroturf

In recent years, political forces have turned their attention to seeding their interests at the local level. "Astroturf" groups posing as grassroots organization representing parental interests are working to establish themselves on school boards and other local positions to influence policy. In May 2021, former advisor to President Donald Trump, Steve Bannon, announced on his podcast, "the path to save the nation is very simple—it's going to go through the school boards." Bannon was merely echoing the earlier sentiments of Ralph Reed of the conservative Christian Coalition. Reed stated, in 1996 "I would rather have a thousand school board members than one president and no school board members" (Zimmerman, 2021). Both emphasized a focus on building support at the local level, and in down-ballot races typically garnering little public notice (Nierenberg, 2021).

Ballotpedia has noted an increase in activist-driven recalls of school board seats to create openings (Nierenberg, 2021). The Ohio School Boards Association noted a 50 percent increase in the number of school board candidates in 2021, many running for the first time. Paul Beck, a political science professor at the Ohio State University, notes the role of nationwide efforts, some supported by Koch Industries funding, to fill boards with conservative representatives (Ingles, 2021). Diane Ravitch cautioned against the rise of "astroturf," groups engaging in local education issues and school board races. "When an alleged 'grassroots,' 'family-led' group of 'ordinary moms' begins their existence with a budget of more than $1 million, you can be certain there were no bake sales. Look, look, look to the Waltons or some other funder of astroturf groups" (Ravitch, 2021).

Southlake, Texas

One example of likely astroturf influence is Southlake, Texas, which may be recognized as a leader in the battle against antiracism efforts. Responding to a student-created viral video with racist content, the Carrol Independent School District took steps, as reported in an NBC podcast, to build a greater level of student respect and acceptance of diversity. Pushback from conservatives in the community rose to the level of lawsuits against school board members, a restraining order against development or implementation of the diversity plan, and a change in the composition of the school board.

A group leading the opposition, Southlake Families PAC, committed to "Judeo-Christian values," was not a grassroots movement. It was formed by the local Republican Party and raised $250,000 to support local candidates.

Their model has been credited with influencing similar efforts elsewhere in the country. Among their strategies was a stated opposition to "critical race theory," which they conflated, inaccurately, with a laundry list of hot-button issues of race, gender, and sexuality (Hixenbaugh, 2021).

Critical Race Theory

In the early 2020s, CRT was introduced as a school issue. Conservatives claimed that CRT was "being taught" in elementary schools and was divisive and racist, intentionally blaming White children for America's history of slavery. There were claims of subversion and Marxist indoctrination.

While it is true, and often pointed out, that CRT derives from graduate-level legal frameworks, it has also had a place in education research. In education research, critical theory urges the inclusion of the life stories of marginalized groups in order to confront "historical illiteracy" that serves to maintain social inequities (Taylor, 2000).

Conservative activist Christopher Rufo, however, found the term itself to be a handy pejorative replacement for terms like "political correctness" and "cancel culture," in fighting cultural wars. He mined footnotes in corporate antiracial bias trainings in order to cherry-pick supposed links to Marxist thought and introduced the term for conservative use.

Its connotations are all negative to most middle-class Americans, including racial minorities, who see the world as "creative" rather than "critical," "individual" rather than "racial,' "practical" rather than "theoretical." Strung together, the phrase "critical race theory" connotes hostile, academic, divisive, race-obsessed, poisonous, elitist, anti-American (Wallace-Wells, 2021).

Rufo attracted the attention of the Trump White House and was soon invited to assist in drafting an executive order aimed at limiting the way that federal contractors could address race in diversity seminars (Wallace-Wells, 2021). As a result, many states enacted vague legislation to ban the teaching of various topics believed to be a part of "Critical Race Theory."

Lindsey Love, the first Black school board member in Chandler, Arizona, remarked on the conflation of issues. "It's all morphing into the same thing," she noted. "You hear people comparing children being masked to slavery and referring to mask supporters as Marxists." A father addressing the school board opined, "Mask mandates, forcing vaccines, canceling prom, limiting graduation, critical race theory. The list goes on. When is enough enough?" (Berkshire, 2021)

An examination by *EdWeek* of proposed and enacted state legislation, considered to be "anti-critical-race-theory" bills, identified five categories of focus:

1. "Divisive" or "racist or sexist" concepts
2. Other rules related to discussing identity

3. Bans on "action civics"
4. Curriculum transparency requirements
5. Prohibitions against teachers showing bias

EdWeek sourced much of the language found in the bills to the Executive Order issued by former President Donald Trump (and overturned by President Joe Biden), and various conservative political advocacy groups, including the Heritage Foundation and ALEC (Schwartz, 2021).

A Columbus Dispatch editorial suggested a motive, noting that "these bills are not about protecting children from critical race theory, but they do create a boogeyman people fear" (The Dispatch Editorial Board, 2022). Lindsey Love expounded on the motive for the creation of such boogeymen. "There's this constant refrain that our schools are broken, that they're liberal indoctrination camps." This, she claims, sets the stage for parents to look for options outside of public schools (Berkshire, 2021).

Online "Influencers"

A new wrinkle in the formation of public opinion, with a powerful capacity to drive local action, is the emergence of online "influencers." The Internet has provided multiple venues, and echo chambers, for communication by persons with a wide range of qualifications. Success is measured in "clicks" and "followers," and some are "monetized" by advertising. While YouTube may well be a great way to share handy household tips, caution is warranted in seeking expert advice on complex topics.

But many are drawn by the comfort of finding "communities" of people who agree with them (often maintained by "blocking" involvement of others). Such echo chambers provide useful "crowdsourcing" tools to overwhelm local issues. Online campaigns have targeted LGBTQI+-inclusive events held in schools and libraries, and in some cases posed sufficient threats to result in cancellations.

A Pride Prom, scheduled to be held in a Jacksonville, Florida, public library was cancelled following a telephone campaign organized by vlogger Elizabeth Johnston through her Activist Mommy Facebook page. She urged her substantial cadre of national followers to call the library and "express your disgust that this perversion is taking place in a taxpayer funded library." The library cited security concerns as the basis for their decision (DiMichele, 2019).

A Columbus, Ohio PTA found itself under attack when it announced an afterschool movie-themed event hosted by two local drag queens, dressed as Disney characters. The free event, part of a month-long readathon, was broadly supported by parents and school staff. The event was cancelled when the school was flooded with calls, emails, and negative reviews from anonymous sources, believed to be from outside of Central Ohio, recruited through unidentifiable Twitter accounts. An Ohio library was also forced to cancel a "Drag 101" theater workshop for teenagers following a campaign of threats. Former Ohio House Speaker Larry Householder, with some influence over library funding, wrote to the Ohio Library Association expressing his opposition to such events (Neese, 2020).

Like CRT, issues involving the rights and inclusion of students, and families, who are gay or transgender, provide a useful boogeyman. Online echo chambers serve to both amplify fears and to organize broad, and threatening, campaigns.

Big Walnut Local Schools, Sunbury, Ohio

A prime example of school board controversy happened in a rural/suburban school district north of Columbus, Ohio. In the fall of 2021, three new school board members were elected to the five-person board. In campaigning for election, one candidate who was elected listed issues such as age-appropriate academics, rejection of "therapeutic" learning that is emotionally manipulative, and "woke" curriculum (Friends of Alice Nicks, 2022).

In the spring of 2022, these new board members faced a routine renewal of the district's membership in the Ohio High School Athletic Association (OHSAA). This awakened fears of Association policies regarding participation by transgender students. Some opponents suggested that trans-athletes would over-run girls' athletics. Locker room issues also came up. The prospect of not being able to participate in statewide sports competitions if membership was discontinued led the community to react strongly. Hundreds of high school students walked out of class in protest and parents who strongly supported the sports programs let their voices be heard. After reviewing a letter from the OHSAA, pointing out both safeguards in their policy and the tiny percentage of trans-athletes, the school board voted unanimously to rejoin the association. Said one parent, "I just want to see our kids being put at the forefront of the decisions of this board, not politics. I don't want to see our kids being used as political pawns. That's not what they're here to do" (Herchik, Halperin, & Griffin, 2022).

COMMUNITY ENGAGEMENT FOR COMMUNITY GOOD

Federal programs in education since the 1960s have tended to require community support and engagement. While we have seen how several of these requirements have changed over time to focus more specifically on individual parent support for their own children, some have maintained a broader focus. These include early childhood and vocational education.

Early Childhood Education

Head Start and Early Head Start are undoubtedly the largest and best-known sources for community-based early childhood education. These federally funded programs provide services through 1,600 public and private nonprofit and for-profit agencies. Of interest here is the long-standing focus on involving parents not just as service recipients, or learners of parenting skills, but also as advocates within their homes, schools, and communities. The various centers across the United States must include parents as members of advisory committees but may also identify additional parent contributions, such as serving as a liaison to the local community (The National Center on Parent, Family, and Community, 2019). As noted earlier, the role of community liaison is included in Epstein's parental roles, codified as a part of federal education funding, and seldom operationalized.

Career and Technical Education

Career and technical education present fertile ground for mutual interaction between communities and education systems. When education systems fail to engage with local industry, skills gaps are likely to emerge between graduates and employer needs.

Tri-Rivers Career Center in Ohio worked with local industry to identify and respond to a manufacturing skills gap. The result was Robotics and Advanced Manufacturing Technology Collaborative (RAMTEC), which opened in 2013. Working with local industry to identify needed skills was fundamental in creation of the original site in Marion, Ohio. State funding assisted in expanding the model to other locations around the state. Engaging with industry was the key to developing curriculum and identifying needed tools and machinery. Many high school graduates find that they are immediately employable, and the centers provide training for adults seeking new skills (Tri-Rivers RAMTEC, 2018).

STEM education is another area where schools and local communities have built mutually advantageous relationships. Appalachian communities in Ohio and West Virginia, for instance, have lost jobs because of the decline in the coal industry. There is a strong need to grow the local work force and talent pool in emerging new industries and to rebuild regional economies. Partnerships between local entities and curriculum developers assist with cultural relevance and teacher training. Materials can be enhanced through regional field trips. Teleworking opportunities, enhanced during the COVID-19 pandemic, also hold promise for geographically isolated communities that fear loss of family members who attain higher education.

EMERGING METHODS FOR BUILDING CIVIC ENGAGEMENT

The current mood of the country is one more heavily focused on individualism, "I," than community, "we" (Putnam, 2020). We see this in calls for individual "opt out" policies regarding coursework and educational content. A controversial Florida education bill, aimed at limiting the teaching of topics related to gender and sexuality is titled Parental Rights in Education—with the intimation that individual families can set certain educational parameters for their own children (even at a cost of the exclusion of other families and individuals). However, such individualism is not destiny. It is possible for communities to organize around common concerns in ways that allow warring camps to find some greater good to which they can commit. In some cases, schools can lead, and in other cases schools can choose to join with others.

As noted in the power and inclusion discussions earlier, defining parents and communities as too troubled, or otherwise incompetent, to deserve, want or participate in meaningful engagement, serves as a powerful protection against the possibility of losing social or political power. Much research into civic engagement has therefore focused on individual barriers to participation (socioeconomic status, race, ethnicity, cultural differences). Well-meaning educators may conclude that external factors well beyond their control are responsible for a perceived absence of parental and community presence. They may see themselves as benevolent actors in excusing the lack of relationship. Such assumptions, however, also mask the role of engagement structures themselves in maintaining social inequities, building on unexamined biases of the designers of public participation opportunities (Clark, 2021, p. 363).

Some Examples of Community Engagement

For educators to move outside of the geography of school buildings to find the community that lies beyond requires first some internal work to let go of a belief that school superintendents are solely responsible for the quality of education in their schools. This belief not only sets up an impossible responsibility for superintendents, and their faculty, but it also "leads to alienation and irresponsible public behavior" (Getting Out of the Box, 1999, p. 135). When the public, or parental, voice in planning and accountability for education is denied, tantrums at school board meetings (or down votes on operating levies) should not be surprising.

When the Community Is Allowed to Come In

Moving outside the schoolhouse doors to find community (or welcoming others to come in) is seldom a trip down some yellow brick road to a happy Land of Oz. One example is the experience of Madres Unidas in Oakland, California. A parent-led community group, organized by the Oakland Coalition for Community Action, successfully lobbied their district for the creation of a bilingual community school organized around social justice. A new school resulted from their eight years of advocacy. In the process of making decisions preparatory to the school opening, however, it was clear that parents and teachers had subtle, but important, differences in defining community and social justice.

The teachers held an understanding of social justice that did not recognize the life experiences of the immigrant mothers who had spurred the school's creation. They objected to the name the parents selected for the school, which emphasized community, while advocating for something more in line with their own understanding of justice—focused on individual heroes. However, they also leaned on the parents, many of whom spoke little English, to recruit sufficient English-speaking students to ensure a bilingual experience. As teachers were hired to staff the new school, they tended to see the parents as having responsibility for life outside the building (such as recruiting English-speaking families), while holding to authority over "school" (Dyrness, 2011, pp. 86–87).

Another experience is more positive. An Ohio school district superintendent inherited a picture of Jesus in a school, hung fifty years earlier in memory of a former superintendent. The American Civil Liberties Union (ACLU) demanded removal and the district's attorney confirmed the legality of their stand. The superintendent was deluged with letters and calls. One, wholly defensible option, would have been to remove the picture and issue a statement regarding the legal requirements.

Instead, the superintendent provided a series of opportunities to hear public opinion. Opinions were widely varied, some ugly. Some recounted personal experiences of religious discrimination. The superintendent's role was to listen, just listen. Through listening, he was able to identify a unifying theme, that of sadness, a loss of heritage and values commitment. It was this that provided the context as he moved the picture from the school to a local church, held a ceremony in honor of the former superintendent, and convened an effort to define community values.

The grounding provided by this effort was helpful as the district faced another, weightier decision, that of building a second high school, which would divide the student body. A substantial process of listening led to a different solution, an expansion of the existing high school, which would then be subdivided into four school communities. This served to maintain unity and a sense of community—both important community values (Irish, 1999).

The communities in these examples differ from one another. Each community, however, consisted of a population having varied, and in some cases strongly held, beliefs and opinions. Community is perhaps best defined as those beyond the school building who share a concern for education. Engagement requires multiple skills and activities, but perhaps the most important is that of listening and honoring the opinions of those in the community.

COMMUNITY ENGAGEMENT GROUNDED IN LOCAL CONDITIONS

Some, when considering community engagement, think in terms of enticing various local service providers to co-locate within a school building (or nearby). Such providers might be envisioned as providing health care, dentistry, counseling, or perhaps even tutoring to students. Such "supportive" services are generally regarded as solving problems that the educators have diagnosed as barriers to students learning and progressing through the curriculum.

Such visions fall short of community engagement on several fronts. First, they seldom provide for the experts within "school" to go beyond either the geography of their building or their committed areas of expertise as they engage with other professionals already working, often similarly siloed, with their students. Educational professionals often work from a viewpoint that students come to school bearing burdens created by others, which require the expertise of others to resolve (Singleton, 2015, p. 11). Should health-care professionals, for instance, point out a lack of physical activity through the school day, the educators may think in terms of an add-on, afterschool program, rather than considering ways to incorporate movement into their teaching.

Such service-focused visions also tend toward gathering "experts," that is professionals, into planning groups to respond to some need they have defined. Should any parent or other "community" voices be considered, they are frequently brought in as an audience to consider plans already arrived at by others. This leads to a "majoritarian" dominance, with assumptions that overlook structural inequalities that pose barriers to learning while accepting myths of parental incapacity or disinterest in education. Also missing when the "counter stories" of parents and others are not heard is the recognition of strengths and skills existing in families and communities (Dyrness, 2011, p. 4).

Friere emphasized a need for humility when engaging in dialogue with an intent to create change.

> How can I dialogue if I regard myself as a case apart from others—mere "its" in whom I cannot recognize other "I"s? How can I dialogue if I consider myself a member of the in-group of "pure" men, the owners of truth and knowledge, for whom all non-members are "these people, or the great unwashed?" (Freire, 2003, p. 90)

This is not to suggest that educators are universally ignorant of structural inequities of the systems and communities within which they teach, or other life experiences of parents or community members. Kozol notes the conversations with teachers and administrators who recognize enduring racial and economic segregation, and its negative impact, but feel constrained from advocacy by prevailing views within their communities (Kozol, 2005, pp. 219–221). To the extent that authentic marginalized voices are not brought to the planning table, there is substantial likelihood that they will not be effectively represented, even by educators who have heard and understand their stories.

Comer describes collaborative changes to school culture as a preferred response to various issues often deferred to experts to "fix" through "work" with individual students, or their families. He shares his experience using a School Planning and Management Team, to infuse principles of child and adolescent development into school improvement planning aimed at improving academic achievement. His team included a broad representation of staff: teachers, psychologists, social workers, special education staff, and parents. Prevention-focused, the work centered on creating a school culture supportive of healthy student development. A move from control and punishment, implemented by the collaborative group, brought positive changes in student behavior with fewer students being deemed as candidates for individual interventions (Comer, 2009, pp. 17–18).

Comer describes his experience in bringing parents into the Planning and Management Team. An initial school year brought out many disagreements and mistrust. However, as relationships were built, parents were effectively involved in school governance, including the Personnel Selection Committee, in addition to more traditional tasks of organizing social programs. Parents participated in setting major curriculum concerns, which included teaching basic skills as well as teaching pride in belonging and pride in contributing (Comer, 1993, pp. 130, 150). Such broad involvement in setting and understanding curricular goals at a macro level may provide insulation against demands for parental review of all lesson plans, with opt-out/veto ability for individual students.

An Asset-Based Community Approach

In the tumultuous, racially focused school year of 1968–1969, East High School in Columbus, Ohio, a *de facto* segregated Black public school, won state athletic championships in both basketball and baseball. Team members also managed, despite barriers to acceptance of Black students in colleges— including in athletics—to do well in higher education. The story of the stellar East High Tigers, told in *Tigerland*, focuses extensively on the work of coaches and principals to identify and coordinate assets within a racially segregated neighborhood characterized by poverty, vulnerability, and denial of many basic rights.

Assets culled by Principal Jack Gibbs included entrepreneurs serving the Black community, local ministers with national connections (including hosting the Reverend Martin Luther King), a thriving Black newspaper, and the family support of parents whose employment often precluded their attendance at school athletic events. Coach Bob Hart identified an informal athletic feeder system in the Peer Club. The club, consisting of Black men whose race had prevented them from following their own talents into professional teams, sponsored a little league team that provided early training to promising young athletes (Haygood, 2018).

Recognition of such community assets is easily obscured in needs-based approaches to community engagement. Not only does such a deficit focus prevent "the experts" and decision makers from seeing potential working capital, but it is also dispiriting and alienating to the communities being targeted for "help." "Imagine raising children under tough economic circumstances and on top of that be hearing a constant stream of negative messages about you as a parent or negative comments about your community, culture or religion" (Miller, 2017, p. 77).

The State of Michigan provides an example of positive collaboration in their response to 1997 amendments to the IDEA, viewing parents as assets, rather than deficits. The Act promoted involvement of parents of students with disabilities in Positive Behavior Support training. By deliberately including parents with teachers in intensive training, the state discovered that the included parents enhanced the value of training for the professionals. The state ultimately moved to include parents as trainers. The role of parents was thus transformed from that of being the "content" of training to co-learners. In so doing, the professionals discovered a benefit from the parental experience beyond the school walls (Ballard-Krishnan et al., 2003).

The Michigan example suggests that a more open view toward parent inclusion has benefits for professionals as well as families and students. It is, however, drawn from a niche set of families, making generalizations difficult. Other research has shown that the assets parents may bring are not equitably recognized. Middle-class educated parents may be viewed more positively by educators, and their contributions more welcome. Schools may need assistance in building relationships with lower-income parents by working through community-based organizations. Such organizations (a frequent community asset) may offer the advantage of not only leveraging relationships between families but also assist in mediating trust issues between educators and parents (Warren et al., 2009).

Community Organizing for School Reform

Designing new, and more equitable, engagement structures requires both cultural humility on the part of those who traditionally create such opportunities and a willingness to include marginalized groups in planning. Cultural humility consists of designers of engagement structures being willing to examine themselves and their frames of reference in order to understand how their own experiences and biases color their problem definitions and conceptions of what engagement might look like (Clark, 2021, pp. 364, 372; Holley, 2016, p. 52).

The Kirwan Institute for the Study of Race and Ethnicity at the Ohio State University provides a set of principles for authentic civic engagement:

1. Embracing the gifts of diversity
2. Realizing the role of race, power, and injustice
3. Radical Hospitality: Invitation and Listening
4. Trust-Building and Commitment
5. Honoring Dissent and Embracing Protest
6. Adaptability to Community Change. (Holley, 2016, p. 23)

Many of these principles are present in Mauricio Miller's Family Independence Initiative, which focuses on supporting naturally occurring networks of families in working through solutions to economic problems together. Instituting this approach not only requires recognition of (and placing trust in) the gifts within those networks, but it also requires training staff not to step in with "help" in making wise (according to their values and experiences) decisions, but rather to focus solely on gathering data on various impacts, such as employment and earnings (Miller, 2017, p. 130). Kirwan recognizes the importance of such "horizontal" networks in "bridging" social capital, a necessity in moving from traditional to more inclusive structures of engagement (Holley, p. 30).

Effective community engagement must be broadly inclusive. It must also be responsive to localized conditions, as understood by citizens generally, as well as educators and other professionals. Further, effective community engagement requires an emphasis on discovering strengths and resources, rather than just compiling needs and problems, of a community. Without such an asset-based focus, which includes parents as assets, any needs assessments must lead to a search for resources beyond the community, rather than nurturing local assets to be responsive (Kretzmann & McKnight, 1993, pp. 352–353).

Doing things differently than they have been done in our own country requires an acknowledgment of the enormity of the problem of poverty. Two-fifths of the population is impoverished. No "program" implemented by educators has the power to change this. Change will require community, or collective, action. Building communities with such capacity requires professionals to share control and encourage agency (Miller, 2017, pp. 127–129)

An Annenberg Institute study examined the impact of community-based school reform efforts. The study noted that "continuous and consistent parent, youth and community engagement produced through community organizations both generates and sustains these improvements." The research noted both capacity for successful learning environments and higher student educational outcomes (Mediratta et al., 2008). It is important to distinguish between community organizing, which involves power-building and a base outside of school, and more traditional parent organizations that serve a public relations function in support of existing school structures and practices (Gold et al., 2004, p. 58).

Annenberg also identified several characteristics of effective engagement initiatives:

- They were inclusive and dialogue-driven.
- They sought meaningful and long-term improvements in schools.
- They attempted to establish common ground and broad consensus around complex and controversial issues.
- They featured an atmosphere of candor and trust (Rodriguez & Villarreal, 2003).

Networking for Growth and Resilience: International Models

The OECD is a rich resource of data relating to education, economics, and governance across many countries internationally. One topic of study over time has been the development of resilient and sustainable systems of education, connected to localized skill needs and changing economic realities. With the advent of COVID-19, they were well-poised to gather data about education responses across a range of countries.

As a general rule, the time to build resilient systems is before a time of crisis. The OECD model for resilient systems of education relies on both empowering educators to "lead rich learning processes," and positioning schools at the center of networks to support student needs for services and to provide ongoing learning for teachers to stay current with changing technologies, and the like (Organisation for Economic Co-operation and Development, 2021).

An analysis across forty-three education systems internationally found that those best poised to counter learning gaps on return to school buildings following COVID-19 shutdowns were those with strong networks in place prior to the disruption. Citing the potential of such linkages to "open the black box" of what happens in classrooms and foster transparent systems of accountability, OECD advocates for networks that both extend the classroom into the community and create space for the community within the operation of the school. "Strengthening mechanisms for the co-creation of education policies and processes is also necessary in order to meet the needs, passions and hopes of all students more fully" (Organisation for Economic Co-operation and Development, 2021).

OECD offers some examples of international education systems having formal processes focused on parent engagement. Australia has a national parent engagement network that employs research to identify effective strategies to build capacity. Strategies include preservice teacher training and professional development. Ireland supports parents with family literacy initiatives and homeschool liaisons to empower adults in student's homes (Organisation for Economic Co-operation and Development, 2021).

Multiple countries engaged Internet providers to ensure student access to lessons during quarantine and shutdowns. As education systems return to more-accustomed configurations, they can build on these networks as they face learning gaps.

OBSERVATIONS

Faced with shouting on many sides, it is tempting to suggest carving the education pie into ever smaller and more specialized slices, each designed around the needs and desires of some specific group. This leads to some interesting questions. Who has responsibility for the leftovers (and there are always leftovers)? Are there belief systems that represent a bridge too far to be accommodated by public education, and more importantly, recalling historical segregationist efforts presented as "parental choice," what are they? Can accountability for quality be maintained across an increasingly diverse landscape of special interest schools? Can rural and sparsely populated areas even contemplate such accommodation? Or, alternatively, can we consider better means of fostering authentic parent involvement and community collaboration around issues of education?

One place communities might start is to focus on early childhood education. Head Start services are already available to low-income parents. But the need for education prior to kindergarten cuts across income levels. It also overlaps with the need for childcare while parents work. Although educators expect early childhood experiences to prepare children for later learning, parents, particularly mothers, have additional concerns, such as hours to fit with a work schedule and perhaps transportation. Working parents, particularly women, have been impacted by COVID-19-related changes to their employment, enhanced by closing of childcare centers, schools' transition to online classes, and erratic start-up of in-person classes (Miller, 2021).

Moving forward, in a post-COVID-19 world, a community approach to early childhood education will need to consider family childcare as well as learning needs. There may be new lessons to consider based on the pandemic experience. Might employers be urged to consider a continuation of flexible hours or teleworking, for instance.

Every community has many similar opportunities to nurture collaborative efforts to impact education. Rather than exclusive focus on the parent-teacher-student triad within schools, attention must be paid to encouraging "social capital" between and among parents beyond school. Community-based organizations can provide important linkages between parents and schools as well as building groups of parents. Such groups, operating outside of school systems, are critical to building and sustaining school reform (Warren et al., 2009, p. 2213).

The focus on community-based organizing for school reform is an important departure from the notion of "bringing in" experts from various fields to address student and family deficits that are believed to stand in the way of educators from being successful. Rather, the approach works to build on and develop agency and strengths within the community itself, in order to advocate for and support school reform. This will require a shift away from the "I" focus, as noted by Putnam, to a "we" focus. This shift, however, is necessary and appropriate for growth and development of a system of public education in a democracy.

REFERENCES

Auerbach, S. (2007). From moral supporters to struggling advocates: Reconceptualizing parent roles in education through the experience of working class families of color. *Urban Education*, 250–283.

Ballard-Krishnan, S. A., McClure, L., Schmatz, B., Travnikar, B., Friedrich, G., & Nolan, M. (2003). The Michigan PBS Initiative: Advancing the spirit of collaboration by including parents in the delivery of personnel development opportunities. *Journal of Positive Behavior Interventions*, 122–126.

Berkshire, J. C. (2021, June 22). *Culture war in the K–12 classroom*. The Nation. https://www.thenation.com/article/society/culture-war-classroom-teachers/.

Clark, J. K. (2021). Designing public participation: Managing problem settings and social equity. *Public Administration Review*, 362–374.

Comer, J. P. (1993). *School power: Implications of an intervention project*. New York: The Free Press.

Comer, J. P. (2009). *What I learned in school: Reflections on race, child development and school reform*. San Francisco, CA: Jossey-Bass A Wiley.

Congressional Research Service. (2009). *Parental involvement provisions in the Elementary and Secondary Education Act (ESEA)*. Washington DC: Congressional Research Service.

Cooper, C. W. (2009). Parent involvement, African American mothers and the politics of educational care. *Equity and Excellence in Education*, 379–394.

DiMichele, A. (2019, June 24). *Library cancels sold-out Pride Prom event*. The Florida Times-Union. https://www.jacksonville.com/story/news/2019/06/24/jacksonville-library-cancels-sold-out-pride-prom-event-says-it-cant-provide-adequate-safety/4826911007/.

The Dispatch Editorial Board. (2022, January 23). *Our view: Critical race theory bills would poison future at the expense of kids*. The Columbus Dispatch. https://www.dispatch.com/story/opinion/editorials/2022/01/23/editorial-ohio-bills-ban-critical-race-theory-poison-future/6579974001/.

Durand, T. M., & Secakusuma, M. (2019). Negotiating the boundaries of parental school engagement: The role of social space and symbolic capital in urban teachers' perspectives. *Teachers College Record*, 121(2), 1–40.

Dyrness, A. (2011). *Mothers United: An immigrant struggle for socially just education*. Minneapolis: University of Minnesota Press.

Freire, P. (2003). *Pedagogy of the oppressed*. New York: The Continuum International Publishing Group, Inc.

Freng, A., Freng, S., & Moore, H. A. (2006). Models of American Indian education: Cultural inclusion and the family/community/school linkage. *Sociological Focus*, 55–74.

Friedan, B. (1997). *The feminine mystique*. New York: W. W. Norton & Company, Inc.

Friends of Alice Nicks. (2022, May 23). *Home*. Alice Nicks for Big Walnut School Board. https://www.alicenicks.com/.

Getting out of the box. (1999). In W. G. O'Callaghan (ed.), *The power of public engagement: A beacon of hope for America's schools* (pp. 147–157). Manhattan, KS: The Master Teacher Inc.

Gold, E., Simon, E., Mundell, L., & Brown, C. (2004). Bringing community organizing into the school reform picture. *Nonprofit and Voluntary Sector Quarterly*, 54–75.

Haygood, W. (2018). *Tigerland*. New York: Alfred A. Knopf.

Herchik, M., Halperin, E., & Griffin, D. (2022, April 27). *Big Walnut schools to stay in state sports organization after questioning transgender policy*. NBC4i. https://www.nbc4i.com/news/local-news/sunbury/big-walnut-schools-board-raises-concerns-about-ohsaas-transgender-athletes-policies/.

Hixenbaugh, M. (2021, November 2). *Diversity plan opponents win control of school board in Southlake, Texas*. NBCnews. https://www.nbcnews.com/politics/elections/diversity-plan-opponents-win-control-school-board-southlake-texas-rcna4337.

Holley, K. (2016). *The principles for equitable and inclusive civic engagement*. Columbus: The Kirwan Institute for the Study of Race and Ethnicity at the Ohio State University.

Ingles. (2021, October 22). *School board races are hotly contested this year*. The Statehouse News Bureau. https://www.statenews.org/government-politics/2021-10-22/school-board-races-are-hot-this-year.

Irish, C. M. (1999). Working through the fear (and creating a culture of engagement). In W. G. O'Callaghan (ed.), *The power of public education* (pp. 159–169). Manhattan, KS: The Master Teacher Inc.

Kozol, J. (2005). *The shame of the nation*. New York: Crown Publishing.

Kretzmann, J. P., & McKnight, J. L. (1993). *Building communities from the inside out: A path toward finding and mobilizing a community's assets*. Chicago, IL: ACTA Publications.

Ladd-Taylor, M. (1995). *Mother-work: Women, child welfare and the state, 1890–1930*. Ubana and Chicago: University of Illinois Press.

Lott, B. (2001). Low-income parents and the public schools. *The Society for the Psychological Study of Social Issues*, 247–259.

Mediratta, K., Shah, S., McAlister, S., Fruchter, N., Mokhtar, C., & Lockwood, D. (2008). *Organized communities, stronger schools*. Providence, RI: Annenberg Institute for School Reform at Brown University.

Miller, C. C. (2021, May 17). *The pandemic created a child-care crisis. Mothers bore the burden*. The New York Times. February 5, 2022. https://www.nytimes.com/interactive/2021/05/17/upshot/women-workforce-employment-covid.html.

Miller, M. L. (2017). *The alternative: Most of what you believe about poverty is wrong*. Kindle Edition: Lulu Publishing Services.

Moy, A. (2022, February). *State board books*. Publiceducation.ohio.gov. http://public.education.ohio.gov/StateBoardBooks/2022%20-%20Board%20Books/February%20-%202022/Public%20Participation/Ambor%20Moy%20Testimony.pdf.

The National Center on Parent, Family, and Community. (2019). *Families as advocates and leaders*. Boston Children's Hospitals. February 5, 2022. https://eclkc.ohs.acf.hhs.gov/sites/default/files/pdf/rtp-advocates-leaders.pdf.

Neese, A. W. (2020, February 9). *Columbus school's PTA cancels "drag queen story hour," citing safety concerns, harassment.* The Columbus Dispatch. https://www.dis patch.com/story/news/education/2020/02/09/columbus-school-s-pta/1741862007/.

Nierenberg, A. (2021, October 27). *The conservative school board strategy.* The New York Times. https://www.nytimes.com/2021/10/27/us/the-conservative-school-board-strategy.html.

O'Connor, C., Robinson, S. R., Neal-Jackson, A., Hope, E. C., Hengen, A., & Drotar, S. (2019). *Race-making in schools of choice: Teacher narrative construction of the Black interloper.* Teachers College Record. https://www.tcrecord.org/Content. asp?ContentID=22700.

Organisation for Economic Co-operation and Development. (2021, November 22). *3. Strengthening resilience at the broader learning environment level through strategic networks and empowered education staff.* Education Policy Outlook 2021: Shaping Responsive and Resilient Education in a Changing World. https:// www.oecd-ilibrary.org/sites/ca34a20a-en/index.html?itemId=/content/component/ ca34a20a-en#section-d1e10669.

Pew Research Center. (2019, January 24). *Public's 2019 priorities: Economy, health care, education and security all near top of list.* Pew Research Center. https://www. pewresearch.org/politics/2019/01/24/publics-2019-priorities-economy-health-care-education-and-security-all-near-top-of-list/.

Putnam, R. D. (2020). *The upswing: How America came together a century ago and how we can do it again.* New York: Simon and Schuster.

Ravitch, D. (2021, April 5). *Maurice Cunningham: The rise of Astroturf rightwing "parent groups".* Diane Ravitch's Blog. https://dianeravitch.net/2021/04/05/ maurice-cunningham-the-rise-of-an-astroturf-rightwing-parents-group/.

Rodriguez, R. G., & Villarreal, A. (2003, November–December). *Community and public engagement in education: Opportunity and challenge.* Intercultural Development Research Association IDRA Newsletter. https://www.idra.org/resource-center/ community-and-public-engagement-in-education/.

Rogers, J., Lubienski, C., Scott, J., & Welner, K. G. (2015). Examining the parent trigger as a strategy for school reform and parental engagement. *Teachers College Record*, 117(6), 1–36.

Schwartz, S. (2021, July 19). *Who's really driving critical race theory legislation: An investigation.* EdWeek. https://www.edweek.org/policy-politics/ whos-really-driving-critical-race-theory-legislation-an-investigation/2021/07.

Singleton, G. E. (2015). *Courageous conversations about race: A field guide to achieving equity in schools.* Thousand Oaks, CA: Corwin.

Sorensen, M. E. (2013). *A case study in online parent community in an educational environment* (Doctoral dissertation). Ann Arbor, MI: ProQuest LLC.

Taylor, E. (2000). Critical race theory and interest conversion in the backlash against affirmative action: Washington State and Initiative 200. *Teachers College Record*, 539–560.

Thompson, G. L., Warren, S., & Carter, L. (2004). It's not my fault: Predicting high school teachers who blame parents and students for students' low achievement. *The High School Journal*, 5–14.

Tri-Rivers RAMTEC. (2018, August 2018). *Tri-Rivers RAMTEC addresses manufacturing skills gap*. Tri-Rivers Career Center. https://tririvers.com/tri-rivers-ramtec-addresses-manufacturing-skills-gap/.

Van Der Wal, L. (2020). *Parent-teacher relationships and the effect on student success*. Iowa: Northwestern College.

Wallace-Wells, B. (2021, June 18). How a conservative activist invented the conflict over critical race theory. *The New Yorker*.

Warren, M. R., Hong, S., Ruben, C. L., & Uy, P. S. (2009). Beyond the bake sale: A community-based relational approach to parent engagement in schools. *Teachers College Record*, 2209–2254.

What is Bronfenbrenner's ecological systems theory? (2019, May 3). The Psychology Notes Headquarters. https://www.psychologynoteshq.com/bronfenbrenner-ecological-theory/.

Woyshner, C. (2003). Race, gender and the early PTA: Civic engagement and public education, 1897–1924. *Teachers College Record*, 520–544.

Zalaznik, M. (2022, March 16). *Family engagement is more important than ever: How K–12 leaders are responding*. DA District Administration. https://districtadministration.com/k-12-school-leaders-respond-parent-family-engagement-more-important-than-ever/.

Zelman, S. (2021). Informal interviews with 103 Ohio superintendents. Unpublished study by the author.

Zimmerman, J. (2021, September 9). *Why the culture wars in education are worse than ever before*. Politico. https://www.politico.com/news/magazine/2021/09/19/history-culture-wars-schools-america-divided-512614.

Chapter 5

School Governance in America

WHO CONTROLS AMERICAN EDUCATION?

Who has responsibility and authority over public education? Parents? Teachers? School administrators? Elected school board members? State legislators? U.S. Congressional representatives? The state or federal departments of education? Everyone? Public governance of public education is quite complicated.

Within the public are many contradictory interests. As an example, some people claim that education, and as a result society, is diminished when there is no sanctioned prayer in schools. Others humorously say that so long as there are sports competitions and academic assessments, prayer in school will always exist. Still others have argued all the way to the Supreme Court that there should not be any official prayer in school because the U.S. Constitution specifically states that "Congress shall make no law respecting an establishment of religion." This one issue alone reveals how complex it is to govern public education.

This chapter explores public school governance in the United States from the intentions of the Founding Fathers as written in the Constitution through the growth of state and local agencies and federal oversight. It explores changes to the regulatory roles of the federal, state, and local governments and considers the ongoing tensions between local control and the need for standardization as well as the balance between equitable access and high quality. In defining different education stakeholders, the ongoing interactions between school governance and the political forces of government are revealed.

The U.S. Constitution

The ratification of the U.S. Constitution in 1788 marked the movement from a confederation of individual states to the birth of a new nation. As certain as that change is regarded from the vantage point of today, it is important to recall the sense of risk that must have been experienced for states to agree to some degree of submission to a new federal government. The powers of the federal government, therefore, are carefully delineated, with the clarification that all others that are not mentioned remained with the states. Education was not mentioned as the purview of the federal government. Education, then, is a state responsibility in the United States.

The American system of government incorporates multiple means of diversifying power. Not only are multiple authorities granted to the states, but the federal government is based on three co-equal branches (executive, legislative, judicial) designed to serve as checks on one another. States generally mirror the federal system of checks and balances. Although the federal government has national concerns, the state systems are not designed to create policies of cohesiveness across all states but rather to provide for a multiplicity of voices that reflect the citizens of each state and a broad marketplace of ideas.

A Thorough and Efficient System of Education for Common Ideals

Acting on the primary role for education assigned to states by the U.S. Constitution, most state constitutions mention their responsibility for "a thorough and efficient system of education" or other similar language. Any national system that affects states requires that each state buy into it.

Although the states are granted responsibility for education, the state role has not negated all possibility for federal involvement or local oversight. For example, in the 1800s, the federal government required, as part of the land grant system, that each community establish a local school. These schools were supported by tuition and operated under local, not federal, control. In addition, despite federal Supreme Court desegregation orders from the 1950s to the 1970s and some district consolidations, the states left much of the educational policies to local districts.

From the 1980s to the present day, governors, legislatures, and state courts have taken a more aggressive role in creating systems based on equitable access to quality education, a national goal. Mechanisms developed include academic content standards, assessments, and accountability. There have been attempts to improve adequate and equitable funding of school districts. Various choice options have been funded in attempts to improve outcomes through a competitive "marketplace" of education. Each state has charted its own course to meet federal goals.

As outlined in this book's Introduction, Horace Mann, regarded by some as the father of public education, coined the term Common School. Mann was an ardent supporter of what we recognize today as universal public education. Mann's vision of the Common School was intended to make education available to rich or poor alike across the nation. Education for all students regardless of race, sex, or class was intended to achieve a base level of literacy but also to support adherence to a common set of American ideals. Still, the definition of such ideals was and is a state matter.

Charles Glenn in 1988 offered a critique of Mann's concept. Glenn referred to the Common School as a single state-approved pattern. While agreeing with the importance of free education and that the state should set clear expectations for every child, he differed with Mann's vision for a common set of ideals. Whereas Mann included civic virtue, facts, and intellectual skills in his education reform, Glenn argued that this does not allow for personal family convictions in a diverse pluralistic society (Glenn, 1988).

The attempt to create a single "common" vision has resulted in public education in the United States being plagued by continual philosophical differences. Some of these have dealt with the role of religion in public education, pedagogical concerns such as reading and math wars, and various enduring hot-button issues surrounding sex education, free speech, and the teaching of science and history in classrooms. For example, Eurocentric views of history/arts/literature have not only overlooked other cultural contributions, but they can also lead to social support for enduring cultural mythologies and racial prejudices. The very notion of common ideals tends toward cultural genocide, such as experienced in the American Indian Boarding Schools.

Understanding the American system of education, or rather the fifty-plus systems of American education, requires consideration of the changing landscape of various players over time.

STATE GOVERNANCE OF EDUCATION

As states took responsibility for education, they established governing bodies to adopt policies and organize state systems to promote education and serve the needs of students, families, and educators in each state.

State Departments of Education over Time

As outlined in the Introduction of this book, the education system of the United States developed over time. State-governing agencies developed in response.

1812–1890

Throughout the 1800s after the Constitution was adopted and during the periods of Education in a New Nation, the Common School era, and throughout Reconstruction and Industrialization, as outlined in this book's Introduction, state departments of education were established in each state. At first, these departments were advisory, but after the Civil War, with the expansion of public education, they became more powerful and developed the foundation for state educational systems, consolidating forces for education that included teachers, legislators, and parents. The departments of education were strongly influenced by social and economic movements.

1890–1946

During the Progressive era of American education history, with the acceptance of compulsory education and the need to enforce attendance, maintenance and operational functions of the state departments of education were strengthened.

1947–1964

Multiple issues arose in public education during the Cold War era. These included the capacity needed by urban and rural schools to provide for universal compulsory education. In response, states worked to consolidate and reorganize school districts, with a particular focus on providing a greater number of services to rural students. School financing also became a significant priority for state departments of education. In addition, national pressure to provide technical training for industrial expansion was addressed.

1965–1980

As part of the Equal Education Opportunity era of American education history, state departments of education were overhauled as they responded to federally defined needs for social, economic, and demographic changes in local schools to meet demands for greater student achievement in science and mathematics. They also became responsible for ensuring that minimum standards were met to combat inequities and students with special needs were addressed.

1980–Present

State departments of education were changed again by the 1983 publication of "A Nation at Risk." As a result, states have taken on a greater responsibility for public dissemination of test data and holding districts accountable for achieving Adequate Yearly Progress toward academic proficiency goals. These responsibilities have forced state departments of education to address both technically and politically challenging roles (Roe & Herrington, 2022).

Overview of State Roles in Education

Education is one of the largest areas of state government spending. States have organizing bodies that play different roles in education. These bodies are defined in each state constitution and have specific responsibilities related to public education.

Governors

Governors are popularly elected and serve as a state's chief executive officer during a term of office. A governor's power over education varies from state to state, in accordance with the state's constitution. For education, a governor makes appointments, signs legislation related to education, and is responsible for enforcing it.

Governor's Cabinet

Governor-appointed cabinet members advise the governor on policy, which may include educational issues.

State Superintendent

Variously known as Chief State School Officer or Commissioner, the Superintendent is typically the head of a state's department of education. The state superintendent carries out the educational policies of the board of education, including legislative actions.

State Department of Education

A state's department of education is part of a state's executive branch with a mission to promote academic achievement in the state. It serves as the administrator of a state's public schools. State departments of education interpret and facilitate legislation relating to education, including state education budgets.

State Board of Education

The state board is typically a nonpartisan policymaking body for academic standards, curriculum, instructional materials, assessments, and accountability.

State Legislature

Each state's legislature is responsible for writing state laws relating to educational policy, budgeting, and spending allocations.

State Judiciary

The system of courts settles disputes related to education.

Governors

Although some may think that the governor of a state has authority over education during his or her term in office, his or her powers in that arena are limited. In the spring of 2020, it was the governors across the country who announced school building closures due to the pandemic. But although governors have used the bully pulpit, as George Wallace did in 1963 when he stood at a schoolhouse door to block the entry of two Black students and stop the desegregation of schools, historically, governors have left key education decisions to local and state boards of education.

As a result of the economic crisis of 1982, however, governors saw education as a factor in addressing a weak economy and a rise in global competition. Sensing an unmet need, they formed a policy agenda hoping to reap "political support and influence as a primary reward" (Henig, 2013, p. 36).

In the 1980s and 1990s, the NGA helped support governors through technical assistance delivered by highly qualified staff. The NGA helped to make education both a national and a state public issue. Given the national and state focus on education, governors challenged the traditional authority of state boards of education, and their state school superintendents.

Southern governors took the lead with an interest in improving education in their states. They understood the importance of a high-quality education system for improving their state's economic development. Many of these governors later carried out their school improvement agenda at the national level. Henig points out that most governors in the 1990s followed the Southern governors' lead. Most governors mentioned the importance of education in their State of the State addresses. Many also proposed educational reform policies and programs. However, in this new role, governors found themselves in conflict with the agendas of state superintendents, appointed by state boards of educations or state-elected superintendents of education, who are independent of state boards of education (Henig, 2013, p. 36).

The variability of different state governance structures makes a difference in implementing education reform. States differ from one another in the number and size of districts and the extent to which state legislatures and governors respect local control. Therefore, it is important to understand at the state and local levels the different state governance structures and how education reform can or cannot work within these structures (Dahill-Brown, 2019).

By the late 1980s, governors who wanted more power over education found themselves trying to challenge the traditional roles of the boards of education and state superintendents. Governors saw them as possibly competing or blocking the governor's educational reform agenda. Governors understood that they needed to compete with elected state superintendents and elected state boards of education that had their own constituencies and individual and state policy priorities.

Governors were able to increase their influence on education by expanding their ability to appoint state superintendents. From 1980 to 2005, the nation went from five governors appointing state superintendents to fourteen governors with appointment responsibility. In addition, governors moved to control the selection of members of state boards of education. In 1997, Ohio's Governor George Voinovich convinced the legislature to change the composition of the Ohio State Board of Education from twenty-three elected positions to eleven elected positions with eight gubernatorial appointees. The chairs of the Senate and House Education Committees also now serve as ex-officio members of the State Board of Education.

"A Nation at Risk" helped governors legitimize their enhanced role in education (Henig, 2013, p. 39). However, even before "A Nation at Risk," governors such as Bill Clinton of Arkansas, Bob Graham of Florida, James Hunt of North Carolina, Richard Riley of South Carolina, Tom Kean of New Jersey, and William Winter of Mississippi realized the relationship between education and the economy. They sensed an economic pressure beginning to develop from global competition.

Different governors in the same state place different emphases on educational policy. In Ohio, Governor George Voinovich supported a strong investment in early childhood education. Then came Governor Taft with a strong reading initiative. Governor Strickland supported, but never got passed, a school funding initiative. Governor Kasich supported educational innovations and statewide mentoring. Governor DeWine has funded social and emotional learning (SEL) and supports. Districts jump through hoops and compete for funds based on whatever agenda is current. Educators overwhelmed by "the flavor of the month" frequently wait to see which changes will last.

Remember that the founding belief articulated by Horace Mann was that state boards should be nonpartisan to ensure continuity of educational policy and balance the power of government. Governors' powers to appoint board members and, in some states, board chairs increased in thirty states. A primary role for governors in educational policy is still strong in most states.

State Superintendents

State superintendents of education may also appear to have the authority over education in a state. They are known by various titles, depending on the individual state's constitution or legislation. They can be known as superintendents of public instruction, commissioners of education, directors of education, or secretaries of education. They are represented nationally by the Council of Chief of State School Officers (CCSSO).

State superintendents come to their positions in one of the three ways: elected by citizens of their state, appointed by a state board of education, or appointed by the governor. State superintendents do not necessarily require an educational background. Elected superintendents have been lawyers, state legislators, and communications experts. Many superintendents have come to the position with experience as local superintendents of schools. A few come from higher education or extensive experience in state government. In most states, they serve as the administrative head of the state's department of education.

The primary role of the state superintendent is to serve the interests of school districts and students and to ensure equal educational opportunity and equity. Superintendents who are appointed by a state board may face reappointment every time a new board is convened. They are only as powerful as the support of the board that appointed them. If they are appointed by a governor, they serve at his or her pleasure and cannot afford to alienate any of the governor's stakeholders. Elected superintendents must raise money for statewide campaigns and convince their constituencies that they are meeting the state's needs.

Regardless of how superintendents come to their position, they all must work with media outlets to promote their educational agenda. They must work with their state's congressional delegation to ensure the state's federal funding and their views are represented in national debates. Variability in government from state to state makes a difference in state policy (Dahill-Brown, 2019).

In all states, state superintendents, regardless of how they came to the position, are accountable to multiple authorizing environments. They must work in partnership with the governor if they want their educational agenda to be implemented. They must establish a good working relationship with legislative leadership to support their legislative agenda. They must have a strong relationship with the attorney general's office to ensure adequate representation in federal and state courts.

State Departments of Education

Today, each state, U.S. territory, and Washington, DC has a department of education that has been granted its powers and responsibilities by a state constitution. Each is headed by a superintendent and coordinates activities with local school districts and federal and state agencies. In recent years, state departments of education have moved from a primary focus on regulatory compliance to provision of technical assistance and support for academic and other student-focused areas. Departments of education are justified by state constitutions and legislation. The departments within each state department of education help form the legislative agenda for their state boards by providing data on the conditions of education in the state. They also serve a quasi-judiciary role among local districts and other interested parties. For example, departments may be responsible for approving territory transfers, mediating special education disputes, and adjudicating educator licensing decisions. The role of state education departments is also shaped by the changing landscape of federal legislation.

Historically, state departments of education have also been given responsibility for other functions where there was no other state agency to do so. Some state departments have accepted authority for operating schools for the deaf and blind and for overseeing interscholastic sports, teacher placements, community colleges, and library services. This expansion of expectations can lead to agencies being understaffed. Employees who are funded by state and/ or federal funds must interpret and facilitate the implementation of various federal and state laws through regulatory processes.

In the 1960s and 1970s, many retired local school superintendents were employed by state departments of education. Working for the department was a prestigious position, and salaries made the position even more attractive. From the 1990s to the present day, however, department of education budgets and salaries are no longer competitive with many well-to-do suburban school districts.

Today, in response to federal funding requirements state departments of education are focused on statewide strategic planning to meet the needs of all students and try to provide support to districts that serve vulnerable students and families. In an age of new technology, they may provide networking opportunities and professional development for educators. Again, there is great variability in the sizes of departments of education and their budgets.

In the 1990s two books questioned the capacity of state departments to implement this new important mission of supporting low-performing schools (Lusi, 1997; Madsen, 1994). In Ohio, the legislature questioned the ability of the state department of education to support the lowest-performing districts, resulting in the creation of the Academic Distress Commissions (ADCs). The commissions were intended to govern poorly performing school districts for five consecutive years to troubleshoot and improve outcomes. ADCs were tasked with appointing district CEOs to develop strategic plans to improve performance. Plans and implementation were approved and monitored by the

ADCs. Unfortunately, the legislation did not eliminate or clarify a new role for district boards of education. Believing that they still had control over districts created conflict that inhibited the new CEOs from focusing on district improvement. A lack of demonstrated success has led to the Ohio legislature slowly dissolving the ADC mechanism with control and responsibility returning to the local school board.

In some states, like Massachusetts, educational consulting firms have been contracted by the state departments of education to provide support to the lowest-performing districts. These consulting firms work with districts to build staff capacity for improving education outcomes.

COVID-19 has recently demonstrated the stresses on federal and state safety net systems. Cohen and Hill's book, *Learning Policy*, documents that those teachers who consistently implemented state policy at the local level had better outcomes for students. Most teachers lacked access to support for learning new practices that the state policies required (Cohen & Hill, 2001). Again, there is a disconnect between what the state proposes and the state and regional capacity, such as education service centers, to provide the professional expertise to educators to implement new initiatives. Therefore, education reform is uneven among districts, given the variability of resources at the state and local levels for implementation.

Some hold that decision-making processes inside bureaucratic structures hamper the implementation of policy by under-resourced departments with limited personnel. In addition, many state agencies across the country do not reflect the racial and ethnic makeup of their state (Madsen, 1994).

State Boards of Education

In 1826, Horace Mann as former president of the Massachusetts Senate was appointed to lead a state board of education. Establishing a board outside the legislature was intended to divorce education from general gubernatorial and legislative politics. Soon after, twenty-six states emulated Massachusetts's example in creating their own state boards of education. These state boards were designed to engage in important discussions about educational policy without partisan infighting.

State boards of education around the country today have different types of authority. Some are part of the state department of education, while others are independent. Minnesota and Wisconsin do not have state boards of education. The New Mexico public education system has the only state advisory board (Education Commission of the States, 2022). Some state board members are elected, while others are appointed. Some boards, like Ohio's, have a hybrid membership of elected and appointed members. The role of state boards of education differs across the country, depending on state constitutions and state legislative authority.

The National Association of State Boards of Education (NASBE) is a membership organization of state board members. It helps support the capacity of state boards in policy development and national networking. It is the lobbying arm to Congress for state boards of educations. According to NASBE, the state boards of forty-five states adopt learning standards for all students. In thirty-one states, states boards have primary authority over state assessment systems. Most boards establish high school graduation requirements, determine educator certification requirements, establish district and school accountability policies, and accredit local districts (National Association of State Boards of Education, 2022).

In contrast to Mann's vision of a state board that operated separately from political concerns, governors and state legislators have in recent years become increasingly interested in having an active role in education. Many state legislators have adopted market-based views as discussed earlier and have come to see their state departments of education as bureaucratic and inefficient, justifying legislative activity.

Some state boards of education reflect cultural trends. Ohio presents an example. In July 2020, the Ohio State Board of Education responded to a summer of national focus on racial bias in public policy following the murder of George Floyd with the adoption of a resolution condemning racism. The resolution directed districts and the department to examine curricula for bias and provide anti-bias training to department employees. This resolution sparked hours of public testimony that accused the board and the department of endorsing CRT, prohibiting the teaching of our country's founding documents, encouraging white children to feel guilty, and leading schools to communism, socialism, or Marxism.

By October 2021 the composition of the board had changed, and the resolution was rescinded, replaced by a resolution that "condemns any standards, curriculum, or training programs for students, teachers, or staff that seek to divide or to ascribe circumstances or qualities, such as collective guilt, moral deficiency, or racial bias, to a whole race or group of people" (State Board of Education of Ohio, 2021).

Two appointed board members who failed to support the new resolution were informed that they would not be confirmed as required by the Senate and were asked by Governor DeWine to resign. Former state board president, Laura Kohler, wrote in an editorial in the *Columbus Dispatch* that "politics, not meeting the needs of children, are driving the educational policy these days. And anyone who doesn't get on board, even fellow Republicans, may be escorted from the arena" (Kohler, 2021).

State Legislatures

A state's legislature creates all the laws related to education in a state. The governor signs or vetoes the laws, and the department of education implements new legislation. State legislatures typically have education committees that consider matters concerning education in the state. They may pass laws related to free speech, privacy, school records, vaccinations, compulsory education, corporal punishment, graduation requirements, and what can and cannot be taught in school.

State Judiciaries

When disputes arise over laws or implementations of education laws and practices, the state judiciary system is responsible for solving the dispute. An issue may start on a local level and if one party files a suit, it can escalate to local and then to state court.

LOCAL CONTROL

The early development of "thorough and efficient" state systems of education relied heavily on local efforts to locate or build facilities, set curriculum, identify funding sources, and hire personnel. Local districts created governing systems to accomplish these tasks. They typically include these organizing bodies.

School Districts

Districts that are established by state education agencies to serve a particular geographical area may include one or many schools to meet the needs of the population.

District Superintendent and Administrator

Local boards of education appoint or hire a person to oversee the management of the district.

District Board of Education

District boards comprise elected or appointed members who address educational issues related to the school district.

School Principals and Administrators

Within each school district, the school board approves the hiring of principals who oversee the administration of each school in the district.

Teachers

Teachers are hired by school administrators and approved by the school board to oversee classroom activities with students.

Parents

Parents can serve a variety of roles in a school district. They can volunteer to help a teacher or with school activities. They can be members of a Parent-Teacher organization or appear as an advocate at school board meetings.

School Districts and District Superintendents

School districts are the creation of the state legislatures. In some states, such as Virginia, each county is a designated school district. In other states, counties may be broken into separate school districts. Large cities may be divided into individual school districts. Like town or county governments, school districts are established as local government units that operate under state law with authority over public school operations and policies. They may be independent or part of the local government.

The consolidation of schools in the mid-twentieth century significantly changed particularly rural school districts that banded together to provide more comprehensive programs and services. During this period, states moved to consolidate districts that were small and inefficient. District consolidation created an upheaval and is still resented by some districts and communities today.

Until the 1980s, state government left key decisions about K–12 education to local government (Henig, 2013, pp. 36–37). In most of the 15,000 school districts in the United States, a district superintendent is hired by the local school board. The superintendent is elected by voters of only a small number of districts. The role of the superintendent is a complex one. They have many authorizing environments. They must answer to the board, parents, their professional staff, and the community at large. Like state superintendents they need to develop many community-based partnerships with religious organizations, nonprofit youth development groups, town or city mayors, and county officials.

Superintendents must lead their boards in strategic planning to address equity issues, academic achievement, and faculty development. Successful superintendents possess skills that assure good school board relations. They run the day-to-day operations of the schools, and they oversee transportation, building projects, and maintenance. The superintendent must understand state and school budgeting (Zelman, Interviews with 101 Ohio Superintendents).

Most state constitutions and legislation grant states authority over school districts in areas such as control over teacher education and certification, school calendars, compulsory education, and financial support to the local tax base.

Sarah Dahill-Brown describes the problems of the perception of local control. She points out that states can dissolve or create local school districts. As noted, Tennessee and Louisiana recently created recovery school districts. These districts contain low-performing schools now overseen by state authorities (Dahill-Brown, 2019, pp. 194–196).

Superintendents have been stressed by the COVID-19 pandemic, which has led to divisive community politics. The former superintendent of Palm Beach County said that "there was something shifting that forced us to deal with the politics way more than we ever did before. Democracy is messy. I think COVID brought out the hyper messiness." One superintendent reported receiving threatening letters and had a security team during COVID-19. He was called a child abuser because he mandated masks, his equity policies were questioned, and he was compared to a Nazi general. Superintendent Dan Domenech stated:

> We see a large number of educators, including principals, that are leaving the profession, and it is going to be a long-term problem. It's a matter of threats. It's a matter of politics. It's a matter of being able to do the job they feel they are able to do to protect children and staff. (Santiago & Weisfeldt, 2022)

Local School Boards

Local school boards are regarded by many to be best suited to implement policies that affect the day-to-day operations of a school district. The notion of local control implies that elected school boards throughout the United States are to govern "without the interference of state and local officials." Sarah Dahill-Brown notes that most elected school board members are not educators (Dahill-Brown, 2019, pp. 194–195). In this view the role of the local school board is to empower the district superintendent and central office staff to support teachers, principals, and parents who best know their children. The community, the school board, and the superintendent engage together in educational decision-making to provide best outcomes for students (Dahill-Brown, 2019, pp. 194–195).

Historically, school board elections have been nonpartisan and based on the individual qualities of the candidates. According to John Chubb, school board elections once were "political backwater" and "low visibility affairs," typically losing the spotlight to elections of city or town mayors or councils. In the 1990s and early years of the current century this remained the case. Some school boards even had difficulty recruiting candidates to run for office. Incumbents frequently ran uncontested (Chubb, 2001, pp. 24–25).

Chubb was not the first academic to criticize school boards. Seymour Sarason in 1999 argued for abolishing school boards and giving a greater voice in educational policymaking to teachers, parents, and the community (Sarason, 1999). He makes a strong case that new governance structures should emerge that address the question: What is the purpose of education? In addition, Howard Good in 2006 demonstrated that even with individuals who come on the board with good intentions, local and personal powers play, and their lack of knowledge of education put the boards' worth in doubt (Good, 2006).

Currently across the country, individuals who support a political agenda have been running for school board seats. As commented in *The New York Times*, Republicans particularly have used school board elections to politicize CRT and the teaching of civil rights history as campaign issues (Nierenberg, 2021). The 2021 elections suggest that school boards are no longer a "political backwater," but a political tool.

School board meetings have turned ugly as some parents, or other parties, shout, threaten, and interrupt respectful discussions on masking, vaccinations, remote learning, and the teaching of American race relations. The National School Board Association (NSBA) on September 29, 2021, wrote to President Biden requesting federal investigation and assistance when anger and threats follow school board members beyond school walls. Four states' school board associations, Missouri, Pennsylvania, Ohio, and Louisiana, countered by withdrawing from the NSBA (Staver, 2021).

School boards are no longer seen by the public as institutions that debate professional salaries, collective bargaining agreements (some states), district contracts, budgets, and strategic plans. The COVID-19 era has aroused a level of parental anger and suspicion that school boards are either simply incompetent in the face of challenges or have a nefarious agenda that is not in the best interests of children and education. Some districts still debate sex education, with new wrinkles having to do with LGBTQI+-inclusive materials. Others request reviews of required (or available) school literature. Transgender issues in athletics and bathroom use have been contentious (Nierenberg, 2021).

The Republican Party has capitalized on the dissatisfaction of parents regarding COVID-19 responses and culture war issues. Ballotpedia, a non-partisan digital encyclopedia of American politics and elections, observed efforts to use fears of CRT to unseat eighty candidates out of 207 school board candidates that they followed. Some suggest that this is a Republican strategy to influence mid-term 2022 elections and reclaim suburban districts that they lost in the 2020 presidential election. Senator Ron Johnson from Wisconsin stated, "Take back our school boards and our city councils" (Nierenberg, 2021).

Conversations with school board members at the Ohio School Boards Association meeting in November 2021 revealed that many believe non-partisan school board elections will no longer exist. Reminded of contested school board elections in Ohio from anti-tax partisans, they reported that school board elections remain a political issue. Anti-tax issues frequently arise in districts that have many students who attend religious and private schools. Parents of private school students may run for the school board to vote against putting a levy on the ballot (OSBA, 2021).

Political pundits believe that education was a factor in the successful 2021 Republican governor's race in Virginia and contributed to the narrow victory of the Democratic governor in New Jersey. School superintendents are very concerned about the politicization of local school board elections. They are angry that "dark money" by plutocrats may have jeopardized their jobs. They understand the importance of focusing the board on educational strategic planning to address the education of the whole child. Board politics, however, have become a tremendous distraction.

While superintendents felt that political divisions within their community over the handling of COVID-19 issues represented a no-win situation, the majority was concerned about children's safety and educational performance. They quickly worked with their boards to assure that their students had food as well as access to technology and the Internet so that they could continue their education. They developed plans to deliver education either wholly online or combined with some face-to-face arrangements. In some cases, they opted to continue schooling as usual.

Many superintendents relied on their assistant superintendents or curriculum directors to use new or emerging technologies to facilitate learning. They also had to educate their boards about how these technologies could support meeting the needs of individual students, but the technologies could not replace teachers. They are beginning to focus on technology integration across pre-K–12. Most school districts in Ohio now have an electronic device for every student. School board meetings have taken an unusual toll on superintendents. Many superintendents are thinking about early retirement, rather than waiting for contentious boards to retire them (Zelman, Interviews with 103 Ohio Superintendents).

Parental Community Control: A Subset of Local Control

In the turbulent 1960s, a community control movement hit large cities. Minority parents were frustrated that large districts were not adequately educating their children and called for an enhanced voice and influence. In 1964, a community-organized student walkout succeeded in bringing about a limited busing program for desegregation in New York City schools (*The New York Times*, 2019). By 1969, a decentralization bill established thirty-two elected community school boards across the city with responsibility for oversight of elementary and middle schools. A system of proportional representation ensured diversity on the boards (More Equitable Democracy, 2020).

Chicago, faced with multiple fiscal and management crises, instituted a system of locally elected school councils in 1988. One feature of the system granted substantial autonomy to school principals. By 1995, confronted with a failure to improve fiscally or educationally, the mayor was granted authority to appoint a single board resulting in increases in academic outcomes and in graduation rates (Welsh, 2021).

Oakland, California, in 2000, responded to the voices of over 2,000 parents, community organizers, and faith-based groups at an action to demand the establishment of "New Small Autonomous Schools." This event and the commitment that followed marked the beginning of a journey bringing together *Madres Unidas* as an external community group with the official governing entities of a school and district (Dyrness, 2011, pp. 6–7).

One weakness of formally decentralized governance was exemplified in broad controversy over the publication of *Children of the Rainbow* by the New York City Central Board in 1991. This 440-page resource was intended to provide curricular support to teachers presenting multiculturally sensitive lessons on tolerance. At the behest of groups lobbying the Central Board, approximately three pages were included to respond to the issue of same-sex families. Other groups, meanwhile, lobbied community school boards in conservative areas and were successful in arousing substantial opposition to perceived "dangerous information about sodomy" and a "homosexual conspiracy." Various boards adopted resolutions modifying use of the guidelines. The Central Board responded by voting not to renew the contract of Chancellor Joseph Fernandez (Karp, 1995).

The New York experience demonstrates the vulnerability of widely decentralized authority. The heightened sensitivity to aggrieved voices also renders such localized authorities susceptible to manipulation. As various anti-gay groups targeted the New York Community Boards, rather than the Central Board, recently, other radical-right groups have sought election to seats on local school boards. A study by People for the American Way identified hundred such candidates in two Southern California counties, with a third of them winning seats. Ralph Reed of the lobby Christian Coalition urged that such candidates not divulge their affiliations (Karp, 1995).

While few "on the front lines" in education have ever appreciated the work of "the central office," there remains a certain efficiency in the ability of a strong leader to make decisions and handle crises. When Michelle Rhee became Washington DC's first chancellor appointed by Mayor Fenty, there followed a period of reform resulting in academic gains for students. Yet problems remain in terms of equitable access and enduring achievement gaps. Further, the leadership style of Rhee and other rapid reformers failed to generate the broad support needed to continue progress (Mead, 2017).

FEDERAL GOVERNANCE

During the 1950s and 1960s, the federal government's role expanded due to the Cold War between the United States and the Communist Bloc countries. During this period, the NDEA changed the federal relationship to state and local authorities. As our economy became more global, there were increased tensions between the United States and the Soviet Union. The tensions influenced the perception of a need for this bill. The act focused federal education spending from Congress on ensuring that students would be capable of defending our democracy and on assuring a well-qualified workforce to compete globally (Corcoran & Goertz, 2005).

The National Defense Justification

The most significant event credited with reshaping public expectations and federal involvement in what schools could and should accomplish was the 1957 Soviet launch of Sputnik. The 1958 NDEA helped to fund major math and science curriculum projects and extensive teacher training, as well as foreign language labs in high school. The NDEA did not mandate these programs but incentivized states and districts to implement them. Dahill-Brown notes that this federal act

> set a precedent for targeted federal assistance, spurred matching investments from local and state communities, presaged the outcomes of 1964 debate over general vs. categorical aid, included provisions that supported the expansion of testing to identify gifted students, and raised concerns about curriculum and standards more broadly. (Dahill-Brown, 2019, p. 83)

This legislation set the tone for many reauthorizations that began to address equity issues through increasing federal aid to poor students and denying federal funds to those states that refused to apply.

Despite the NDEA, most Americans during the 1950–1970s continued to believe in the philosophy of local control of schools. They believed that their local school board and superintendent should set educational policy and budgets for their schools. They fostered democratic localism and individualism without any connection to state interest.

Equality and Civil Rights Considerations

Chapter 3 discussed the Supreme Court decision, *Brown v. Board of Education*, decided in 1954, which in many ways framed the equity debate that we are still having today as a nation. That Supreme Court decision increased the federal role in ensuring students' civil rights, arguing that the equal protection and due process clauses of the Constitution entitled students to equal access to education and appropriate educational programs (Dahill-Brown, 2019, pp. 80–82). The launch of Sputnik occurred just a month after the Little Rock Nine were escorted into Central High School to integrate the school district.

As urban districts came under Supreme Court pressure to desegregate during this time, an enhanced federal presence began to emerge in education. The ESEA of 1965 provided federal funding to equalize educational opportunity for low-income students as a part of the War on Poverty. The NAEP was put in place in 1969 to track student achievement at the national level and, particularly, to measure achievement gaps between demographic groups. These actions at the federal level led urban districts to enlarge their administrative capacity to ensure compliance with a new set of expectations. This tended to override vested community interests in setting educational policy.

In 1975, the federal government passed the Education for All Handicapped Children Act that affirmed the right of education for all students, regardless of ability (Taylor & Zelman, 1979). Students with special needs could no longer be denied a high-quality public-school education. The act required states to establish a Child Find program designed to reach out to such students and provide an adequate level of education appropriate to the disability. The federal government only provided 40 percent of the needed funding, and states were required to provide the rest to ensure that students were appropriately educated, alongside their typical peers, in the least restrictive environment.

Concern for International Competitiveness

During the period of the 1970s and 1980s, as the nation focused on both the NAEP measures and the international comparisons possible through the

OECD, there were concerns about the governing structures of education. Governance reforms of the 1970s and 1980s included school-based councils, parent selection of principals, enhanced community input on instructional programs, community control of schools, mayoral control over school boards, and the shifting control of federal and state government entities. However, this era of governance reform did not improve American student learning when compared to other Western democratic countries. Further, the tinkering did not significantly improve equal educational opportunity for all students (Organisation for Economic Co-operation and Development, 2021).

In 1979, under the Carter administration, education was separated from the Department of Health Education and Welfare and made a cabinet-level agency. This move reduced policy opportunities and funds that could be leveraged from health and human service programs. Federal restrictions impeded the leveraging of state and federal funds. Interagency rules are complex and made it difficult for states or local governments to receive waivers and show accountability for the use of these funds.

Accountability for Leaving No Child Behind

When Bill Clinton became president in 1992, he worked for standards-based reform that provided states resources to develop and implement state academic content standards to promote high learning expectations for all children. Legislation made funds available to local school districts, through their states, for school improvement and professional development. Most states took advantage of these funds.

During Clinton's years in office, the 1965 ESSA was reauthorized as Improving America's School Act. The act required each state to develop a single set of academic standards for all students, reduce bureaucratic processes, and document how they were using the funds. The law also helped to fund charter schools, safe and drug-free schools, professional development in math and science, and increases to bilingual and immigrant aid and education technology.

More specifically, the ESSA reauthorization gave more aid to Title I programs. In contrast to earlier versions, it also had stronger accountability measures for states, comparing outcomes for disadvantaged students to those of other students. Many states and districts simply overlooked this requirement. However, the requirement did lay an important basis for evaluating the intended impact of the federal dollars in terms of student achievement and graduation rates. The testing and reporting requirements were not widely followed by states. States and districts did not use data to formulate improvement strategies for students lagging their peers (Dahill-Brown, 2019, pp. 90–93).

During the George W. Bush administration, ESSA was reauthorized as NCLB. This was a bipartisan bill with the late Senator Ted Kennedy and Speaker of the House John Boehner working together with the president to assure passage. This version puts in place accountability for all subgroups of students. Testing data were reported for students receiving special education, ELs, those with low socioeconomic status, and minority populations.

NCLB required states to set goals (AYP) for achieving academic proficiency by all subgroups within five years. Annual achievement testing was required in grades 3–8 in reading and mathematics. State government officials were widely dismissive of the possibility that all subgroups could achieve proficiency. Many states set low progress goals for first years with steep improvement down the road. They hoped that reauthorization of the law would alter the requirement to meet the standards that they set. This did, in fact, happen.

After No Child Left Behind

In 2009, newly elected President Barak Obama announced a competitive grant fund for states called RTTT. Eligibility required states to link student achievement data to teachers, providing annual professional evaluations. State accountability systems were to include and place significant emphasis on these teacher evaluations. A further prerequisite to be considered for funding was for state applicants to participate in developing and adopting what became the Common Core academic content standards for mathematics and English language arts.

While nineteen states received funding, the response to teacher evaluations based on student performance on assessments created a furor. Not only did teachers and their unions object but also parent groups, fearing undue pressure on students, blamed the Common Core for creating an unhealthy educational environment. Objections took the form of complaints that local control was being lost and that students were being over tested, along with suspicions of government indoctrination of students through setting curriculum. As a result, many states rejected cooperation with the Common Core, returning to state-created standards and assessments

During the Obama administration, states wanted to be relieved of the academic achievement and gap-closing requirements of NCLB, which had frustrated many stakeholders at the local and state levels. States applied for waivers to various requirements. The waivers started a backlash against state testing as well as against the federal role, which was perceived as dictating states' educational policy. Many forgot that before NCLB states did not disaggregate or publish student achievement data or hold districts and schools accountable for student learning. No Child Left Behind may have been the most important piece of civil rights education for students ever passed.

State superintendents of education believed that NCLB shone a light on equity and helped them require poor-performing districts to pay attention and improve accountability for all vulnerable students and families. However in the next re-authorization of ESEA, the Every Student Succeeds Act (2015-2016) eliminated the accountability requirement of AYP. The keys to improvement, however, have proven to be elusive. And, to be fair to those on the front lines of education (who in 2022 face a third year of uncertainty and unprecedented stress because of COVID-19), individual classrooms, schools, and even districts are limited in their ability to bring about systemic improvement. Education is a systemic affair with historic roots that have included inequitable access. These historic structures have proven very difficult to overcome. Further, education exists in a larger economic system that in the United States sets no lowest bar of expectations in the realms of such basics as income security, health care, and housing. Some of our students live lives of continual crises that drain focus from learning.

SCHOOL FUNDING

Very few individuals understand how their school districts are funded and the source and rationale for these various funding streams. This section will explain the basic concepts of school funding. Some classic state court cases from Massachusetts, Ohio, Texas, and New Jersey are described in the appendix. Readers may develop an appreciation of attempts to use state and federal funding to create equitable access to education and some of the barriers to achieving that end.

Unlike Western European countries, the American education system relies heavily on local property taxes to fund its schools. Most districts in the United States also receive state funding, depending on the wealth of the district. State funding aims to equalize resources across local districts having vastly different property wealth and income levels. Federal dollars, which account for about 10 percent of the school funding, are distributed to states to allocate to local districts based on a variety of criteria. Federal funding frequently aims to support equity and civil rights compliance.

State and Local Funding

Combined state and local taxes account for about 90 percent of the public-school funding, including charter schools (Baker, 2018, p. 103). In recent years, some states have moved toward shifting public funds to private schools and homeschooling.

State formulas generally distribute funds based on district wealth. District wealth may be defined differently from state to state, but most states have a formula to take into consideration individual and commercial property values. A state formula considers the ability of the district to pay for adequate services. The definition of what is "adequate" may be based on the average of districts in the state or the lowest cost districts in the state.

The formula may also reflect the wages and cost of living across various geographical areas in the state, which indicate how much tax burden local citizens can bear. Different student needs, such as special education, bilingual education, and socioeconomic status, are recognized as the cost of education in districts, and needs are not evenly distributed. Some states assume responsibility for building construction or a share of transportation costs based on factors like the geography of the local district.

State school aid also needs to be understood in context of the variable state tax policy in the fifty states. States may allow or limit the taxing capabilities of local districts through such mechanisms as millage caps or automatic rollbacks in response to increases in property values. Some districts are permitted to tax local income, while others may be prohibited from doing so. Some districts, particularly in high wealth areas, have established foundations as an additional funding stream.

State funding generally seeks to achieve equity in the face of inequitable resources and needs across a spectrum of urban, suburban, rural, and other districts. In facing the inequities, the task of defining "adequacy" falls to legislatures as they attempt to respond, through budget allocations, to an uneven playing field. The question of what constitutes an adequate education has been the subject of multiple legal filings and court cases.

Adequacy: How Much Is Enough?

Bill Gates and many others have fostered the belief that "the U.S. spends more on schools than any society in human history" and that as we put more money in schools, our academic achievement has remained flat. Bruce Baker takes a closer look at education spending as well as U.S. achievement data over time. Much of the cynicism regarding the relationship between spending and achievement dates to a 1986 meta-analysis by economist Erik Hanushek. Later refinements to Hanushek's work eliminated some unreliable studies from the analysis, resulting in a stronger conclusion that financial investment in education does track positively with academic achievement. Baker was also able to consider tightening of education budgets through the 1980s and 1990s, leading to a picture of stagnant overall funding rather than dramatic increases. This stagnation in spending co-occurs with similar stagnation in achievement measures particularly in closing gaps between demographic groups (Baker, 2018, pp. 3–5 and 33–35).

Baker explains that when more money is given to schools, districts usually spend it on personnel and salaries. Human resources matter for high-quality education. Despite some progress, American teacher salaries are still less competitive with other professions than they are in Western European nations. Salaries affect teacher quality. Competitive compensation is needed for a more qualified teacher workforce (Baker, 2018, p. 227).

Education finance expert, Marguerite Roza, suggests that districts using federal COVID-19 relief money for short-term personnel positions such as summer school or tutoring have chosen a wise use of these dollars. She also notes that targeted raises in difficult-to-fill positions and one-time incentives such as moving expenses to attract personnel may not be sustainable (Hess, 2021).

In 2011, the Obama administration formed a national equity commission to explore funding inequities in the United States. It was clear from this report that high-poverty districts spent more per student than did low-poverty districts. However, such aggregate data mask important regional differences in labor and other costs. More important are more localized comparisons such as urban areas with their surrounding suburban rings as the competition for quality teaching staff is a significant factor in being able to meet student needs. This is even before factoring the enhanced cost of educating students having higher needs because of lower family income (Baker, 2018, pp. 117–119).

Examples of Good and Bad State Funding

No state funding formula is perfect. In the school choice discussion in chapter 3, there have been some serious inequities, for example in 1917 when states in the South spent only $0.29 on Black students for every dollar spent on White students. If school funding is based on property taxes, wealthy districts will always provide more school funding than impoverished districts.

According to Baker, Massachusetts and New Jersey have some of the best funding formulas to provide sufficient levels of funding for all students. It turns out that Massachusetts and New Jersey, two of the highest-performing states on the NAEP, have benefited from state court rulings on school finance.

By contrast, Illinois and Pennsylvania have regressive formulas, but state courts have refused to act (Baker, 2018, pp. 117–119). Since the 1990s, Ohio's school funding system has been declared unconstitutional four times by the Ohio Supreme Court, but the legislature has yet to adequately overhaul the system. Judicial oversight is important.

Baker suggests that state and the federal governments should collect data and monitor the equity and adequacy of states' school fiscal systems. The annual reports of state departments of education should report how the conditions of state funding address issues of educational equity and adequacy, as well as the allocations of federal aid to the general public (Baker, 2018, p. 206).

Federal Funding and the Influence of Court Decisions

Federal funding accounts for 10 percent of the overall education spending (Baker, 2018, p. 1). As noted earlier, federal dollars have attached compliance expectations that impact educational policy. ESSA gave dollars directly to poor districts and funded state departments of education staff to monitor their use. This reinforced a strong compliance culture in state agencies. The federal government requires that federal funds not supplant existing state funding but rather provide an expansion or enhancement. States are therefore required to show maintenance of their own effort in receiving funds for new programs.

In addition to such direct funding, Supreme Court decisions have defined various state and district spending obligations for education. Other chapters in this book discussed how the Supreme Court decision of *Milliken v. Bradley* (1973) exempted suburban districts from taking responsibility for the desegregation of urban schools. As a result, "white flight" to the suburbs created rings of mostly white, well-to-do suburban school districts surrounding mostly minority urban districts with declining property value and income levels.

In 1973, the U.S. Supreme Court in *Rodriguez v. San Antonio Independent School District*, 411 U.S. 1, held that the U.S. Constitution does not provide a right to equal educational opportunity based on students' relative wealth or poverty. In other words, this meant that education is not a fundamental right under the U.S. Constitution and that wealth is not a suspect classification. However, this opened the door for cases challenging the equity or adequacy of public school funding to proceed under state courts. By the 1980s, state courts were faced with cases charging that districts with low property wealth and a low-income population had fewer resources to spend on education than richer suburban school districts. Two-thirds of all such cases that won in the state courts were based on language in state constitutions such as "thorough and efficient," "a sound basic education," or "adequate education." There has been some legal action or lawsuit in most of the fifty states to address education funding disparities. See appendix A for more court cases.

COVID-19 Funding

In response to the education impact of COVID-19, the America CARES Act has provided $189 billion to states for education. The purpose of this money is to replenish funds that districts spent on health and safety requirements of COVID-19 as well as to enhance technology, equipment, and Internet services. Additional services are intended to help districts get students back on track. Some districts have used this money to develop summer school programs, tutoring, tele-counseling, longer school years, teacher shortages in special education, retention bonuses, and stipends for teachers who take on extra work (Hess, 2021).

The funding, however, came with little regulation regarding how dollars were to be spent. Education finance expert, Marguerite Roza, expressed concern that this one-time infusion of money could bring a disruptive "fiscal cliff," if it was used to postpone needed staffing changes in districts previously facing declining numbers. She highlighted some good fiscal practices, such as those followed by Atlanta, Denver, and Chicago, which gave a portion of this money directly to schools so that the principals in the community could address what students needed (Hess, 2021). While the global pandemic has been devastating to school districts and families, the requirement of engaging communities based on community needs might stimulate more innovation and educational equity.

International Comparisons

One way to think about American education is to compare it to the education systems in other countries. In his critique of the Common School, Charles Glenn leads us to investigate how Western European countries govern their school systems and lays the groundwork for a new governance structure for America to better achieve choice on how we educate our children. Glenn's ideas are also supported in Ashley Rogers Brenner's book, *Pluralism and American Public Education: No One Way to School*.

Brenner challenges our education and governmental structures and contributes to the vision of a new pluralistic regional education system governed by the states. Brenner argues that one of the main reasons the Common School system is failing to meet its goals is that it does not embrace pluralism, which other democratic countries have done. In her definition of pluralism there is a more expansive definition of public schools to include government support of private and religious schools with strong accountability (Brenner, 2017, p. 20). She believes that we can change the structure of our public education system. Such changes would mitigate against uniformity and mediocrity and achieve better outcomes for students. Families, therefore, would not have to compromise the inherent normativity of schooling and would be encouraged to think more deeply about educational outcomes for their children (Brenner, 2017, p. 21).

OBSERVATIONS

The country's founders feared a tyrannical and centralized government. Further, while the Articles of Confederation failed to create sufficient cohesion in some critical areas (such as taxation to pay for the Continental Army), the confederated states saw themselves very much as individual entities. In bridging these realities to arrive at a new constitutional government, there was great concern for the ability of the states to maintain cultural identities and authority in areas outside of those considered critical for national defense and survival. Education was among those duties and responsibilities that fell to the states.

State policies as well as federal policy around equity issues have sometimes fueled culture wars among states and local districts and between states and the federal government. Issues at all levels have been debated around common core standards, student and teacher accountability, and state takeover of low-performing schools. Furthermore, states' and districts' implementation of state and federal policy vary from state to state, depending on the geography and size of districts in the state; the number of rural, urban, and suburban districts; and the wealth of the districts.

State government structures differ from state to state with varying degrees of responsibility for governance by governors, state superintendents, and state board roles and authorities. In the past forty years, some governors have taken more of an interest in education because of its impact on the states' economy and on globalization. Governors change as the result of state constitutions and elections. Different governors in the same state place different emphasis on policies.

Horace Mann, echoing concerns by Noah Webster and Abraham Lincoln, believed that children must be taught at an early age to revere liberty, thus creating the concept of the Common School. All students, no matter their socioeconomic status, were to go to a public school grounded in the values of democracy, where they would receive a "common" or standard, level of education.

The Common School notion, however, is embedded in a historical, physical, and social environment that reflects a diversity of resources and limitations. Common School values were intended to replicate the ideals of a power elite and dampen the impact of immigrant values and beliefs. But education is also a social institution. It interacts with political, economic, family, media, and educational interest groups. We cannot understand education unless we understand the interactions of political and social systems on education. We have documented the impact of federal housing and banking policies on segregation and white flight to the suburbs.

The aspirational vision of a values-based common education for all has been impeded by multiple realities. While many of Mann's supporters endorsed education as a tool for the assimilation of immigrant children, insulating against the potential influence of "foreign" ideas, the notion of universal access to education has remained problematic. Education was systematically denied to the enslaved population lest they become empowered to oppose their status. This denial continued, again systemically, following emancipation, as a means of preventing economic competition with Whites. The legal reality (*Plessy v. Ferguson*) that transpired was one of separate and unequal education for Blacks and Whites throughout the South.

Throughout the North, where much of the responsibility for public education was ceded to local boards and local funding, access to a "common" education was uneven. In addition, not all immigrant groups embraced the notion of assimilation. Recall the German language schools in Columbus, Ohio, created in response to a population eager to maintain their mother tongue but also to contribute German methods of education to their adopted country (Uhas-Sauer, 2019). German methods, at the time, were more progressive than in the United States.

Such curricular and values-laden differences have been solidified by economically (and racially) segregated neighborhoods and school districts created by post–World War II federal housing policy. The resulting statewide "systems" of education with assignments based on students' residence have not produced quality education for all let alone any commonality of either academic curriculum or implicit (or explicit) values.

The neighborhood school, from which few parents, until very recently, have had alternatives, has become the site for renewed culture wars and arguments over school governance. The notion of a "common" education has never been without controversy. Common schools came into being as blatantly Protestant, incorporating Biblical content along with daily recitation of prayers and verses. Anti-Catholic teaching was permissible. The objections of Catholic families frequently took the form of advocating for the inclusion of Catholic teachings, or alternatively, for public funding for Catholic schools (Hunter, 1991, pp. 198–201).

While schools are not currently the site of Protestant versus Catholic battles (owing to the 1963 court decision removing prayers and religious teaching from public education), there remain organized voices calling for religiously inspired curricula and decrying their perception of immoral or at best amoral education within public schools (Hunter, 1991, p. 197). This tension invokes strong feelings among parents and the community about what needs to be taught and how it is taught. Conflicts arise over the multiple purposes of education: civic values, liberal arts, career and technical education, and collective bargaining versus right-to-work laws. The question before us is whether our systems of education can respond to such a diversity of beliefs and whether the notion of a "common" school structure, with neighborhood-based attendance zones, is the right one to do so.

Our schools are a microcosm of what occurs nationally and at state and local levels. We are now more divided politically and culturally than at any time since the Civil War. Traditional education interest groups have lost presence and influence. Such traditional interest groups as teachers' associations and unions, the business community, statewide administrative and school board groups now contend with various partisans, plutocrats, and influencers in federal-, state-, and local-level educational policy debates.

Many hold a nostalgic view of the neighborhood school and American democracy engaging in citizen participation. Such nostalgia often creates a barrier to state attempts to overcome funding inequities and student academic achievement gaps. As noted in chapter 3, many local districts are outgrowths of racially discriminatory housing and banking policies. While such policies have been legally struck down, many vestiges remain, particularly in demographics and property values. Local property taxes contribute significantly to school funding in most states.

Increasing compliance powers of federal and state agencies over local school districts during the past thirty years have not increased educational outcomes or significantly closed achievement gaps between our highest- and lowest-performing students. Governing structures at the state level reflect the current state of national politics. The most important question of what is good for students of any state has not been adequately addressed. Our current education governance and finance system may well be considered broken, reflecting the political divisions and cultural wars of our nation.

Experience suggests that merely tinkering with governance structures has not had a major impact on learning for all students. Therefore, we need to understand our current governance and imagine a new system reflecting and incorporating differences in educational philosophies and vested interests. This could serve to mitigate against the culture wars that have taken up residence in our schools.

Identifying the common ideals our nation has for its education system is essential. Educational governance needs to provide ways that we can amicably work together to explore and mediate educational options and philosophies.

REFERENCES

Baker, B. D. (2018). *Educational inequality and school finance: Why money matters for America's students*. Cambridge, MA: Harvard University Press.

Brenner, A. R. (2017). *Pluralism and American public education: No one way to school (education policy)*. Palgrave Macmillan.

Chubb, J. (2001). The system. In T. M. Moe, *A primer on America's schools* (pp. 15–42). Stanford, CA: Hoover Institution Press Publication.

Cohen, D. K., & Hill, H. C. (2001). *Learning policy: When state education reform works*. New Haven, CT: Yale University Press.

Corcoran, T., & Goertz, M. (2005). The governance of public education. In S. Fuhrman, & M. Lazerson, *The public schools (institutions of American democracy)* (pp. 25–56). New York: Oxford University Press.

Dahill-Brown, S. E. (2019). *Education, equity, and the states: How variations in state governance make or break reform.* Cambridge, MA: Harvard Education Press.

Dyrness, A. (2011). *Mothers United: An immigrant struggle for socially just education.* Minneapolis: University of Minnesota Press.

Education Commission of the States. (2022). *50 state comparison K–12 governance.* Education Commission of the States. https://www.ecs.org/50-state-comparison-k-12-governance/.

Glenn, C. (1988). *The myth of the common school.* Amherst: University of Massachusetts Press.

Good, H. (2006). *Inside the board room: Reflections of a former school board member.* Lanham, MD: Rowman & Littlefield Publishers, Inc.

Henig, J. R. (2013). *The end of exceptionalism in American education: The changing politics of school reform.* Cambridge, MA: Harvard Education Press.

Hess, F. (2021, November 10). *Ed finance guru Marguerite Roza on how schools can best spend COVID aid.* Education Next. https://www.educationnext.org/ed-finance-guru-marguerite-roza-on-how-schools-can-best-spend-covid-aid/.

Hunter, J. D. (1991). *Culture wars: The struggle to define America.* New York: Basic Books.

Karp, S. (1995). Trouble over the rainbow. In D. Levine, R. Lowe, B. Peterson, & R. Tenorio, *Rethinking schools: An agenda for change* (pp. 23–36). New York: The New Press.

Kohler, L. (2021, November 10). *Former Ohio school board member Laura Kohler: "Not resigning was not an option".* The Columbus Dispatch. https://www.dispatch.com/story/opinion/columns/guest/2021/11/10/ohio-education-board-member-laura-kohler-resignation-anti-racism-resolution/6338167001/.

Lusi, S. (1997). *The role of state departments of education in complex school reform.* New York: Teachers College Press.

Madsen, J. (1994). *Educational reform at the state level: The politics and problems of implementation.* Milton Park, UK: Routledge.

Mead, S. (2017, April 20). *The Capital of Education Reform.* US News and World Report. https://www.usnews.com/opinion/knowledge-bank/articles/2017-04-20/michelle-rhee-set-national-example-of-education-reform-in-washington-dc.

More Equitable Democracy. (2020, August 24). *NYC community school boards: Dispatch from New York City.* More Equitable Democracy. https://www.equitabledemocracy.org/nyc-school-boards/.

National Association of State Boards of Education. (2022). *About state boards of education.* NASBE. https://www.nasbe.org/about-state-boards-of-education/.

The New York Times. (2019, July 18). *The myth that busing failed (podcast transcript).* The Daily Show. https://www.nytimes.com/2019/07/18/podcasts/the-daily/busing-school-segregation.html.

Nierenberg, A. (2021, October 27). The conservative school board strategy. *The New York Times.*

Organisation for Economic Co-operation and Development. (2021). *OECD*. Education at a glance 2021: OECD indicators. https://www.oecd-ilibrary.org/education/education-at-a-glance-2021_b35a14e5-en.

Roe, W. H., & Herrington, C. D. (2022, May 9). *State departments of education: Role and function*. Education Encyclopedia. https://education.stateuniversity.com/pages/2447/State-Departments-Education.html.

Santiago, L., & Weisfeldt, S. (2022, February 1'). *Dealing with schools in the pandemic made him lose 50 pounds and collapse. So this superintendent got out*. CNN. https://www.cnn.com/2022/02/01/us/school-superintendents-quitting-pandemic/index.html.

Sarason, S. (1999). *Parental involvement and the political principle: Why the existing governance structure of schools should be abolished*. San Francisco, CA: Jossey-Bass Inc.

State Board of Education of Ohio. (2021, October). *Resolution to promote academic excellence in K-12 education for each Ohio student without prejudice or respect to race, ethnicity, or creed*. Ohio Department of Education. http://public.education.ohio.gov/StateBoardBooks/2021%20-%20Board%20Books/October-2021/Member%20Proposed%20Resolutions/Item%2013%20-%20Resolution%20to%20Promote%20Academic%20Excellence%20-%20Final%20-%20Certified.pdf.

Staver, A. (2021, October 27). Ohio School Boards Association cuts ties with national group over Biden "terrorism" letter. *The Columbus Dispatch*.

Taylor, K., & Zelman, S. (1979). Open the schoolhouse door. *Children's World*.

Uhas-Sauer, D. (2019). *A history of Columbus schools, 1806–1912*. Teaching Columbus. https://www.teachingcolumbus.org/a-history-of-columbus-schools-1812-1912.html.

Welsh, K. R. (2021, April 2). An elected school board is a big risk for Chicago. *Chicago Times*.

Zelman, S. (2021). *Informal interviews with 103 Ohio superintendents*. Unpublished study by the author.

Chapter 6

A New System of Education: Starting from Scratch

RENOVATING AN AILING SYSTEM OF EDUCATION

Throughout its history, the United States has worked to improve and fix its ailing system of education. At times the country has made great strides and at other times much effort has been put forth with minimal results. With the pandemic crisis, our nation is at a critical juncture. One 2020 survey indicated that as many as 44 percent of teachers plan to retire within two years (Will, 2022). At the same time, online education has provided realistic opportunities to address specific needs. The country is hungry for an educational system that will prepare future citizens for a positive, productive, and profitable tomorrow.

As Lincoln said one month before signing the Emancipation Proclamation:

We can succeed only by concert. It is not "can any of us imagine better?" but "can we all do better?" The dogmas of the quiet past are inadequate to the stormy present. The occasion is piled high with difficulty, and we must rise— with the occasion. As our case is new, so we must think anew, and act anew. We must disenthrall ourselves, and then we shall save our country. (Glass, 2017)

To build an education system for the future, all of us must think and act anew. We must disenthrall ourselves of the status quo. We must agree on a vision for education for our nation. This vision should center the needs of children and their families, within the national need for lifelong learners to support a sound economy and ecology. This will require challenging the vested interests that we outlined in the Preface, that of professionals, parents, producers, publishers, politicians, plutocrats, and partisans. In order to move from our current state, we will need to come together to craft this new vision of public education that prepares our children for a complex changing world full of uncertainties. We can prepare them to confront a landscape of new liabilities, as well as assets, such as climate change, emerging technologies, artificial intelligence, and changing geopolitical power structures. Our next system of education needs to address issues of equity, diversity, equal educational opportunity, and coherent governance structures that align federal, state, and local roles.

The first five chapters this book describe our historical journey leading to the current system of American education. We have defined five areas that we must address: curriculum and instruction, the teaching profession, school choice, community engagement, and governance and finance. In the Observations at the end of each chapter, we outlined those issues that must be addressed in building improved structures.

This chapter proposes a provocative model that may provide a way, with a firm understanding of our past, to think anew about American education. We propose a pluralistic model, drawing on features of our current system augmented by research into successes in other developed countries. We propose this new system for debate and discussion. We will also offer ideas of how states may move to implement new structures, even in our current, highly contentious atmosphere.

To build our model, we propose a private-public partnership to fund national competitions to implement new pluralistic education systems. Such systems will mobilize our ingenuity and apply emerging technologies to resolve the issues we have highlighted. Our dream is not the only possible vision for moving forward, but we hope that it may provide the basis for a new conversation about the direction of American education.

FROM COMMON SCHOOLS TO PLURALISTIC SYSTEMS

Horace Mann introduced the notion of a system of common schools to provide universal access to a common body of academic knowledge, grounded in a set of American values. As we have traced the history of American education, we have observed multiple changes and challenges to the content of such education as well as barriers to universal access. And yet despite obvious differences in access, content, and outcomes of our public education, we have held tenaciously to a belief that American education provides equally and equitably. Further, we continue to believe that it is possible for our system to adhere to a common system of values, beneficial to all. And yet the evidence indicates otherwise. Our vision of a common system leads us to deny the reality that schools and districts differ widely in the needs of students, the resources to meet their needs, and their success in doing so.

In this chapter, we suggest that a new model of public education is called for. In looking at the history of American education, it is clear that no single leader, group, or entity, has had a blueprint for the success of education in our democratic society. Simply raising standards with high-stake assessments is not the answer. Neither is lowering standards and reducing accountability as Virginia experienced when they moved away from rigorous standards, regulations, and testing and found that Virginia student scores on the NAEP dropped and students were falling behind their peers in other states (Virginia Department of Education, 2022).

Any system must reflect and be responsive to a wide variety of needs and interests of the population. We must commit to all American children, no matter where they live or what their ancestry, having the opportunity to reach their full potential. We are suggesting a move from our historic dedication to a false belief in commonality to a vision of pluralistic systems of public education.

A Pluralistic System of Public Education

A pluralistic system is not a single federal or state government takeover. It is not allowing a group of anxious parents to dictate what will or will not be taught in schools. It is not a privatization of education with no accountability.

We define a pluralistic system as having a multiplicity of schools that incorporate a range of education best practices and provide families and students with options. A pluralistic system may allow two or more sources of authority to co-exist, which affirms our nation's democratic principles and addresses the need for a strong accountability system that demonstrates academic outcomes. It would support and encourage educational innovation through new models that respect different beliefs, conditions, and lifestyles of diverse populations. The system creates a strong human resource system for the profession and encourages robust community engagement and civic participation. These best practices address the five problematic issues described in this book.

We support Ashley Rogers Berner's definition of pluralism as "changing the structure of public education so that state governments fund and hold accountable a wide variety of schools, including religious ones" (Berner, 2017, p. 3). This new structure would help an increasingly diverse and divided American population to choose schools that meet their educational needs.

For a pluralistic system to be successful, we must challenge our current norms in education. New norms are needed to consider government funding for private and parochial schools within clear accountability parameters and build upon what we have learned from our history of our current fragmented system. With a vision that centers on the needs of children, their families, and the population, our challenge will be to work with all vested interests that have a stake in our current educational system, the professionals, parents, producers, publishers, politicians, plutocrats, and partisans that include lobbyists from higher education, business, health, and human service providers, technologists, labor, legislators, parents, religious leaders, and taxpayers.

Noted scholars such as Mark Tucker, Linda Darling-Hammond, Charles Glenn, and others have discussed the possibility that a pluralistic system aligned with American values and clear aims could enrich the intellectual, civic, social, and moral lives of the next generation of Americans.

Our proposal for an accountable pluralistic system is based on a 2015 book by Paul Hill and Ashley Jochim, *A Democratic Constitution for Public Education* (Hill & Jochim, 2015). Hill is a research professor at the University of Washington State of the Center of Public Education. Jochim is a research analyst at the Center. In their book, the authors note a need for a new structure to respond to demonstrated limitations of state departments of education or local boards of education in improving poorly performing public school districts or schools. Meanwhile, poorly performing charter and voucher schools have received state dollars with little state oversight, accountability, or proven success.

Challenges

Upgrading our educational system will not be easy. There are significant challenges that must be faced. Such an inclusive change process was suggested by Francesca Gino in *Rebel Talent: Why It Pays to Break the Rules at Work and in Life* (Gino, 2018). She cites numerous stories and studies about new ways of doing things that derive from breaking the rules to design more successful and challenging systems. We agree with Gino that "to make an omelet you have to break some eggs. While this is easy, the omelet will have more success in crafting a clear recipe—which eggs, when, how, blended with what" (NPR, 2018).

Accommodating Multiple Perspectives. Meaningful change requires bringing everyone to the table. Multiple perspectives are needed to provide a system of quality choices with clear philosophical and educational rationale. Quality options should be reflected across a range of school missions, core beliefs, and principles.

Accountability. The pluralistic system we propose must not only support student and family choice but also be accountable for educational quality and democratic values. There must also be a quality human resource system for the teaching profession that is accountable for ensuring that the best people are in place to create a more perfect educational system.

School Member Requirements. The unique feature of the model being proposed is the option of inclusion of multiple models of public, private, and parochial schools into the public school system supported by federal and state dollars. Inclusion in this pluralistic model of public education would require various demonstrations. Included schools would be required to support core democratic values, such as equity and inclusion of demographic groups and commitment to civil rights and civic political discourse. Schools would also be required to meet standards of quality. This could include curricular oversight, monitoring of outcome data (discipline, graduation, assessments, employment, or higher education of graduates), facility review, and professional development.

Disruption. A system that moves away from our legacy of entrenched residentially based districts (with underlying resource inequities) may serve to interrupt some of our thorniest educational issues—particularly those that drive poor achievement and outcome gaps between groups. There is hope that such a new system could help to heal some national divides and improve upon and address the underlying structural and educational problems that we have identified in this book. A new system could disrupt the inclination to "return to normal" and revert to practices that were not successful in the past.

BENEFITS OF PLURALISM

Moving from the illusion of a common (equal and equitable) school to a pluralistic system has a number of advantages.

Equitable Funding. This type of system provides public funds that allow parents to access a range of high-quality school choices, supported by government funding, oversight, and accountability.

School Choice. A pluralistic system of education can provide for the development of unique systems of curriculum and assessments and allow schools to teach according to distinct missions. Different types of schools can help to stimulate creativity in educator training programs, new parent organizations, restructuring of traditional educational professional organizations, and new emerging civic organizations for oversight of the system.

Accountability. Bringing various schools, such as private/parochial and charter schools into a regional system of oversight provides a greater opportunity to hold these schools accountable for academic outcomes. A pluralistic system with a sound accountability structure can expand the availability of high-quality school choices for students and families. It can provide for better "matches" between family aims and their chosen school's mission. It also creates opportunities for parents to explore different educational philosophies.

Relevant Research and Development. This system would clarify the role of the state as a major funder of students and monitor of system effectiveness. The state and federal roles would have a stronger investment in research and development and report back the results to the field of education and the public so that the research can be actualized. Pluralism encourages individual self-expression and stimulates innovations in methodologies, teacher training programs, and school funding and tax policies.

Transparency. Schools would be required to articulate their mission, values, and methodology and make them public. These practices provide more transparency than our current public school system. A well-functioning pluralistic system should ease culture wars, by providing space for various viewpoints within a broad educational environment.

GOVERNANCE AND FINANCE IN A PLURALISTIC SYSTEM

The most comprehensive change we are proposing involves the school governance and financing, which was the issue explored in chapter 5, "School Governance in America." We recommend a wholesale restructuring of the current government roles in education. To build a more effective system of educational governance and finance for the future, we need to rethink the roles of federal, state, and local governance. The goal of this change is to provide more policy coherence and justify greater funding of the education enterprise, including a stronger role for research and development. Equitable and rational school governance requires changes in the current government processes at the federal, state, and local levels through such mechanisms as federal, state, and local advisory boards and local community control of schools in large urban areas.

The proposed system offers some possible responses to issues we have raised, but this is still an embryonic concept. We offer it to our readers to stimulate thinking about how we might come together to develop a more accountable pluralistic system than is currently in place.

Pluralistic Systems in Other Democratic Countries

Other democratic countries have pluralistic systems of schools supported by the government. In these societies, the government provides a fixed percentage of the cost to operate nongovernment schools. These percentages are typically quite high, often above 80 percent. Funded nongovernment schools in most Canadian provinces, French-speaking Belgium, Ireland, and Italy allow for hiring teachers on the basis of their belief systems, in accordance with the school's mission (Berner, 2017, pp. 20–21). The Netherlands, Northern Ireland, and England, within constraints, also allow schools to hire on the basis of beliefs, and fund "belief-oriented, teacher training programs" (Berner, 2017, pp. 20–21).

While the common school notion of a single set of values and curriculum was also adopted across European countries, over time the notion has been challenged in France as chasing an impossible ideal of universality, requiring a highly bureaucratic administrative system, and in the end failing to meet the needs of a diverse population of learners. The Netherlands, with a long history of religious (Protestant and Catholic) and secular schools, has recently seen a movement toward "freedom of education," inclusive of nonsecular schools, as being supportive of parental choice (Glenn, 1988, pp. 264–276).

To find the best teachers, countries with pluralistic systems often set high admission standards for teachers to qualify for teacher training programs. These standards are in line with the needs of schools for faculty who support the schools' ideals. Admission requirements are established in a variety of ways. Some countries like Norway and Slovenia feature open admissions. The Netherlands and French-speaking Belgium, by contrast, allow religion-based or philosophically based admissions but require that the programs beliefs have been clearly and publicly articulated in advance. France forbids admissions based on religion or philosophy but requires an agreement to support the mission of the school. Many European countries fund private and parochial schools using a model of funding that follows the student. This is strikingly similar to the U.S. precedent set by *Zelman v. Simmons-Harris* in 2002 (Berner, 2017, pp. 21, 56).

A Pluralistic Model for American School Governance

Our proposed model for school governance involves the following features.

Oversight. Some American states are well suited to considering a strong pluralistic system of governance with funds going to religious, private, and public schools. Such a transformation would require government to establish strong oversight over a common set of standards, curricula, and assessments, while allowing schools to teach the material according to their distinctive missions. Building on the work of Hill and Jochim, a pluralistic system would support different types of schools with new governance and funding structures and require transparent demonstration of rich curriculum instruction and assessment, with a strong human resource system for educators. Such a system has models available in some best practices of Western European countries. Transformation may well begin with an examination of school finance, governance, and educational policy in countries with highly successful systems.

In urging a pluralistic system, it is prudent to consider a regionalized system of private, parochial, and public schools, including existing charters and alternative schools for which people have used vouchers. There may be a role for homeschooling and pod collaboratives and other new innovative school designs, which currently receive government funding. These schools would accept public funds with clearly established responsibility for defined education outcomes. Establishing systems regionally would assist in disrupting the long history of districts distinguished by income and ethnicity.

School Choice. A new system of governance at regional levels within a state would focus on creating a menu of options providing meaningful choice among public, private, and parochial schools. Regional authorities would have responsibility for ensuring sufficient high-quality capacity to educate all students within their region. Funded sufficiently by the state and federal governments, an experimental regional model could be researched and evaluated by independent researchers to measure parent satisfaction, policy coherence, and strong educator involvement in meeting the needs of all students within the regional jurisdiction.

Funding Sources. Clearly such an experiment would need a strong infusion of educational funding at the state and local levels. One barrier to garnering such an infusion is that the average parent or citizen does not understand the complexities of school funding or how weighted school funding translates into services and resources for their child. State departments of education audit districts on general categories of funding. Actual cost data studies are often ignored, not advertised, or not done.

This new model may require eliminating the local property tax to be replaced by a state tax and a stronger infusion of federal funds, in order to help equalize school funding. This is particularly important because over the past thirty years, voters in states have placed limits on how much can be spent by local and state sources (Berne & Stiefel, 1994, p. 10). As an example, in interviews of over hundred superintendents in the state of Ohio, most see their function as a fundraiser working to convince their communities about the importance of funding a high-quality education (Zelman, 2021). This distracts their focus from improving teaching and learning for their students, educators, and community. Property tax issues will continue to be the focus of many state school funding court cases until we take on this antiquated and inequitable structure and change it.

Eliminating the local property tax with a statewide property tax in every state could provide resources to be distributed based on student needs. The state would not fund districts but, instead, fund students. As Hill and Jochim suggest, each student would have a "backpack" of funding that would follow the student from school to school (Hill & Jochim, 2015, pp. 30–31). Our current system could be replaced with a new system of state-level weighted school funding based on special needs of the students including socioeconomic status, bilingualism, and special education needs. It would be the responsibility of the state to regularly conduct cost studies to adjust funding. Each school would be required to report back to the state how the dollars were spent through an available high-tech reporting system. Such accounting should mimic individual online banking accounts where data are updated in real time. Per-child spending could also be made available for parents to better understand what resources were available for their children.

By moving to an equalized statewide funding system, superintendents would not have to spend time convincing the public to support local property taxes. Parents of students in private or parochial schools would not be pitted against public school parents over tax levies. A regionalized system could result in greater levels of school integration by interrupting existing segregated districts and attendance zones. Schools would contract with this new authority and be held accountable for demonstrating closed achievement gaps and high academic student performance.

In addition, to build a pluralistic system, we will need coherent government structures at the state level that define complementary roles among governors, state boards of education, and state departments of education. We must provide sufficient funding for state departments of education to monitor and provide technical assistance to regional structure to assure equity and prevent fraud and abuse of the system.

The federal role in education should be to provide federal dollars, as appropriate, to fund students directly, not districts or schools.

Regionalized Governance. We suggest making education governance more coherent by moving from a local-level governance structure of school boards to a regionalized governance model. This new model would have a civic education council (CEC) representing multiple stakeholders and would hire a Chief Executive Officer (CEO) to be accountable to the CEC. This officer could not own or operate schools, but rather would manage the portfolio of different types of schools in the region. An imagined portfolio would include innovative models, public schools, and private/parochial schools that would be required to join if they accept students funded by state dollars. The advantage to parents is that participating private and parochial schools would be fully state-funded and affordable to all. At the level of current districts, more autonomy should be granted to educators to exercise professional knowledge and judgment and not constrained by central office bureaucracy or excessive governmental regulations.

In addition to providing funding for students, a primary federal role in education would be in research and development to support the work of the CEOs. An agency like the National Institute of Health should be created with substantial funding for basic and applied research in education. The federal role would include reporting the conditions and status of education in all fifty states. Data must be usable and transparent for the public as well as state policymakers and educators.

Pluralism and Curriculum and Instruction

In chapter 1, we discussed the challenges inherent in choosing curriculum and methods of instruction. There are many controversies in American education, such as whether to teach basic academics or to incorporate the needs and interests of the whole child; tensions between neighborhood identity and racial balance; sex education versus abstinence; career and technical education versus the liberal arts; the history of civil rights versus denial of institutional racism; and multicultural education versus Western culture.

The controversy over teaching SEL provides a specific example of the challenges faced by people making school curriculum choices. Although SEL has been established in state and national curriculum standards, in 2022, the state of Florida rejected math textbooks because they included SEL strategies. SEL is seen by some as usurping parents' responsibility. Others argue that it takes time away from academic subjects. Although many conservatives approve of character education in line with traditional values, they reject SEL as indoctrination, fearing that some teachers would insert their own political bias. Some are concerned about shallow, superficial approaches to SEL, or culturally based efforts to "fix" minority children, making them compliant to the structures of school, rather than examining the role of structures themselves in impacting behavior.

The reality is, however, especially after the pandemic, that children are desperate for social and emotional engagement and need some form of social and emotional education. Any learning is difficult without community-building, learning routines, active listening, identifying emotions, learning how to share, how to behave properly, and treat each other fairly. "It is through these practices—not in spite of them—that virtues are taught" (Grossman, 2022).

Before the pandemic, through the reauthorizations of ESSA, the nation attempted to improve the current system of curriculum and instruction with a focus on national standards, assessments, and accountability, but many parents, teachers, and districts have been frustrated by this effort.

Pluralism provides no magic bullet to the resolution of any of the curricular or cultural battles that we have seen across the history of American education. Care must be taken to avoid endorsing an "anything goes," or "every school for itself" approach in the name of pluralism or diversity. Inherent to the success of a more pluralistic system will be a willingness to come together to define broad areas of agreement, as well as permissible areas of divergence. Such a coming together, to be effective, must be broadly representative and inclusive. The possibility exists of resolving cultural tensions by offering many high-quality options within an environment that both defines commonalities and respects differences.

In America, we believe that schools should educate students to be good citizens in a democracy and have knowledge, skills, and depositions to participate in making the American economy strong and vital. With a new pluralistic system, there would be a portfolio of a variety of public, private, parochial, and innovative new models that clearly define their vision, mission, and goals. Each school, in order to receive public funding, would sign a multiyear contract with their regional CEC. The contract would include the school's vision, mission, goals, and philosophy of education. The school would be required to publish its entire curriculum, including the scope and sequence of its academic content. The modes of instruction and assessments would be explained in lay terms. This transparency would help parents to select schools that reflect their philosophies for their children's education. Each curriculum would align to state academic standards. Academic outcomes would be measured by state assessments as well as school assessments.

This new system would provide parents with transparent knowledge of curriculum, teaching methods, and how their children will be assessed. This information should help parents make informed choices and think deeply about the education outcomes for their children. In a system of enhanced family choice, educators may be encouraged to better engage with families than is presently the case.

All schools in a new pluralistic system need a rich curriculum covering English language arts, mathematics, science, world languages, music, art, physical education, and health. State standards at developmentally appropriate student level should be developed in the aforementioned subject matters. Multiple modes of assessment for state standards should be encouraged.

Educators in this new system can focus on providing high-quality curriculum and instruction. Rather than having a central district office control the purchasing of the curriculum and assessments, each school would be responsible for deciding what curriculum materials, including new emerging technologies, would best align to the school's mission and individual student needs.

Pluralism and Technology

As revealed during the COVID-19 pandemic, all students need access to their own personal technology devices and easy access to Internet services. Students and teachers should have access to new emerging technologies that personalize student learning and give teachers and students immediate feedback on student success. Teachers must receive ongoing support for the adoption of new mechanisms as they emerge.

Technology access equates to greater school choice. With synchronous and asynchronous online classes, students could have access to a wide range of instruction and virtual learning experiences, as well as engage in discussion, group work, and assessment remotely or in groups onsite.

Pluralism and the Teaching Profession

In chapter 2, we noted that educators in other democracies are more valued and honored than those in the United States. Unlike in this country, teachers' salaries are equal to those in other professions, and teachers spend time planning and collaborating on education lessons. Entrance requirements to highly sophisticated teacher educator preparation programs are selective with excellent support systems for beginner teachers.

In America, we have failed to meet the professional needs of teachers through adequate compensation and their needs for ongoing support for planning time and collaboration with their colleagues. As a result of COVID-19, public support for educators in this country is declining, while demands are increasing, and educators are leaving the profession. On the state and local levels, we do not have a strong human resource system for the profession. We lack best practices in how we recruit, train, and retain our educators. A simple, albeit costly, shift in teachers' workload could provide some immediate balm to overwhelmed teachers (and improve student outcomes). Fewer classes (or time with students) coupled with "more time in the day to plan, grade, and collaborate with colleagues" (Klein, 2022) would begin to bring us in line with practices in other countries.

In the current system, state and district central offices set general policies that may not be successful for some schools. For example, governance at federal, state, and local levels hold districts and schools accountable for academic results. This sounds like a good idea but has led to unintended consequences. Focusing only on test scores often results in restricting the professional judgment of educators seeking to provide a rich liberal arts curriculum for their students. Furthermore, rather than putting more resources into building the profession through better educator training, professional development and salaries comparable to other professions, some states require that teacher evaluations link to student assessment results. This policy led teachers to do extensive student test preparation. In addition, individual teachers have been concerned about their jobs and reputations.

In a pluralistic system, all school professionals could be accountable for academic achievement. Educators would have strong incentives to collectively make their schools successful. If schools are not successful, they could be closed or eliminated from the tax-supported system, leaving teachers out of work, and their professional reputation tarnished.

In the system we envision, approved curriculum and assessments could encourage the use of multiple measures of student growth and performance. This would provide educators an enlarged space within which to exercise their professional judgment, matching curriculum, methods, and materials to their students in order to achieve and demonstrate high academic performance.

In a new pluralistic model, a different set of competitive forces could support good teaching, such as enhanced teacher salaries, supported by enhanced state and federal funding—which could be directed where the need is greatest. This would assist in moving away from a current condition in which wealthy suburban districts easily attract highly desired experienced teachers, leaving other areas with a revolving door of inexperienced staff. From a macro view, we need a highly qualified education workforce, capable of teaching in a variety of different schools.

Teacher Preparation and Development

To arrive at a successful pluralistic system, new and highly selective teacher training programs would be required to train teachers in order to staff a variety of schools based on different philosophies. Traditional schools of education might present different types of programs to respond to this need. States could develop grant programs for schools and training institutions. Hill and Jochim recommend a problem-solving, rather than prescriptive, orientation to curriculum development and educator training. This allows greater flexibility in meeting emergent needs (Hill & Jochim, 2015, p. 15).

Within this context, there would remain a number of common goals. Successful educator training programs would ensure that teachers are well educated in all liberal arts disciplines, in addition to those they will teach. Teachers must emerge with a knowledge of the major constructs of their own discipline, and how their discipline constructs its own knowledge. These programs would need to establish partnerships with a variety of schools to develop theories of action and conduct research in methods, particularly action research leading to an understanding of methods appropriate for a range of learners.

Programs should provide future teachers with experience in successful school, as well as following their graduates to best understand their ability to support student and school success. Through such ongoing relationships, programs would have the opportunity to support customized professional development, peer collaborations, mentorships, research opportunities, and the ability to network professionally with other educators. Of particular importance is that programs reinforce democratic values and the civil rights of all students.

Teachers and Schools

In a pluralistic system, policymakers would need to see the value of the teaching profession in preserving our democracy and supporting workforce development. Policymakers would then be expected to develop at the state, region, and school an aligned educator comprehensive human resource system from recruitment to retirement. A pluralistic system would place the onus on professionals to support their students ahead of answering to a central office bureaucracy to meet high qualification standards.

In our restructured education system, schools would be challenged to:

- use the freedom and resources to do whatever it takes to make their students successful;
- form multiple collaborations across schools to purchase human resource supports such as teacher recruitment, benefits, and evaluation systems;
- create differentiated roles and responsibilities across the teaching profession;
- develop staff internally to meet various emerging needs. An alternative route to a specific certification might involve providing evidence to the state that an individual is capable of meeting the needs of the students at the school;
- provide educators access to strong human resources, including ongoing professional development;
- use emerging technologies to support learning for students, educators, parents, and the community;
- make clear how they are using federal and state funds to equalize school salaries to other professions; and
- compensate teachers similarly to other professionals.

Pluralism and School Choice

As discussed in chapter 3, most states have some form of school choice through programs such as vouchers, charter schools, state scholarships, and interdistrict transfers. These various options suffer from a lack of strong accountability systems. We have also seen the rise of largely unregulated homeschooling enabled by state relaxation of homeschooling requirements. As a result of COVID-19, more state legislatures are pursuing bills to allow new or expanding private school options. These options increase the eligibility for vouchers and tax credit scholarships (Spurrier et al., 2022).

But our overall system of education, viewed at the macro level, remains inequitable. The hope of systemic improvement resulting from the creeping expansion of publicly funded school choice, despite some recent successes, has largely not been realized. Culture wars grounded in disagreement over what a universal model of public education should include have resulted in a spate of legislative actions. These legislative demands regarding what must (or cannot) be taught have resulted in haphazard policies throughout public education and make the public system a target for various political interests.

The push for increased school choice with public funding has intrigued conservatives as well as liberals, for differing reasons. Conservatives tend to operate from a combined distrust of government regulation and faith in markets to provide an improved education "product." On the other hand, while many liberals have worked against public funding for school choice, others have seen choice as providing "a way out of failing schools," for marginalized groups. Jack Jennings suggests in his book, *Presidents, Congress and the Public Schools: The Politics of Education Reform*, that the Democratic party must respond with what they are for, rather than what they are against (2015, p. 221). While generally liberals do not support school choice, they must be proactive in advocating for the systems of students who attend poorly performing schools. We must all advocate for all tax-supported educational institutions (including vouchers, school scholarships, and charter schools) to subject to a rigorous accountability system to support high-quality education for all children.

Our current system of education has given lip service to the argument that poor and minority students should have equitable distribution of opportunity, resources, and outcomes to assure success in a democracy. Minority, lower- and middle-class parents do not have the breadth of choices available to them needed to make such equity a reality. The reality is that all children are unique. No school can be all things to all students. In our current system, opportunities are not available to cultivate the wealth of all student talents, abilities, and learning preferences.

Federal and state governments should support research, evaluation, and incentives for innovation and report results across the nation, districts, and state. Whether a state has large or small districts, structures should be in place to provide choices across a range of high-quality education options for all families, based on the needs of their children. Providing such a range of options at the local level may prove more inclusive of diversity than current attempts to meet all needs within every building. While Jennings, is still hopeful that over time a strong federal investment will come, our children cannot wait. Jennings gives good advice when he states, "advocates for public schools should take lessons from charter school advocates. They know what they are against, but not what they are for" (Jennings, 2015, p. 221).

A pluralistic system that provides multiple accountable choices would allow for a deeper discussion of education philosophies without making the public school a battleground. As Berner points out, there are three major questions facing educators and parents: What is the nature of the child? What is the purpose of education? And what is the role of the teacher? To choose the appropriate education for their children, all parents must think deeply about these issues (Berner, 2017, pp. 8–9).

Parents will answer each of these questions in many different ways. The lack of meaningful, accessible, and affordable school choice options mitigates against thoughtful discussions of education philosophies. In our present system, parents' frustrations are vented by disgruntled and marginalized "customers" of our public system. These frustrations become embattled policy debates at all levels of government. These debates distract from the more serious need to provide the best education possible for students and their families.

In the pluralistic system model we propose, parents and children would be regarded as important stakeholders. Their voices would be respected by school boards and regional councils. They would be included, at the ground level, in planning and decision-making, including decisions regarding facilities, curriculum, and personnel. Such involvement need not require every parent in every possible set of decisions. As Comer and Haynes note, parents arrive with a range of interests and comfort levels (Comer & Haynes, 1991). This should not be used as an excuse for denying involvement options to parents who are interested.

As our pluralistic systems mature, we anticipate the availability of diverse education options around the state that articulate a clear mission, vision, goals, and curriculum. These schools would also be held accountable for the quality of their education, but also their success of their students. This will require strict attention to such criteria as inclusion (to avoid "cherry-picking" students) and ability to maintain a consistent student body over time. Government entities can offer support to families making informed choices regarding the fit of a particular school to the needs of their student. Entities could provide banks of school information, including student achievement and discipline data and approaches to education. Schools that accept state funding would be held accountable for academic results, in addition to meeting various health and safety and related criteria. Schools that fail to measure up would lose public funding. New organizations would be developed to guide families to make informed decisions based upon different schools' curriculum and academic performance.

Private, public, and parochial schools would still exist without federal or state funding, should they choose. Private and parochial schools would have the option of not accepting state funding. Public school districts could choose to stay intact. Over a ten-year period, we need to provide evidence that a pluralistic system can mitigate against cultural wars; create exciting new partnerships; and change educational structures, roles, and responsibilities to address a more coherent system. Research and advocacy will be the key. We should look at the work of Bryk, Gomez, Gronow, and LeMahieu that borrows the ideas of improvement science to give us guidance in designing our new system (Byrk et al., 2015).

School choice options would move from discrete programs with little oversight to an accountable pluralistic system. This pluralistic model would include charters, vouchers, state scholarships, interdistricts transfers, private and parochial schools, homeschooling, and pods.

Pluralism and Community Engagement

The pluralistic system of curriculum and instruction and school choice discussed earlier also leads to a new vision of community engagement. The essence of our democracy is community and civic engagement. We need to break down the barriers between formal and informal education and build on our community assets, engaging the community with its solutions.

In our current system, as a result of COVID-19 and political operators, there is a great deal of dissatisfaction with our schools and districts. Prior to COVID-19, schools were perceived as a stable institution for working parents. With the issues of opening and closing, hybrid versus in-person, and masks versus unmasking, parents could no longer trust the stability that was inherent in a school schedule. Data show that many parents opted out of our public schools and enrolled their schools in parochial schools, which tended to stay open during the pandemic (Spurrier et al., 2022). Parents with financial resources hired tutors or placed their students in private school pods, hiring teachers to teach the curriculum to small groups. While historically parents have supported their local schools, school support is starting to wane, and parents want a greater voice in their schools. In addition, political partisans funded by outside money capitalized on this dissatisfaction in recent school board elections, as described in our governance and finance chapter.

Larry Cuban in *Confessions of a School Reformer* reminds us that public school students spend less than 20 percent of their total hours in school (Cuban, 2021). To fully educate our children requires strong family and community engagement and partnerships to guide students' development. A regional system may have greater access to a range of community assets to provide opportunities to guide our students into adulthood. Opportunities can include youth development organizations, health and human services, and workforce development linked to regional economies.

Compared to Western European countries, the United States has fewer government-provided health and human services or programs to relieve income insecurity. Countries with such safety nets, such as Finland, have been able to coordinate their work with that of schools. In this country, we have had some success in developing "full-service schools" by partnering with various private, or occasionally public, entities.

In order to build upon this in our new model, schools will need to adopt a greater sense of humility regarding such partnerships. An effective pluralistic model should not view full-service schools as a way of fixing students, making them better fit the existing school structure, or enticing parents into the building. Such efforts are better viewed as opportunities for schools to become a greater part of the community as a whole. Rather than focusing on "opening the schoolhouse door," and expecting the community to walk in, there is a critical need for educators to open the door and walk out into the neighborhood.

A new model must respect the autonomy of human beings and the duties and rights of citizens' living in a democracy. To preserve our democracy, we must remember an important tenet of political science about the need for citizen participation in community-based organizations. Political scientist Robert Putnam in two recent books discusses the unprecedented collapse in civic and social organizations in American life (Putnam 2015, 2020). In rethinking how schools are to be redesigned, we must support parents' and students' abilities to participate in public service.

In a pluralistic system, schools that rely on family choice for students would be more likely to nurture meaningful opportunities for interaction with parents. Modeling community engagement through relationships with parents helps to develop norms that support our democracy. In our new design, opportunities for public service and models of dealing respectfully with conflict should be addressed.

Ohio's Kirwan Institute also remarks on the collapse of civic engagement, noting an economic component driving a wedge between potential civic partners.

The growing divide between the haves and have-nots in the civic engagement environment mirrors the growing divide in our communities. The decline in civic life is occurring alongside a widening wealth gap and a shrinking middle class, where more and more Americans are struggling to make ends meet. In our more disadvantaged communities, decades of neglect and disinvestment, along with economic and racial inequality, have robbed these communities of healthy civic engagement supports. This results in bleak engagement environments that often separate vulnerable residents from opportunities to make a difference in their communities. (Holley, 2016, p. 14)

Transforming our systems of education will require a transformation of our engagement practices in order to overcome decades of exclusion, conflict, and a resulting mistrust of government and authority. Among the necessary tools to be employed must be the recognition and inclusion of critical stakeholders throughout the process—from earliest planning stages on forward. Families and educators form a core of critical stakeholders and may be represented by such traditional groups as unions and school-based parent groups (such as PTA). However, a full range of community-based organizations, from mental and physical health advocacy to ethnic heritage groups, chambers of commerce, social justice advocates, city councils and mayors, library patrons, religious leaders, and philanthropic organizations should be brought to the table, in order to build past existing mistrust and isolation and ensure that transformation can endure. Not only will such widely inclusive planning provide access to multiple resources in the community, it will build the foundation for community engagement in the ongoing work of the regional governance system, to work within the new structure, suggesting improvements and monitoring the fairness of the location of schools.

The schoolhouse door needs to be open to the community. But the professionals inside need to pass through the same door to engage the community outside. We need to break down the barriers between formal and informal education and encourage two-way communication with parents and community stakeholders to revitalize economic and community development based on regional assets.

HOW A PLURALISTIC MODEL COULD WORK IN AMERICA

Under the U.S. Constitution, a new school governance model would work at the state level to bring a more accountable pluralistic system to state government school choice policies. Hill and Jochim make it clear what this new democratic constitutional governance system should accomplish and avoid. First, it must be established by state statute. Second, the statute would create a new local authority that would provide a structure to implement the new system locally and manage the establishment and implementation of the new system with strict accountability and oversight. A good education governance system must achieve many things, including satisfaction of all its stakeholders. This new system must be efficient, equitable, transparent, and accountable and must foster democratic, American principles (Hill & Jochim, 2015, p. 22).

Over the past twenty years, many states have implemented elements of a pluralistic system. States have supported school voucher programs, charter schools, and private school scholarships. But most state choice programs lack accountability and are discrete programs, lacking a coherent system. States' legislative research arms should study other democratic countries' high-performing systems to draft legislation to improve upon their current policies.

This book includes valuable references to many works of American researchers who carefully examined best practices of pluralistic systems in other democratic countries. Jal Mehta, Robert B. Schwartz, and Frederick M. Hess, for instance, edited *Futures of School Reform*, which contains essays that could guide policymakers to build a more accountable system. They describe the rapid growth of educational policy in Finland and the rapid progress that was made over a twenty-year period of time (2012, p. 23). Mehta in his article "The Courage to Achieve Our Ambitions" describes the underlying frustrations in trying to change our current system. A question is posed by Ben Levin, "Why should we consider creating a radical new system when there are proven ways from international leaders to take from the existing systems" (p. 193)?

While their book of essays suggest that American school reform should learn from best practices of other countries and reassemble our current system, they neglect to consider how our current disjointed governance system on the federal, state, and local levels inhibits consistent policies. Our education governance needs to clarify the roles and responsibilities of the federal, state, and local levels to accommodate an accountable pluralistic model. Many other countries that have these best practices have coherent governance structures that support strong pluralism. As we have discussed in chapter 5, there is much disjointedness and overlap in education governance in this country. A new governance model must be implemented at the state level to permit all parents regardless of income to choose the best schools for their children.

In our pluralistic school model, these governance roles would be redefined.

Governor

During a ten- or fifteen-year demonstration of a new system, changes in governors are to be expected. Education systems, such as Finland, managed to reinvent themselves over a twenty-year period by garnering bipartisan support of politicians and citizens of their country. Reinvention of a public education system requires strong support from all stakeholders, who will support the governors who support research and development of the new system.

State Legislature

The role of the state legislature would be to establish this system through legislation. The state legislature would establish a CEC. Its composition (elected or appointed), powers, and limitations should be spelled out clearly in statute. The legislature would establish the school regions in the state and approve weighted per-pupil funding every two years.

While districts ought to have the option of coming under the regional authority, the state legislature might want to include in its education legislation a requirement for a persistently poorly performing district school to move under the governance of the regional structure.

A critical role for state legislatures will be to ensure financing of the new system. This would rely on a portable, weighted allotment per student. Amounts should be adjusted by the legislature at periodic intervals based on ongoing cost studies.

A legislature may well also want to establish a new commission to oversee results of the system and make reports to the legislature, governor, and state board of education. They might also choose to include this as an expansion of duties of the state department of education. A team of researchers should come from a variety of education, social service, and finance and process quality backgrounds. Qualitative reviews of progress will be important. If there are federal investments, reporting should also include any required by the federal government.

Start-ups and innovation can be messy. Therefore, a formative evaluation should guide the needed mid-course corrections and provide clear and transparent progress monitoring. We do not want to dismiss new experiments too quickly. Rather use data to further innovate and make informed decisions, making use of emerging knowledge as available.

State Department of Education, State Board of Education, and State Superintendent

A state department of education and state board would maintain similar roles to those they now have. They would be responsible for setting academic content standards, various operating standards, oversight of licensing, and distribution of state funds. They would serve as liaison between the legislature and local authorities to assist in understanding the legislation, provision of mandated training, and support for implementation. The legislature may choose the state education department as the appropriate entity to oversee research and development.

District/Region Board of Education

The CEC as defined by the state legislature would serve as the local education authority. The statute should describe the role of a CEO to be hired by the CEC. The CEC would limit the jurisdiction of a variety of private, public, and parochial schools within its catchment areas. It may serve in place of school boards for schools or districts that want to join this new movement. Charter schools, voucher schools, and private and parochial schools that accept government funding would go under the CEC authority (Hill & Jochim, 2015, pp. 24–48). Building on Hill and Jochim system, private and parochial schools who accept public money would be governed by this new authority but could have a relationship with their current boards.

The CECs should be subject to checks and balances that would be described in the statute. Their central focus would be on improving school performance for all schools under its jurisdiction.

The local CEC would consist of twelve to fifteen members. It could be completely elected from a specific geographical area or appointed by state and local officials and representatives of select interest groups. The members could also include high school students and educators who are not employed by the regional governance authority. It could be a hybrid model of five elected by citizens from the geographical area that the CEC covers; five appointed by state board of education and the state superintendent and mayors in the encompassed area; and five appointed from vested interests such as business, labor, and higher education. Initially, terms would be staggered over a seven-year period. Board members would serve for not more than seven years. The CEC would not be an employer except for the CEO, whom the CEC could remove for cause.

The CEC would review school financial audits that would be transparent to ensure that the money supported students that it was intended to support. The CEC would also approve contracts of all schools under its jurisdiction and set criteria to determine whether schools would continue to receive state support. Proposals for whether a school would be part of the system would be solicited and reviewed by the CEC.

The CEC would address the difficulties that small districts and rural schools encounter in providing alternatives to address the needs of individual students and families. A variety of different types of schools with efficient transportation and blended learning opportunities would help to customize students' and families' concerns.

The CEC would also enter into an agreement with the schools to set a common set of multiple measures of school performance to include academic content, skills, and critical problem-solving. The CEC would review data from actual cost studies to determine whether weighted per-pupil funding was used appropriately based on the needs of students in the system.

District Superintendent versus CEO

A main role of the CEC would be to appoint a CEO under contract for at least five years to manage the schools in any district opting to be a part of the new system.

Any current district superintendents who become CEOs of regional systems will find themselves in a distinctly different role. This new role would require skills and the ability to manage a portfolio of schools and assure that this portfolio has sufficient capacity to provide equal and adequate education opportunity to all students in the region.

CEOs would survey parents in the region and work to recruit the types of schools that best serve the students in each area. CEOs must be able to understand education research to compare the outcomes of various schools across the region and state and recruit successful school models based on area needs. They must assure that schools in the region do not discriminate when accepting or not accepting students with special needs or other biases.

Further, the CEO's role would be to help schools form collaboratives to purchase services that best meet the needs of their students and families. Principals would be granted the authority to hire teachers and services to support the profession through recruitment, retention, and retirement. They would be responsible for the development of the school's budget, contracting for needed services, and engaging parents as partners with the school.

The CEC and CEO could raise money through grants and philanthropic contributions.

The CEO would report to the CEC as defined by state statute. The CEO would present to the CEC performance and fiscal data. The CEO would recommend closing low-performing schools and schools that do not meet the criteria set by the CEC. Options regarding conflicts between the CEO and the CEC would need to be spelled out in state statutes authorizing this new system. State legislation should also prohibit campaign contributions to CEC's elected members and should audit school contracts to assure that sweetheart deals are not adopted. The state department of education would also engage decertification of a CEC if the system was not improving student achievement. The statute specifying the criteria to do so should be transparent, given the vagaries of state politics. The CEO would have to manage a portfolio of a variety of different types of schools.

The CEO would engage families in the creation of processes and programs to educate families on school choices available to them within their CEC district. The CEO would help schools link students and families to needed health and human services or job training. Schools would provide data to the state department of education based on their cost studies that linked performance measures and actual costs. The CEO should keep abreast of new emerging education technologies. The CEO could also develop a contract with a qualified university or a research and evaluation organization to provide both formative and summative data and report monthly to the CEC. Semiannual reports would be shared with the state legislature and state board of education to enhance the system and improve checks and balances through clarifying roles and responsibilities. All education decisions at the school level would be left to educators in consultation with families and communities as appropriate.

The CEO could help schools develop collaboratives to purchase services to promote efficiency in budgeting and accounting, human resources, and purchasing. The CEO would work with national, state, and local institutions of higher education, professional unions and/or training institutions, and parent organization to address needs that arise. The CEO would help raise research and development for new models that would be under the regional system (Hill & Jochim, 2015, pp. 49–63).

Principals and Individual Schools

The CEC and CEO would not hire staff, teachers, or principals nor enter into collective bargaining agreements. The CEC would not own school buildings or manage services. Schools would contract for these services. Collective bargaining would take place at the school level. By state statute, the CEO and CEC could not give preferential treatment to any school that did not meet the performance expectations that they agreed upon, which would include a uniform timeline for all schools to demonstrate success.

Teachers

A key aim of a reformed system is to make the education expertise of teachers central. In accepting a mantle of empowerment, some teachers may be disappointed to discover that this does not mean anything goes at the individual teacher, or classroom, level. An expectation is that the collaborative judgment of teachers will not only guide curricular decision-making but also take on responsibility for evaluation of learning outcomes and formulating responses where issues emerge. Some teachers may take on new mentoring roles or provide high-quality professional development to other staff. The exercise of collaborative judgment ought to include the views and input of other, adjacent, experts, such as parents, fiscal agents, researchers, and the overseeing authority (CEC and CEO).

Parents

Planning for such an ambitious attempt at reform should include parents and community members from earliest brainstorming through all that follows. Planners would be wise to identify and work with existing community-based organizations with established relationships. They should also be prepared to discover that parents and members of the community have very different priorities than those brought to the table by various experts.

A private school might feel that it could benefit from state funding and convince its board to enter a contract with this new CEC to increase enrollment and provide students with more opportunities for diversity. Parents may be more concerned with support for the existing district school in their neighborhood, feeling that a diversion of public funds poses a threat. Some parents may place a high priority on respect for diversity, while others are more fearful. Parents with substantial experience of marginalization, particularly in education, may be reluctant to invest time and effort in planning without a demonstration that there is indeed a meaningful place for them at the table.

Implementing a New System: How to Get There from Here?

Implementing a pluralistic model will be challenging. Questions will need to be addressed, and details will need to be worked out. For this, we also need to think and act anew. To promote the best ideas and an inclusive process, we must view this transformation as a collaborative opportunity, rather than a preformed plan to buy into and apply. This means that the first task will be to assemble a broadly diverse group of planners to create a demonstration project.

Funding

One way to start is to bring together venture capitalists, which include state and local government investors, private philanthropists, and social venture capitalists, to put together the needed funds to fund the design and implementation of the new systems. The role of such a group would be to generate excitement for the innovation, as well as provide funds for planning and initial implementation.

Creative and Diverse System Designers

It is important to bring creative people together that represent all spectrums of political thought. This new organization would develop a process to implement a grand competition to design new pluralistic education systems. This organization needs to decide on the appropriate incentives that would encourage a diverse group of people to participate in a competition. They need to develop a communications and marketing system to advertise the competition and put together a staff that can manage an organization which can implement their plan for a pluralistic education system. Staff for this planning group would include a CEO, directors of communication, marketing, data analytics, and legal and political lobbyists. The organization would create an education advisory board composed of traditional and nontraditional educators from the public, parochial, and private sectors, as well as diverse individuals from many fields, including research and evaluation.

One innovative model is seen in the XPRIZE Foundation (XPrize Foundation, 2022). A similar approach could stimulate a competition to develop a pluralistic system of education.

XPRIZE is used to tackle the humanities greatest problems through competition. This competition should provide enough options that would appeal to a diverse group of individuals who want high-quality publicly funded schools available to all parents in geographical areas around the United States. Funding for such an endeavor may require start-up capital to design new systems. Interested parties can apply for a planning grant. The organization will need to establish criteria to evaluate such plans. Criteria should be vetted so that they do not inhibit creativity and innovation. Diversity of the design teams and the feasibility of developing the designs should be considered.

Like the XPRIZE, a grant prize can be $500 million, second prize $250 million, and third prize $100 million. There can also be additional milestone prizes. The winning teams should be able to work with federal and state officials to put into temporary law their model and have a strong independent seven to ten years formative and summative evaluation by a consortium of diverse researchers. We need to evaluate whether these models are effective, feasible, replicable, and scalable.

Public/Private Partnerships

Over the past forty years the support for educational reform has come from major foundations representing both sides of our political spectrum. For example, the Bill and Melinda Gates Foundation focused on building better high schools through their small school initiative. It spent over $2 billion in grants that went to school districts and some charter schools serving minority populations. Ohio was a recipient of this investment. Bill Gates has pointed out that, while traditional school districts grants did not improve achievement in any way, some charter schools did make some gains (Strauss, 2014). There are multiple weaknesses to the approach used by Gates and others. There are suggestions regarding lack of local buy-in and mistrust of an outsider to education making big decisions. However, it must also be noted that such efforts also lack the ability to take on larger systemic changes.

Chapter 5 on governance describes how both federal and state dollars have been used by policymakers in a bipartisan manner. Billions of dollars have been spent by federal and state governments to district on school improvement efforts. To implement a new system of education will require a substantial private/public partnership. Both sectors have a vested interest in the future of American education. Large foundations that have traditionally invested in education represent both sides of the political spectrum. Examples include the Walton Foundation, Joyce Foundation, Ewing Marion Kauffman Foundation, William and Flora Hewlett Foundation, Eli and Edythe Broad Foundation, Annie E. Casey Foundation, and large business foundations such as the Ford Motor, Chevron, and Michael and Susan Dell Foundation. These types of foundations and businesses could form collaborations with community foundations and small, midsize regional foundations to fund a new organization like the XPRIZE. An XPRIZE competition to generate models of accountable pluralism would produce national and state excitement across the country to address COVID-19 malaise and demonstrate the public's creativity and ingenuity.

There could be a public/private partnership with federal and state governments and private funders to create the financial, political, and social capital to introduce a system of pluralism in this country to stimulate new models of funding and governing private, public, and parochial schools. A private/public partnership needs to be developed to fund and test engagement, effectiveness, efficiency, feasibility, sustainability, and replicability of the new system.

Gleaning from best practices of other democratic countries, we can promote out-of-the-box thinking and create a global network with interested individuals in promoting human growth and development.

Perhaps the National Research Council of the National Academies would partner with this new organization. In 2004, the National Research Council published a book: *Learning and Instruction: A SERP Research Agenda*. SERP stands for Strategic Education Research Partnership, which is a partnership with school districts to do research and development on major pressing problems in collaboration with major research institutions (Donovan & Pellegrino, 2004). The field of education needs a strong federal investment. The National Research Council should engage state departments of education, the U.S. Department of Education, and the Institute of Educational

Students to advocate to the administration and Congress for such new funded education structure that helps the federal government invest in basic and applied research to develop a strong, coherent, and financed research agenda.

Who should participate in the competition? Following the work of Francesca Gino, a Harvard Business School professor, we should bring to the table a variety of individuals who are committed to building a new education system (Gino, 2018). These individuals could be government officials, members of the business and labor communities, scientists, architects, technologists, parks and recreation specialists, higher education institutions, religious leaders of all faiths, health and human service providers, city planners, transportation experts, media and communications personnel, nutritionists, librarians, and community organizers. The list can go on and on. The point is that we want multiple individuals who can understand the strengths and weaknesses of the current system but are willing to work with diverse individuals from many fields to create a new pluralistic system. Diverse organizations can put together teams of individuals who represent different fields to design a pluralistic system consistent with democratic principles.

Tools for Managing Conflict

Renovating our education system, given the polarization in America, will not be easy. In so many ways, educational policies promoted by state legislatures are making us more divided. It is time to mobilize a diverse group of people from different professions, religions, and political persuasions to rethink the American educational system without dehumanizing each other. We will need to find ways to locate common ground in a hostile climate.

Amanda Ripley, author of *High Conflict: Why We Get Trapped and How We Get Out*, explains why Americans build walls dividing ourselves from others we believe to be very different from ourselves. She showed how we fail to understand and listen deeply to each other's values and points of view. She tells compelling stories of individuals as well as documenting empirical research about how individuals can leave behind their conflicts that were once part of their core identity. She notes that "there are many ways to create conflict guard rails in politics, and we practice none of them at the national level in the United States"; with each of Ripley's examples and documented research she notes that "all people are complicated. And in high conflict, there is almost always false simplicity lingering somewhere in the narrative. And in that simplicity, no one hears what they don't want to hear" (Ripley, 2021, pp. 246–248).

Ripley provides a model that can be helpful to our reimagining public education. She suggests bringing in mediators to help people start to feel heard so that they could listen. She notes that conflict arises when there is the appearance of only two binary extremes, but structured conversations can clarify assumptions. Further, she talks about how leaders or politicians can be fire starters or conflict entrepreneurs who use conflict for their own political purposes. She, and others believe that people should "go to the balcony" in one's own mind. This allows for a macro view that places larger goals above various disagreements. Listening carefully to one another's points of view may allow us to communicate across political, religious, geographical, and racial divides. She argues to complicate the narrative, so to spark curiosity to make the conflict interesting.

Another way to overcome our conflicts is modeled by The Human Library, a global innovative and hands-on learning platform to "create more inclusive and cohesive communities across cultural, religious social and ethnic differences" (Human Library Organization, 2022). By creating mutual respect and safe places for conversations to prevent conflicts, we can establish a high-quality, accountable education system that will meet the needs of all citizens, an educational system for a future all Americans can embrace with pride.

The education community can respond productively to high conflict. We should transcend the political partisans who have used education (and myths about education) as a political tool. Honest philosophical disagreements can be useful rather than poisonous in rethinking our educational system. We could come together to better understand the complexities of teaching and learning and design systems that will move us toward an accountable pluralism that can meet the needs of diverse children and families. We can take advantage of emerging technologies, changing workforce development opportunities, and the fatigue of a disruptive political culture to respect our differences and develop a new ecology of our current system to stimulate innovation and research that will best serve our democracy moving forward.

Concerns to Address

The system design teams must define the outcomes of the system over a five-to-ten-year period. The following are the education questions that the design team should think about.

Vision

The first consideration of a planning group should be a focus on the vision and purposes of a pluralistic system. This includes not only the high-level, long-term castle in the air that is hoped for but also some notion of immediate steps (and benefits) in order to get there.

Most importantly, a new system must consider how it will socialize individuals for a democracy, as this is always the larger context. New designs must always relate back to the achievement of the purposes of the system. How does the system propose to articulate the purposes to a variety of constituencies and balance the tensions between individual rights, society needs, and system-wide concerns?

Community and Civic Engagement

Planning for a new system of education must be broadly inclusive of all stakeholders. This includes families generally but also requires specific inclusion of groups marginalized by income, ethnicity, education level or a range of other biases. Educators and students of education must also be represented, perhaps through unions, but also educators in various positions beyond the classroom (curriculum directors, academics, administrators, etc.) that may not have union representation.

Inclusion in planning efforts should define "stakeholder" broadly. Public education impacts employers, investors, and developers. They should have an opportunity to contribute. Religious leaders from the community, as well as others involved in the lives of students: community and recreation centers, health and human services workers, all should be welcomed to contribute to this endeavor. Connections should also be sought with decision makers, local mayors, and council members, as well as the state legislators who will need to shepherd legislation to make a new system possible.

Throughout engagement and planning, it will be important to ensure that the process itself does not pose barriers to full participation by all sectors. This will include such elements as time, location, and format of meetings and means by which invitations are offered. Our recent COVID-19 experience has taught us much about how to meet and communicate virtually. This can open paths to engagement, as well as setting up barriers for those who lack devices or Internet access. These barriers are not insurmountable, but they must be considered.

Curriculum

The core of any educational system that justifies its existence is teaching and learning. While certain parameters, such as the setting of academic content standards, will continue to reside within a state department of education, the delivery of content, through curriculum and instruction, is intended in this model to take a range of forms across a diverse portfolio of schools.

A planning group may be expected to outline mechanisms for ensuring the quality of curriculum across schools. Some considerations may include the capacity of the system to include a range of philosophical approaches, individual learning differences, values of families and communities and the needs of employers and others in the community. In designing a system expected to provide oversight for a portfolio of schools, how will the system guard against imbalances and "cracks" that allow some student needs to go unmet? Responses may consider how curriculum are reviewed and by whom. There are many possibilities, from expert review panels to teachers on sabbatical and parent groups.

Accountability and Assessments

The thorny issue of accountability will not go away in a move toward pluralism. If anything, it will become even more prominent. With differing delivery systems for education, assurance of accountability for learning becomes even more critical. Increased public funding for schools once considered to be wholly outside of public responsibility justifies a greater emphasis on the mechanisms of accountability. Planners will need to determine what measures are appropriate, a common bank of state assessments for all? Or might a broader diversity of means, such as portfolios or problem-based challenges, for demonstrating learning, be acceptable? Are there other skills and achievements (collaboration, creativity) worthy of measuring and reporting? And how might results be reported transparently to parents and others?

Other accountability considerations include finances, attendance and discipline, finances and the success of students following graduation. This might include employment, college matriculation, or other postsecondary education. Systems must be in place to ensure that regional authorities, families, taxpayers, and the state department of education have information on which to base their decisions.

Teachers

The critical task of planners will be to ensure that teachers are knowledgeable and supported in their task of teaching. In most states, teachers are unionized, with contracts to spell out many things, from working hours to salaries and benefits to support for professional development. An improved system should be able to offer benefits to teachers, as well as making demands. Might additional planning time, for instance, be offered in exchange for larger classrooms (maintaining a fixed number of students)? Might there be a possibility of offering year-round employment opportunities (with enhanced salaries) in order to use summers for collaboration and planning (taking the place of the so-called "central office" decision-making). While many of these are school-level decisions, planners should be cognizant and consider how best to encourage such changes.

A larger question has to do with the systemic relationship to colleges of education. Planners should be prepared to detail very specifically any differences between what schools need and the training that teachers receive. Planners should also involve existing entities (state departments of education and higher education) in determining needs in relation to teacher licensing and certifications.

School Finance

Building a pluralistic system calls for changes to taxing for and funding of education. Disrupting current inequities will require a substantial (if not total and complete) move away from local property taxes as a major source of school funding. This is easy to say, but very difficult to do, as witnessed in Ohio by four successive Supreme Court decisions ruling that too great a reliance on local property taxes rendered the system unconstitutional. Further, full funding, at the individual student level, of private and parochial school tuition represents a greater expense than that now being covered across our states.

Planners will have to contend with reluctance of legislators to increase education budgets, or the taxes necessary for support. Further, high-income, property-wealthy districts have never shown themselves eager to share. A case will have to be made based on benefits to the state, perhaps in terms of long-term changes to employment, crime, ability to attract business and industry to the state. Planners will also need to gain an awareness of all sources of funding: federal, state, local, philanthropic, and the like, in order to find existing sources that might be repurposed to a good cause.

CONCLUSION

The purpose of this book is to explore five major policy arenas within American system of education: curriculum and instruction, the teaching profession, school choice, family and community engagement, and educational governance and finance. For each of these issues an overview is provided, including the historical roots and the current tensions between different philosophies of education, including conservative and liberal thoughts. Outlined in each of these areas are best practices from other countries that are outperforming the United States on international assessments. While our system has tried to adapt to changing economic, social, and political demands of our time, it has proven inadequate to meet the needs of all students and their families. When there is only one public school system, there is a propensity for unsatisfied customers to attack it. The Common School has produced cultural wars throughout its history and is currently being used as a political tool to lessen our focus on educational opportunity. For two centuries, people have tried to reform this system. Given the political divide that is now a part of our schools at the local level, it is time to say that, despite some gains, our system is currently broken.

Our country can learn much from observing how other democratic countries address the needs of their diverse citizens through an effective and inclusive system of education. Other systems have also confronted culture wars, while encouraging parents to think deeply about what they want from their children's schools and providing a range of viable options supported by the government to educate their children.

In this new system, we must assure that we present a vision for American education that abides by democratic principles and balances the tensions among civic participation, social justice, and individual freedom. We can do a better job in the United States by developing models that can work for all Americans. George Marsden, as quoted by Jonathan Zimmerman states that "in a pluralistic society we have little choice but accept pragmatic standards—that is the codes and procedures of a liberal democracy." Zimmerman ends his book by articulating that "the rest of us should seize this historic opportunity, showing the same willingness to enter into a dialogue with devout believers as they demonstrate toward us. In the end, debating our differences may be the only thing that holds us together" (Zimmerman, 2002, p. 228)

James Davison Hunter, points out in discussing education that there is a trail of ironies. Both sides of the political spectrum appeal to the notion that public schools must promote the common good (Hunter, 1991, p. 224).

Dana Goldstein notes:

> If we accept the limitations of our decentralized political system, we can move toward a future in which sustainable and transformable education reforms are seeded from the ground up, not imposed from the top down. They will be built more upon the expertise of the best teachers than on our fears of the worst teachers. This is how we will achieve an end to the teacher wars. (Goldstein, 2014, p. 274)

We need to seize the moment and pull our country together and reboot to create systems that will work for all Americans. Robert Putnam compares our current times to the economic, political, social, and cultural times of the Gilded Age of the late 1800s. He reminds us that, during that period, income distribution was terribly unequal and Americans were very individualistic and politically divided. But he gives us hope by describing that what followed was the Progressive era that greatly changed education and the quality of life for many Americans. Together we can develop new institutions and civic groups to move us forward as a nation to address an egalitarian agenda (Putnam, 2020).

Americans are currently in a traumatized state from the impact of COVID-19 and domestic and international crises. We need to focus on education possibilities. We hope that our proposal to develop an XPRIZE organization will generate enthusiasm from all sectors of the political spectrum to embrace our American ingenuity and creativity.

We live in a time when new emerging education technologies can improve our abilities to individualize instruction for all students and give educators and students immediate feedback. We need to create new pluralistic models that invest in the teaching professions by creating strong human resource systems. A new system requires equitable funding for students in ways that address their unique needs. We need to redesign the roles of the federal and state governments to support a new regional governance system and engage in community asset-building by listening and learning from the community. We need to build an education system capable of continually evolving to inspire the next generation to value our cultural roots; preserve our democracy; and master the knowledge, skills, and dispositions to solve the complex problems of an ever-changing new world order.

Provided here is a model to discuss and debate and encourage others to engage in a design of an accountable pluralistic system. The model eliminates central office bureaucracy and puts educational decision-making at the school level to empower teachers. The model supports the funding of private and parochial schools conditional on accountability for preserving the civil rights of all children and showing academic results.

REFERENCES

Berner, A. R. (2017). *Pluralism and American public education: No one way to school.* New York: Palgrave Macmillan.

Berne, R., & Stiefel, L. (1994). *The measurement of equity in school finance: Conceptual, methodological, and empirical dimensions.* Baltimore, MD: Johns Hopkins University Press.

Byrk, A. S., Gomez, L. M., Grunow, A., & LeMahieu, P. G. (2015). *Learning to improve: How America's schools can get better at getting better.* Cambridge, MA: Harvard Education Press.

Comer, J. P., & Haynes, N. M. (1991). Parent involvement in schools: An ecological approach. *The Elementary Journal,* 271–277.

Cuban, L. (2021). *Confessions of a school reformer.* Cambridge, MA: Harvard Education Press.

Donovan, S., & Pellegrino, J. W. (2004). *Learning and instruction: A SERP research agenda.* Washington DC: The National Academies Press.

Gino, F. (2018). *Rebel talent: Why it pays to break the rules at work and in life.* New York: Harper Collins.

Glass, A. (2017, December 1). *Lincoln defends his emancipation policies to Congress: Dec. 1, 1862.* Politico. https://www.politico.com/story/2017/12/01/this-day-in-politics-dec-1-1862-268420.

Glenn, C. L. (1988). *The myth of the common school.* Amherst: University of Massachusetts Press.

Goldstein, D. (2014). *The teacher wars: A history of America's most embattled profession.* New York: Anchor Books: A Division of Penguin Random House LLC.

Grossman, N. (2022, May 12). *Schools have no choice but to teach social and emotional skills.* Thomas B. Fordham Institute. https://fordhaminstitute.org/national/commentary/schools-have-no-choice-teach-social-and-emotional-skills.

Hill, P. T., & Jochim, A. E. (2015). *A democratic constitution for public education.* Chicago, IL: University of Chicago Press.

Holley, K. (2016). *The principles for equitable and inclusive civic engagement.* Columbus: The Kirwan Institute for the Study of Race and Ethnicity at the Ohio State University.

Human Library Organization. (2022, May 16). *Human library: Unjudge someone.* Human Library. https://humanlibrary.org.

Hunter, J. D. (1991). *Culture wars: The struggle to define America: Making sense of the battles over the family, art, education, law and politics.* New York: Basic Books.

Jennings, J. (2015). *Presidents, Congress and the public schools: The politics of education reform.* Cambridge, MA: Harvard Education Press.

Klein, A. (2022, May 20). *The teaching profession is "crumbling": What can school leaders do to help?* EdWeek. https://www.edweek.org/teaching-learning/the-teaching-profession-is-crumbling-what-can-school-leaders-do-to-help/2022/05.

Mehta, J., Schwartz, R. B., & Hess, F. M. (2012). *The futures of school reform.* Cambridge, MA: Harvard Education Press.

NPR. (2018). *You 2.0: Rebel with a cause.* The Human Brain. https://www.npr.org/transcripts/631524581.

Putnam, R. (2000). *Bowling alone: The collapse and revival of American community.* New York: Simon & Schuster.

Putnam, R. (2015). *Our kids: The American dream in crisis.* New York: Simon & Schuster.

Putnam, R. (2020). *The upswing: How America came together a century ago and how we can do it again.* New York: Simon & Schuster.

Ripley, A. (2021). *High conflict: Why we get trapped and how we get out.* New York: Simon & Schuster Paperbacks.

Spurrier, A., Graziano, L., Robinson, B., & Squire, J. (2022). *Expanding educational options: Emergent policy trends.* Washington DC: Bellwether Educational Partners.

Strauss, V. (2014, June 9). How much Bill Gates' disappointing small-schools effort really cost. *The Washington Post.*

Virginia Department of Education. (2022). *Our commitment to Virginians: High expectations and excellence for all students May 2022.* Richmond: Virginia Department of Education.

Will, M. (2022, April 4). *Teacher job satisfaction hits an all-time low*. EdWeek. https://www.edweek.org/teaching-learning/teacher-job-satisfaction-hits-an-all-time-low/2022/04.

XPrize Foundation. (2022). *We are XPrize*. XPRIZE.: https://www.xprize.org/.

Zelman, S. (2021). *Informal interviews with 103 Ohio superintendents*. Unpublished study by the author.

Zimmerman, J. (2002). *Whose America? Culture wars in the public schools*. Cambridge, MAs: Harvard University Press.

Appendix A: Pertinent Court Cases

School funding issues have frequently been elevated to the courts. The following is a sampling of school funding cases that have affected school governance and policies.

MASSACHUSETTS: *MCDUFFY V. SECRETARY OF THE EXECUTIVE OFFICE OF EDUCATION*—415 MASS. 545, 615 N.E.2D 516 (1993)

The question before the court in this case was whether the Commonwealth was mandated by the Constitution to provide students with education. Students filed actions against the Commonwealth in 1978 and then amended them in 1990, alleging that the Commonwealth had failed to fulfill its duty to provide them with an education as mandated by the Massachusetts Constitution. The school finance system, they charged, violated the education clause of the Massachusetts Constitution. The Massachusetts Constitution states in part that "it shall be the duty of legislatures and magistrates, in all future periods of this commonwealth, to cherish . . . the public schools and grammar schools in the towns."

The Supreme Judicial Court held that the education clause is not merely aspirational or hortatory but also imposes an enforceable duty to provide education for all its children through the public schools. The court found:

> While it is clearly within the power of the Commonwealth to delegate some of the implementation of the duty to local governments, such power does not include a right to abdicate the obligation imposed on magistrates [the executive branch] and Legislatures placed on them by the Constitution. *Secretary of the*

Executive Office of Education, 415 Mass. 545, 606, 615 N.E.2d 516, 548 (*The State Constitutional Mandate for education: The* McDuffy *and* Hancock *decisions*, n.d.).

OHIO: *DEROLPH V. STATE*—1997-OHIO-84, 78 OHIO ST. 3D 193, 677 N.E.2D 733

In *DeRolph*, the issue before the court was whether Ohio's public elementary and secondary school finance system was unconstitutional. In 1991 the Ohio Coalition for Equity and Adequacy of School Funding, which represented more than 500 school districts in Ohio, filed a suit in the Perry County courts against the State of Ohio for failing to provide adequate funding to educate Ohio students. The districts argued that school systems in areas with higher property values could more easily meet the needs of and provide more opportunities for their students while students in poorer areas suffered. The claim was that the state failed to provide an "efficient" educational system as dictated by the Ohio Constitution of 1851 by relying so heavily upon local property taxes to fund schools.

The trial court's decision overturned an earlier Ohio Supreme Court ruling from 1979, which claimed that Ohio's school financing system was adequate, saying that "public education is a fundamental right in the state of Ohio" and that the state legislature had to provide an improved and more equitable means of financing education.

The trial court's decision was appealed by the Ohio legislature to the Fifth District Court of Appeals, which overturned the decision, stating that they did not have the power to overturn an Ohio Supreme Court decision.

In 1996, the school districts filed an appeal with the Ohio Supreme Court, which agreed to consider the case. This time, the Ohio Supreme Court decided that Ohio's method of funding schools violated the Ohio Constitution and ordered that the state "enact a constitutional school-funding system" (*DeRolph v. State of Ohio*, n.d.).

TEXAS: *EDGEWOOD INDEPENDENT SCHOOL DISTRICT V. KIRBY*—777 S.W.2D 391 (TEX. 1989)

In this case, the Mexican American Legal Defense and Educational Fund (MALDEF) filed a suit against the Commissioner of Education William Kirby on May 23, 1984, on behalf of the Edgewood Independent School District, San Antonio, Texas, citing discrimination against students in poor school districts. MALDEF charged that the state's methods of funding public schools violated at least four principles of the state constitution, which obligated the state legislature to provide an efficient and free public school system. The plaintiffs had many school districts join this case for a total of sixty-seven school districts and numerous parents and students. At issue was the state's reliance on local property taxes to finance its system of public education. The property values varied greatly from district to district. Therefore, there was a huge inequity in funds available to educate students throughout the state. Plaintiffs believed that this method was fundamentally unequal. These differences produced disparities in the districts' abilities to hire good teachers, build appropriate facilities, offer a sound curriculum, and purchase technology.

On June 30, 1984, which was about a month after the plaintiffs filed their petition, the Texas legislature passed a school-reform measure to increase state aid to poor schools. However, the plaintiffs challenged this new law by amending their petition, and on April 29, 1987, the court ruled in favor of the plaintiffs. The court found that the state's public school financing structure was unconstitutional and ordered the legislature to develop a more equitable system by September 1989. The state appealed this decision to the Third Court of Appeals, where the lower court's decision was overturned by a 2–1 decision on the grounds that education was not a basic right and that the existing public-school financing was in fact constitutional. Plaintiffs appealed that decision to the Texas Supreme Court in July of 1989, and in a 9–0 decision the Texas Supreme Court reversed the Third Court of Appeals and sided with the plaintiffs again to order the state legislature to implement an equitable system by the 1990–1991 school year (*The Texas Politics Project: At the University of Texas at Austin*, n.d.).

NEW JERSEY: *ABBOTT V. BURKE*, 206 N.J. 332 (2011)

The Educational Law Center filed a complaint in 1981 in New Jersey Superior Court on behalf of twenty children attending public schools in the cities of Camden, East Orange, Irvington, and Jersey City. The complaint challenged the New Jersey's structure of financing public education under the Public School Education Act of 1975. This case eventually made its way to the New Jersey Supreme Court through a series of decisions. The main argument of the plaintiffs was that the New Jersey's existing method of funding public schools was unconstitutional because it caused significant expenditure inequalities among poor, urban, and wealthy suburban school districts and that poorer urban districts were unable to effectively meet the educational needs of their students.

Overall, *Abbott v. Burke* was a line of cases that lasted twenty-four years and resulted in more than twenty opinions by the state's courts. The New

Jersey Supreme Court ultimately found for the plaintiffs, and in its *Abbott* rulings the Court compelled the state to act so as to reduce inequalities in school funding and make sure that students across the state receive public education in accordance with New Jersey's state constitution (*The history of Abbot v. Burke*, n.d.).

REFERENCES

Education Law Center. (n.d.). *The History of Abbot v Burke*. Retrieved August 16, 2022, from Education Law Center: https://edlawcenter.org/litigation/abbott-v-burke/abbott-history.html

Massachusetts Department of Elementary and Secondary Education. (n.d.). *The State Constitutional Mandate for Education: The McDuffy and Hancock Decisions*. Retrieved August 16, 2022, from Massachusetts Department of Elementary and Secondary Education: https://www.doe.mass.edu/lawsregs/litigation/mcduffy-hancock.html

Ohio History Connection. (n.d.). *DeRolph v. State of Ohio*. Retrieved August 16, 2022, from Ohio History Connection: https://ohiohistorycentral.org/w/DeRolph_v._State_of_Ohio

The Texas Politics Project. (n.d.). *The Texas Politics Project: At the University of Texas at Austin*. Retrieved August 16, 2022, from Edgewood ISD v. Kirby: https://texaspolitics.utexas.edu/archive/html/cons/features/0404_01/edgewood.html

Appendix B: Discussion Questions

Readers, including parents, teachers, administrators, educational policymakers, as well as any stakeholder in the American education system will have questions about the issues we have raised in this book and how they and their schools are or could be affected by them. Appendix B provides a resource of questions that could begin the development of an action agenda in creating a system of education for the future. Parents, policymakers, not-for-profits, and others concerned with education may begin to understand their own schools and districts by asking questions of teachers, administrators, and local school boards.

These questions are divided chapter-wise to focus on the issues addressed in each chapter. They are further divided, as appropriate, into student and parent-, school-, district-, and state-level concerns. There are also some "big picture" concerns, having to do with public policies impacting education on a much broader scale. The Chapter 6 questions relate to the questions designers of the future of education will need to address.

CHAPTER 1: SCHOOL AS WE KNOW IT

Parent- and Student-Level Concerns

- What are children expected to learn in their current grade?
- Does the school publish grade-by-grade expectations by subjects on their website so that parents can find them easily?
- Are there apparent differences between classrooms in the same grade?
- How can parents help their students learn to the standards?
- What kind of support do teachers give to students who have difficulty in mastering the content?

School- and District-Level Concerns

- Does the school and district use the standards developed by the state?
- What role does the school board have in approving standards and enhancing standards to make them appropriate to the school community?
- How do they make certain that there are no gaps between grades (particularly in transitions such as elementary to middle and middle to high school)?

Big Picture Concerns

- Explore the website of the state's department of education.

  - Are the standards published?
  - Are there tools to help parents and others understand the standards (such as grade-level highlights or explanations in layman's language)?

- Several organizations (Fordham, Edweek-Quality Counts, Achieve) evaluate state standards. Look for areas of strength and weakness that they report. How do your state standards compare to those of other states?

CHAPTER 2: ON TEACHERS

Exploring Teacher Certification

Stakeholders reading this book may wish to look into the policy, practice, and impact of certification in their own district or across their state. Following are questions to pursue.

Parent and Student-Level Concerns

- Are all teachers certified to teach at the grade level and in the content in which they are teaching?
- Does the school have a mentoring system for newer teachers?
- How are substitutes certified?
- Does the school have regular assigned substitutes, or do they rotate across an entire system?
- Are there provisions for long-term substitutes to be appropriately certified for the grade and content area they are teaching?

District-Level Concerns

- Does the district participate in any alternative certification programs, and if so, how do they evaluate the program?

- Do teachers complete the alternative certification programs? Do they stay at the school, or in teaching, or do many leave the school or field?
- Are teachers certified by either alternative or state programs required to complete a "clinical," or student-teaching time prior to certification?
- Does the school report card provide information about the number or percentage of teachers teaching outside their certification areas?

State-Level Concerns

- How are teacher certification programs accredited in the state?
- Does the state report numbers or percentages of appropriately certified teachers on state report cards?
- Are there areas of the state where certification appears to be an issue?
- Are teacher standards for certification aligned with student learning standards by grade level?
- Where may the public view the teacher certification standards?
- What requirements does the state have for continued certification?

CHAPTER 3: SCHOOL CHOICE

Parent- and Student-Level Concerns

The same desperation that made vouchers and NCLB transfers attractive (some kids are in bad situations right now and deserve better) is a very real and present one for parents, realizing how short is the window of childhood, and how limited our time to "get it right." Parents do not have the luxury of reformers to consider long-term strategies and big picture concerns. Parents are faced with the current landscape and what it offers to each of their children as individuals. As parents move to exercise their choice, such as it is, here are some critical questions to consider.

The current level of choice provides many options, but not all are of equal, or high, quality. As parents face this landscape of choice, they also have a new and greater responsibility to evaluate and make good choices for their children.

- Some schools stress the arts and others athletics or technology. Getting a good fit is an important consideration.
- Does our children have any categorical learning needs (disability or giftedness) that help to define the best setting for them?
- How does my child learn? Some children follow an orderly process in all things while others are more eclectic. What are their interests?
- Look beyond the building and consider chains of accountability. A private school may have trustees. A charter school may be accountable not only to

a state-approved sponsor but also to a corporate entity. A district school will have a locally elected board. Depending on your state, there may be strong systems of accountability, or not. Knowing this may lead toward or away from some categories of choice.

- Who are the decision makers at the schools I am considering?
- Most states should be able to provide comparative test data. Other important data, if available, might include attendance, discipline, graduation. Red flags might include poor academic achievement—particularly over a long time period, or high rates of suspension or expulsion.
- How well are the schools I am considering educating students?
- What is the "feel" of the school when visiting? Welcoming? Chaotic? Organized?
- Do you see engaged students or are too many unfocused?
- What are students doing? Are there learning activities beyond listening, reading, and writing?
- Who are the decision makers for education in district and state?
- Who else in my area is concerned with education and what can we do together to work toward a more meaningful menu of choices for all students?

CHAPTER 4: ENGAGEMENT

Parent-Level Concerns

Parents and other community members may find themselves on the outside looking in on their local district and schools. Finding an open door may require first joining with others to make a case for inclusion. Some questions may help to guide the process.

- What family and community engagement opportunities does the local district have in place currently? Are they impactful? Are they equitable and inclusive? Are there barriers to inclusion?
- What education-related organizations exist in the community in addition to those provided by the school or district? Are they affiliated with any larger organizations and funders? Do they share a vision that matches with your own?
- What local interactions and influences are you aware of—to either support or oppose? What "issues" are coming before the school board?
- What resources are available to help parents, students, and other citizens understand such issues?

- What are my existing networks? How might they be useful in impacting education in my community? These might include informal connections such as family and friends, or more formally organized groups such as churches, fraternities, or sororities, or even online communities.
- Who can I approach in the school system when there are concerns?

School- and District-Level Concerns

Forward-thinking educators and administrators may already be tuned into the need for a different level of community engagement. Others may not have considered this to be as important as many other details they face on a daily basis. In either case, the following questions may prove helpful in guiding relationships with both families and the community at large.

- What structures are currently in place to engage families and the community in the business of education?
- What barriers might prevent engagement, and can these be removed?
- At what point in planning for change do families and the community have opportunities for input? Early on in defining problems and solutions? "Stakeholder" sessions to review plans prior to implementation? No opportunities?
- What community groups interact with the school/district on a regular basis?
- What is their vision concerning education?
- What other groups in our community might be open to relationship?
- What professional development is available for teachers to strengthen their outreach capacity?
- Are there any identifiable groups of families or others who are not regularly engaged?

CHAPTER 5: SCHOOL GOVERNANCE IN AMERICA

Parent-, School-, and District-Level Concerns

- What are the components of the state's funding formula? Think about whether there are adjustments based on local property wealth and income or percentage of students with disabilities or ELs.
- How does your district funding compare with that of others? Consider per-pupil funding for a comparison. Another good metric is local millage revenue—a district with higher property values can raise more with a lower tax rate than a district with lower property values.

- Does your district have challenges (rural areas may have enhanced transportation needs, others may have high concentrations of students learning English) that are addressed by your state's formula?
- Does your state provide additional funding for things like buildings and transportation? Is this something that benefits your district?
- Is your district funding sufficient to provide competitive salaries for teachers and other professionals?

CHAPTER 6: A NEW SYSTEM OF EDUCATION: STARTING FROM SCRATCH

Teams tasked with designing a new system of education must define the outcomes of the system over a five-to-ten-year period. The first set of questions should focus on the purposes of a pluralistic system.

Vision Questions

- What is the long-term vision of the system?
- What is the immediate purpose, mission, and goals?
- Are the missions, goals, values, and philosophies for individual schools or learning units clear and transparent?
- How does the system propose to articulate the purposes to a variety of constituencies and balance the tensions between individual rights, society needs, and system-wide concerns?

Curriculum and Instruction Questions

- Does the system provide high-quality curriculum to all students?
- How does the curriculum meet the needs of individual students in a learning system?
- Does the system accommodate various philosophical approaches?
- How does the curriculum accommodate individual differences in learning?
- Does the curriculum reflect the values and traits that parents, educators, and students want to develop?
- Does the curriculum reflect the needs and wants of the local community and see the community as a resource?
- How will curriculum content be derived and continuously improved upon?
- What role do experts, students, parents, and the community play in the design and implementation of the curriculum?
- Will the curriculum encourage community partnerships such as mentors and apprenticeships?

- Does the curriculum lead to pathways to higher educations, jobs, and careers?
- Does the curriculum blur boundaries between students' experience in the community's informal educational institutions such as museums and youth development organizations such as Boy Scout or Boys and Girls Clubs?
- What types of instruction does the school encourage?
- Does it encourage whole group, small group, design thinking groups, or individualized instruction?
- What type of technologies are needed to support curriculum and instruction?
- Will the school use social media, blogs, Wikis, and blended/online learning?
- Where will the content and materials of the curriculum come from?
- Will the curriculum reflect the importance of what research suggests regarding a strong liberal arts curriculum that can be delivered in multiple ways to all students?
- Are curriculum and instruction choices available to students and their parents?

Assessment and Accountability Questions

- How does a student demonstrate what he or she learns?
- Are different modes available to the student?
- Are the modes of assessment competitive with continuous problem-based challenges, do portfolios of student work exist, and are they transparent and evaluated?
- Are assessments evaluating entrepreneurial, collaborative, and creative skills?
- Can we create a system where parents and taxpayers have adequate information about school performance measures and fiscal expenditures?
- How do we provide an accountable system that does not inhibit innovation?

Questions about Teachers

- Who will be our educators?
- What training do they need?
- Who will do the training?
- How selective should the trainer be?
- How should we think about differentiated roles and responsibilities within the teaching profession?
- Should we break down barriers between labor and management?
- Can teachers lead schools individually or collectively?
- Are educators in the system role models to the students that can demonstrate integrity, empathy, and moral courage?

- How will educators continually refine their knowledge, skills, and dispositions?
- How will educators collaborate with each other across other educational institutions locally and globally?

Funding Questions

- How can we design a new system of school funding that eliminates the local property tax and provides equitable funding based on student and family needs?
- How do we attract and give incentives to providers who want to create new education alternatives?
- What role do the federal, state, and local communities play in financing these new systems?

Questions about Community and Civic Engagement

- What are the assets our community offers to build on?
- How do we engage families and taxpayers in our community in redesigning a new pluralistic system that builds on community and family strength?
- How do we engage the community and the public to challenge some of the racist, classist, and gender-based tendencies that continually divide our country? (This begs other questions. Who are we? How have we defined community?)
- How might we involve health and human services as member of our planning and visioning efforts?
- How do we form partnerships with early adopters and political leaders to bring about the change that this country needs?

Index

Note: Page number in **bold** refers to tables on the corresponding page.

Abbott Elementary, 70

Abbott v. Burke (New Jersey), 215

Abington School District v. Schempp, 108

Academic Distress Commissions (ADCs), 189–90

access to education: during 18th and 19th centuries, 6–7; during 1960s through 1980s, 24; during Civil War era, 10; during Cold War era, 20–21; during Gilded Age, 12; during Progressive Era, 16; during top-down reform era, 29

accountability, 85, 117, 200–201, 219–22, 247–48

Achieve, 61

achievement, school choice and, 141–43

Activist Mommy Facebook page, 164

adequate yearly progress (AYP), 25, 27, 28, 60, 201

administrators, local governance and, 193

African American Sunday School Movement, 6

Alexander, Lamar, 26

ALTAIR Learning Management, 126

alternative education programs, 73–74

alternative schools, 130

America 2000, 26

America CARES Act, 205–6

American anti-intellectualism, 19, 70, 97

American Child Health Association, 36

American Federation of Teachers (AFT), 16, 20, 75, 89, 123

American High School Today, The (Conant), 37

American Indian community, 2, 160

American Legislative Exchange Council (ALEC), 120, 164

American Recovery and Reinvestment Act (2009), 25

Annenberg Institute, 173

anti-intellectualism, 19, 70, 97

art of teaching, 66

assessment: creation of, 60; future issues regarding, 61–63; introduction to, 33–34; observations regarding, 62–63; overview of, 59–61; pluralistic system and, 247–48

assessment for learning, 60

assessment of learning, 59

asset-based community approach, 171–72

"astroturf" groups, 162–63
asynchronous online learning, 52
attendance zones, 109–16

back-to-basics movement, 27
backward design, 50
Baker, Bruce, 203–4
Bandura, Albert, 69
Bank Street School, 69
Bannon, Steve, 162
basic skills, 35–36
Beat Generation, 17
Beck, Paul, 162
behaviorism, 14, 68–69
Bell, Terrell, 25
Berliner, David, 29
Berner, Ashley Rogers, 219, 232
best practices, 91–92, 98–99
Biden, Joe, 164, 195
Bilingual Education Act (BEA;
    1972), 22
Bill and Melinda Gates Foundation, 242
Bittle, Bruce, 29
Black Lives Matter movement, 41
Blaine, James G., 13
Blaine Amendment, 13, 16
Blue-backed Speller, 5
boards of education: district, 192,
    238–39; establishment of, 7; region,
    238–39; state, 185, 190–91, 237–38
Boehner, John, 201
book banning, 42
Boston Latin School, 3
Brennan, David L., 124
Brenner, Andrew, 118
Brenner, Ashley Rogers, 206
Bronfenbrenner, 152
Brown, Anthony, 43
Brown v. Board of Education, 17, 20,
    23, 81, 113, 114, 199
Bruner, Jerome, 19
Brunson, Quinta, 70
Bryk, A. S., 233
Buchanan, 111–12

Budde, Ray, 123–24
Bureau of Educational Experiments, 69
bureaucracy, 118–19
Bush, George H. W., 26
Bush, George W., 44, 201

Calkins, Lucy, 38
career development, 95–96
career education, 166–67
career ladders, 95–96
Carnegie units, 55, 133
Carr, Peggy G., 142
Carrol Independent School District,
    162–63
Carter, Jimmy, 23, 200
Cat in the Hat, The (Geisel/Seuss), 35
Catholic schools, 109, 208
cell phones, 50
Center for American Progress (CAP),
    83, 96
centralization, 14
CEO (Chief Operating Officer), 225–26,
    238, 239–40, 241, 242
certification, 72–74, 85
change: in needs, 85–86; ongoing, 99;
    resistance to, 43–44
charter schools, 89, 122–29,
    139–41
child abuse, 132
childcare, 58, 175
Child Find program, 199
child labor laws, 11, 13
Children of the Rainbow, 197
Christian Coalition, 162
Chubb, John, 120, 125, 141, 195
civic education council (CEC), 225,
    237–40
civil discourse, 59
Civil Rights Act (1964), 21
civil rights movement, 20, 28, 44
Civil War era, 7–10
classroom management, 68
Cleveland Scholarship and Tutoring
    program, 135–36

Clinton, Bill, 26, 121, 187, 200
Coalition for Responsible Home
Education, 132
Coalition of Essential Schools, 77
cognitive development, 18
Cohen, D. K., 190
Cold War, 17–21, 35, 184, 198
Coleman, James, 21
Coleman Report, 21
collective bargaining, 89, 90
college attendance rates, 1–2
colonial era, 2–4
Comer, James P., 152, 155–56, 160,
170, 232
Committee of Ten, 14–15
Common Core Standards, 27, 45–46,
60–61, 75–76, 201
Common Schools, 7–9, 10, 16, 67,
107–8, 183–84, 206–8, 248–49
communications systems, 98
Community Action Programs, 21
community control movement, 24
community engagement, 165–74,
233–35, 246
compensation/salaries, 84, 92, 99,
204
Comprehensive Child Development Act
(1971), 23
compulsory education laws, 7, 13,
118
Conant, James Bryant, 18, 37
conferences, 87
Confessions of a School Reformer
(Cuban), 234
conflict management, 244–45
conservative progressives, 13, 14
constructivism, 68, 69
continuing education, 86–88
Continuing Education Units (CEUs), 87
core knowledge, 36
Core Knowledge (Hirsch), 27
corporal punishment, 9
cost economies, 116–17
Coulson, Andrew, 119

Council for the Accreditation of
Educator Preparation (CAEP), 73
Council of Chief State School Officers
(CCSSO), 45, 75, 188
Counts, George, 19
COVID-19: assessments and, 62;
Catholic schools and, 109; "COVID
gap" and, 56; disruptions from,
38, 50–52; district superintendents
and, 194; family engagement and,
161; funding related to, 205–6;
homeschooling and, 132; impact of,
250; Internet access and, 57; local
school boards and, 195–96; private
school enrollment and, 233; resiliency
and, 174; teacher retention and, 86;
teacher shortage and, 72; teaching
profession and, 28, 86; telework and,
166–67; unions and, 90
credit recovery, 51, 53, 55
critical race theory (CRT), 40, 41–42,
43, 163–64, 196
Cuban, Larry, 234
cultural humility, 172
*Cultural Literacy; What Every
American Needs to Know*
(Hirsch), 27
curriculum: during 18th and 19th
centuries, 5; during 1960s through
1980s, 23–24; during Civil War
era, 9; during Cold War era, 18–19;
during colonial era, 3; Common
Core and, 45–46; future issues
regarding, 46–47; during Gilded
Age, 11; historic integrity and,
40–44; introduction to, 33–34;
multiculturalism and, 40–44; NCLB
and, 44–45; observations regarding,
47, 63; overview of, 34–46;
for pluralistic system, 226–28;
pluralistic system and, 246–47;
during Progressive Era, 14–15;
sources of, 39–40; standards for, 46;
during top-down reform era, 27–28

Dahill-Brown, Sarah, 194, 198
Dame schools, 3, 5
Darling-Hammond, Linda, 77–78, 79, 91, 94, 95–96, 220
deficit-based views of students, 159
Democratic Constitution for Public Education, A (Hill and Jochim), 220
Denney, R., 17
Department of National Women's Organizations, 154
Derolph v. State (Ohio), 214
DeSantis, Ron, 116
desegregation, 20, 21, 23, 115, 199, 205. *See also* segregation
DeVos, Betsey, 116, 121–22
Dewey, John, 15, 19, 20, 36, 69
Dewey, Thomas, 36
DeWine, Mike, 187, 191
diagnostic assessment, 60
differentiated instruction, 49
direct instruction, 48
disruption, 221
disruptions in instruction, 50–54
distance learning, 52–53
district boards of education, 192, 238–39
district superintendents, 192, 193–94
districts, public school, 109–17, 192, 193–94
diversity, lack of among teachers, 81–82, 99–100
Domenech, Dan, 194
Doyle, Denis P., 121
drop-out recovery schools, 125
Dr. Seuss (Theodor Geisel), 35
Du Bois, W. E. B., 12
Dukakis, Michael, 80
Dyrness, A., 158

early childhood education, 166, 175, 187
Early Head Start, 166
East High School, Columbus, Ohio, 114–15, 171–72
Economic Opportunity Act (1964), 21

EdChoice, 135–36, 138
Edgewood Indep. Sch. Dist. v. Kirby (Texas), 214–15
Edison Schools, 125
EdReports, 54
educational materials: during 18th and 19th centuries, 5; during 1960s through 1980s, 23–24; during Civil War era, 9; during Cold War era, 18–19; during colonial era, 3; curriculum and, 39–40, 43; during Gilded Age, 11; instruction and, 53; during Progressive Era, 14–15; during top-down reform era, 27–28
educational pods, 53, 133
"Educational Quality and Family Choice" (Finn and Doyle), 121
Educational Service Centers, 54
Education for All Handicapped Children Act (1975), 22, 74, 199
education improvement, school choice and, 141–43
EdWeek, 163–64
Eisenhower, Dwight, 37
EL Education, 128
Electronic Classroom of Tomorrow (ECOT), 125–26
Elementary and Secondary Education Act (ESEA; 1965), 22, 37, 105, 155–56, 199, 200–201, 205, 227
Elementary and Secondary School Act (ESEA; 1965), 25
Eliot, Charles, 14
Ellison, Ralph, 17
Empowered Educators: Developing High Quality Teaching, 94
Empowered Educators: Teacher Appraisal and Feedback, 94–95
Empowered Educators: The Teaching Career and Leadership for the Profession, 95–96
empowering teachers, 90–96
engagement: community, 165–74, 246; introduction to, 151–52;

observations regarding, 174–75; parents and, 151–58, 171–72; pluralistic system and, 233–35, 246; politicization of, 161–65; power and inclusion and, 158–61
Engle v. Vitale, 18
Enlightenment, 4–5
enslaved people, 3, 4, 6, 10, 11, 208
Epstein, Joyce, 153, 155, 160, 166
Equal Education Opportunity, 155, 184
equality: during 18th and 19th centuries, 6; during Civil War era, 9–10; during Cold War era, 20; during colonial era, 4; during Gilded Age, 12; during Progressive Era, 16; during top-down reform era, 28
equal opportunity, 117
e-schools, 123
essentialist tradition, 35–36, 37–38, 68
evaluations, teacher, 75–76, 85, 94–95
Every Student Succeeds Act (2015), 25
experiential instruction, 49
extracurricular activities, 14

Failure to Disrupt (Reich), 69
Fair Housing Act (1968), 113
Family Independence Initiative, 158, 172
federal funding, 205
federal governance, 182, 198–202
Federal Housing Administration (FHA), 112
Feinberg, Mike, 127
Fernandez, Joseph, 197
financial pressures, 42–43
Finn, Chester, Jr., 25, 78, 119, 120–21, 138, 141–42
Flesch, Rudolph, 35, 38
flipped classrooms, 50
Florida opportunity scholarships, 136–37
Floyd, George, 41, 191
Ford, Gerald, 22
formative assessment, 60

for-profit charter schools, 124–26
Forster, Greg, 141
Framingham State University (FSU), 67–68
Franklin, John Hope, 40
Freedman's Bureau, 11
Freire, Paulo, 23
Freng, A., 160
Freng, S., 160
Friedan, Betty, 154
Friedman, Milton, 25, 118, 119, 119–20
Friere, P., 170
Fuller, Howard, 133, 135
full-service schools, 234
funding: equitable, 221; pluralistic system and, 241, 248; school governance and, 202–6, 213–15
Futures of School Reform (Mehta, Schwartz, and Hess), 236

Garther, M., 29
Gates, Bill, 203, 242–43
Geisel, Theodor (Dr. Seuss), 35
geographical isolation, 84
gerrymandered attendance zones, 111–12
Gibbs, Jack, 171
Gilded Age, 10–12
Gino, Francesca, 220, 244
Glazer, N., 17
Glenn, Charles, 183, 206, 220
Goals 2000, 26
Golann, Joanne W., 127
Goldstein, Dana, 89–90, 249
Gomez, L. M., 233
Good, Howard, 195
Goodman, Paul, 23
governors, 185, 186–87, 236–37
governors' cabinets, 185
graduation, exams for, 60
graduation rates, 1, 19, 21, 24, 126, 128
Graham, Bill, 187
Graham School, 128–29
Grant, Ulysses S., 13

Green Dot Charter Schools, 157
Gronow, A., 233
"grow your own" programs, 99

Hannah-Jones, Nikole, 110, 113, 114
Hanushek, Eric, 143, 203
Harding, Warren G., 112
Harrington, Michael, 21
Harris, Wendell, 135
Hart, Bob, 171
Haynes, N. M., 232
Head Start programs, 22–23, 166, 175
health concerns, 56, 86
Henig, J. R., 186
Heritage Foundation, 164
Hess, Frederick M., 236
High Conflict (Ripley), 244
higher education: Committee of
    Ten and, 14–15; curriculum
    reorganization and, 19; high schools
    and, 18; Morrill Acts and, 11
high-speed internet, 57
Hill, H. C., 190
Hill, Paul, 220, 223, 225, 229, 235, 238
Hirsch, E. D., Jr., 27, 36
historic integrity, 40–44
Hofstadter, Richard, 70, 97
Holmes Group, 78–79
Holt, John, 23
home ownership, 112
homeschooling, 27, 131–33
Hope scholarships, 136–37
Hopes and Dreams Protocol, 161
Householder, Larry, 165
Human Library, The, 245
human resource system, 65–66
Hunt, James, 79, 187
Hunter, James Davison, 249
hybrid learning, 52

Illich, Ivan, 23
immigration, 11, 16, 208
Improving America's Schools Act
    (1994), 156, 200
incentives for teachers, 82

individual instruction, 49
Individualized Education Plans (IEPs),
    38, 156–57
individualized instruction, 28
individualized learning, 36
Individual Professional Development
    Plan, 88
Individuals with Disabilities in
    Education Act (IDEA), 37, 156–57,
    171
Industrial Revolution, 10–12
influencers, 164–65
inquiry-based instruction, 49
instruction: differentiated, 49;
    disruptions in, 50–54; future issues
    regarding, 56–59; influences on,
    55–56; introduction to, 33–34;
    lesson design and, 50; observations
    regarding, 58–59, 63; overview
    of, 47–56; for pluralistic system,
    226–28; social-emotional learning
    and, 54; special education and,
    49–50; student-centered, 48–49;
    teacher-centered, 48
international competition/comparison,
    18, 45, 62, 76–77, 90–96, 100, 143,
    173–74, 199–200, 206
international tests, 61, 62
invisibility, 160–61
Invisible Man, The (Ellison), 17

Jackson, Andrew, 7
Jefferson, Thomas, 5
Jencks, Christopher, 23
Jennings, Jack, 231, 232
Jenson, Arthur, 21–22
Jim Crow conditions, 111, 154
job satisfaction, 85
Jobs Corps, 21
Jochim, Ashley, 220, 223, 225, 229,
    235, 238
Johnson, Lyndon B., 21
Johnson, Ron, 196
Johnston, Elizabeth, 164
junior high schools, 14

Kasich, John, 110, 187
Kean, Tom, 187
Kelly, Jim, 79
Kennedy, John F., 38
Kennedy, Ted, 201
kindergarten, assessments for entry
    into, 60
kinesthetic/multiple modalities, 48
KIPP Public Charter Schools, 126–27
Kirby, William, 214–15
Kirwan Institute for the Study of Race
    and Ethnicity, 172–73, 234–35
Knowledge is Power Program (KIPP), 83
Kohl, Herbert, 23
Kohler, Laura, 191
Kolderie, Ted, 123
Kozol, Jonathan, 23, 170
Ku Klux Klan, 13

Laboratory School at the University of
    Chicago, 15
Lager, Bill, 125–26
land grants, 110, 182
*Land of the Free: A History of the
    United States* (Franklin), 40
Land Ordinance (1785), 110
leadership, 95–96
*Learning and Instruction: A SERP
    Research Agenda*, 243
Learning Policy (Cohen and Hill), 190
Learning Policy Institute, 99
legislation: during 18th and 19th
    centuries, 5; during 1960s through
    1980s, 21–22; during Civil War era,
    7; during Cold War era, 17–18; during
    colonial era, 3; during Gilded Age, 11;
    during Progressive Era, 13–14; during
    top-down reform era, 25
LeMahieu, P. G., 233
lesson design, 50
Levin, Ben, 236
Levin, Dave, 127
Levine, Arthur, 78
LGBTQI+ students and families, 139,
    164–65, 195, 197–98

liberal progressives, 13, 15
Lincoln, Abraham, 207, 217
literacy rates, 1, 4, 6–7, 10, 20–21, 77
Little Rock Nine, 199
local governance, 192–98
local school boards, 194–98
"Logo," 51
Lonely Crowd, The (Reisman, Glazer,
    and Denney), 17
Lortie, Dan C., 24
Lott, B., 159
Love, Lindsey, 163–64

Madres Unidas, 168, 197
magnet schools, 115, 129–30
management companies, for charter
    schools, 122–23
Mann, Horace, 8, 9, 89, 107, 183, 187,
    190, 207, 218
Manno, Bruno V., 141–42
Manufactured Crisis, The (Berliner and
    Bittle), 29
market-based systems, arguments for,
    117–22, 141
Marsden, George, 249
master's degrees, requirements for, 87
mastery-based programs, 133
*McDuffy v. Secretary of the Executive
    Office of Education* (Massachusetts),
    213, 215
McGuffey Readers, 5, 39
McKay scholarships, 136–37
McShane, Michael Q., 132–33
Mehta, Jal, 236
Mexican American Legal Defense
    and Educational Fund (MALDEF),
    214–15
mid-career certification programs, 74
Miller, Mauricio, 158, 172
Milliken v. Bradley, 115, 205
Milwaukee Parental Choice Program
    (MPCP), 133–35
Mitchell, Lucy Sprague, 69
modeling, 48
Moe, Terry, 120

Montessori, Maria, 36
Moore, H. A., 160
Morrill Acts, 11
Mosely, Paul, 118
Moynihan, Daniel Patrick, 23
multicultural education, 27–28
multiculturalism, 40–44
multiple perspectives, 220

Nathan, Joe, 123
"Nation at Risk, A," 25–26, 28, 76–78, 96–97, 118–20, 184, 187
National and International Assessments, 29
National Assessment of Educational Progress (NAEP), 2, 29, 61, 142, 199
National Association for the Advancement of Colored People (NAACP), 17
National Association of Colored Women, 154
National Association of State Boards of Education (NASBE), 191
National Association of State Directors of Teacher Education and Certification (NASDTEC), 72
National Board of Professional Teaching Standards (NBPTS), 79, 89
National Catholic Educational Association, 109
National Center on Education and the Economy (NCEE), 91–96
National Commission on Excellence of Education, 25
National Commission on Teaching and America's Future, 79
National Congress of Mothers (NCM), 36, 153
National Congress of Parents and Teachers, 153
National Council of Teachers of Mathematics (NCTM), 26

National Defense Education Act (NDEA; 1958), 17–18, 20, 37, 198–99
National Education Association (NEA), 16, 23, 89, 154
National Governors Association (NGA), 26, 186
National History Standards, 40–41
National Institute of Child Health and Human Development, 38
National Reading Panel Report, 38
National Research Council, 243–44
National School Board Association (NSBA), 195
National Science Foundation (NSF), 18–19, 37
National Society for the Promotion of Industrial Education, 15
national standards, 26, 28
Native Americans, 2, 160
neighborhood schools, 113–16, 208
New England Primer, 3
New Teacher Project, The (TNTP), 75, 83
Nguyen, T., 85
Nineteenth Amendment, 90
Nixon, Richard, 22, 23
No Child Left Behind (NCLB; 2001), 25, 26, 44–45, 60, 74, 75–76, 105–6, 130, 157, 200–202
nonprofit charter schools, 126
normal schools, 9, 67–68
Northwest Ordinances (1785, 1787), 116

Oakland Coalition for Community Action, 168
Obama, Barack, 201, 204
object teaching, 9
OECD (Organisation for Economic Co-operation and Development), 62, 90–91, 173–74, 200
Ohio Coalition for Equity & Adequacy of School Funding, 214

Ohio Collaborative for Educating
Remotely and Transforming Schools
Initiatives, 128–29
Ohio High School Athletic Association
(OHSAA), 165
Old Deluder Satan Act (1647), 3
one-room schools, 8
110 Livingston Street (Rogers), 23
online "influencers," 164–65
online instruction, 51–53, 86, 126
Open Enrollment and Transfers,
130–31
open school movement, 23
open-source material, 42–43
opportunity scholarships, 136
Organization Man (Whyte), 17
Other America, The (Harrington), 21
oversight, 223–24

pandemics, innovation and, 34. *See also*
COVID-19
Papert, Seymour, 51
Parental Rights in Education bill, 167
parent advisory councils, 155
parent involvement, 57
Parent Revolution, 157
parents: engagement, 151–58;
engagement and, 171–72; local
governance and, 193, 197–98;
pluralistic system and, 241; school
choice and, 105–6; sidelining of,
158–61
Parent-Teacher Association (PTA), 36,
153–54
parent trigger, 157–58
Partnerships for Assessments of
Readiness for Careers and
College, 61
patronage, 7, 13
pensions, 82
Perpich, Rudy, 123
personal beliefs of teachers, 43
Pestalozzi, 9
phonics, 35, 38

Piaget, Jean, 18, 36, 69
*Pierce v. Society of Sisters of Holy
Names of Jesus and Mary*, 108
Pilgrims, 3
PISA, 61, 62, 143
Plessy v. Ferguson, 13–14, 17, 110, 208
*Pluralism and American Public
Education* (Brenner), 206
pluralistic system: accountability and,
247–48; assessments and, 247–48;
benefits of, 221–22; challenges
regarding, 220–21; community
engagement and, 233–35; concerns
regarding, 245–47; context for,
217–18; curriculum and instruction
for, 226–28; description of, 219–20;
governance and funding for,
222–26; implementation of, 235–48;
introduction to, 218–19; school
choice and, 224, 231–33; teaching
profession and, 228–30
politics, curriculum and, 40
Politics, Markets and America's Schools
(Chubb and Moe), 120
Pondiscio, Robert, 141
Positive Behavior Support training, 171
prayer, school-sponsored, 18, 25, 181
Prentiss, Virginia, 114
preparation and certification for
teachers, 67–69, 92–93, 97–98
*Presidents, Congress and the Public
Schools* (Jennings), 231
Pride Prom, 164
principals, 193, 240
private schools, 107, 108–9, 233
professional development, 53, 57, 85,
86–88, 94, 99, 229–30
professional distancing, 158–59
professional resources, 54
Progress in International Reading
Literacy Study, 62
Progressive Era, 13–16, 68, 90, 184
progressive tradition, 36–38, 68–69,
89–90

property taxes, 202–3, 209, 214–15,
224–25, 248
Public School Education Act (New
Jersey; 1975), 215
public schools: during 18th and 19th
centuries, 6; case for strong, 116–17;
during colonial era, 3; districts
and attendance zones for, 109–16;
during Gilded Age, 11; impact of
choice options on, 137–43; during
Progressive Era, 13, 16; teachers and,
70–75; universal public education
and, 107–8
public/private partnerships, 242–44
Puritans, 3
Putnam, R. D., 175
Putnam, Robert, 234, 249

Quakers, 6
quality control, 117

race: critical race theory (CRT),
163–64; family engagement and,
159–60; private schools and,
109; PTA and, 153–54. *See also*
desegregation; segregation
Race to the Top (RTTT), 25, 27, 45–46,
75–76, 79, 95, 157, 201
Racial Zoning Ordinance, 111–12
Ravitch, Diane, 139, 162
readiness standards, 26
Reagan, Ronald, 24–25, 119–20
Rebel Talent (Gino), 220
reciprocity, 72, 82
Reconstruction, 10–12
Recruiting New Teachers (RNT), 82–83
recruitment of teachers, 80–83, 92,
98–99
Red Scare, 13, 20, 154
redlining, 110–13
Reed, Ralph, 162, 198
reforms: during 1960s through 1980s,
22–23; during Civil War era, 7–8;
during Cold War era, 18; during

colonial era, 3–4; community
organizing for, 172–73; during
Gilded Age, 11; during Progressive
Era, 13–16; regarding teachers,
79–80; standards-based, 200; during
top-down reform era, 25–27
region boards of education, 238–39
Reich, Justin, 51, 69
Reisman, D., 17
religious schools, 3, 4, 13, 107, 208
research and development, 222
resiliency, 173–74
Resnick, Mitch, 51
retaining teachers, 84–90, 98–99
Rhee, Michelle, 198
Riley, Richard, 26, 187
Ripley, Amanda, 244
Robotics and Advanced Manufacturing
Technology Collaborative
(RAMTEC), 166
Rockefeller, David, 82
*Rodriguez v. San Antonio Independent
School District*, 205
Rogers, David, 23
Roza, Marguerite, 204, 206
Rufo, Christopher, 163
rural districts, teacher recruitment and, 80
Rush, Benjamin, 6

salaries/compensation, 84, 92, 99,
203–4
Sarason, Seymour, 195
Schleicher, Andreas, 91
Schmidt, Benno, 125
Schmidt, William, 44–45
school boards, politicization of, 162
school choice: historical context
for, 107–16; impact of on public
education, 137–43; introduction to,
105–7; market-based systems and,
117–22; observations regarding,
143–44; options for, 122–33;
overview of, 27; pluralistic system
and, 221, 224, 231–33; public

schools and, 116–17; vouchers and, 133–37
school districts, 192, 193–94
school enrollment rates, 1
school funding, 202–6, 213–15, 222–23, 224–26
school governance: federal, 182, 198–202; funding and, 202–6, 213–15; introduction to, 181–83; local, 192–98; observations regarding, 206–9; in pluralistic system, 222–26; regionalized, 225–26; state, 182–92
School Planning and Management Team, 170
school principals and administrators, 193, 240
Schoolteacher: A Sociological Study (Lortie), 24
Schrag, Peter, 23
Schuknecht, Ludger, 91
Schulman, Lee, 96
Schwartz, Robert B., 236
scope, 34
Scopes, John T., 14
Scopes trial, 14, 161
"Scratch," 51
Scripting the Moves (Golann), 127
Search for Common Ground, A, 41
seat time, 55, 126
segregation, 9–10, 11, 13–14, 17, 20, 81, 110–16, 208. *See also* desegregation
sequence, 34
SERP (Strategic Education Research Partnership), 243
sexuality, curriculum and, 41, 43
Shanker, Al, 89, 123–24
Sizer, Theodore, 77, 97
Skinner, B. F., 14, 69
SLANT approach, 127
Slums and Suburbs (Conant), 18
Smarter Balanced Assessment Consortium, 61

Smith-Hughes Act, 15
social-emotional learning (SEL), 54, 86, 187, 226
social isolation, 54
social skills, 54
Socratic method, 69
Southlake, Texas, 162–63
special education, 49–50
spoils system, 7, 13
Springer, M., 85
standardized testing, 28, 29, 60, 201
standards-based reform, 200
State Academic Content Standards, 26
state achievement tests, 60
state boards of education, 185, 190–91, 237–38
state certificates, 72
state departments of education, 183–85, 188–90, 237–38
state governance, 182–92
state judiciaries, 186, 192
state legislatures, 186, 192, 237
state standards, 44–45
state superintendents, 185, 188, 237–38
state universities, educator preparation/certification and, 67–68
STEM education, 166
Strickland, Ted, 187
student body characteristics, 85
student-centered instruction, 48–49
summative assessment, 59
supportive services, 169
Swann v. Mecklenberg County, 114
synchronous online learning, 52

Taft, Bob, 187
Teach for America, 74–75, 78, 83
TEACH grant program, 76
teacher appraisal systems, 94–95
teacher colleges, 9
teacher education and accreditation standards, 28
Teacher Incentive Fund (TIF), 76
Teacher Wars, The (Goldstein), 89

teacher-centered instruction, 48
teachers: art of teaching and, 66;
assessment and, 60; curriculum and,
39, 43; demographics regarding,
81–82, 99–100; empowering,
90–96; human resource system for,
65–66; importance of quality of, 65,
75; improving quality of, 75–80;
lack of diversity among, 81–82,
99–100; local governance and,
193; number of, 65; observations
regarding, 96–100; pluralistic system
and, 240–41, 247–48; preparation
and certification for, 67–69, 92–93,
97–98, 223, 229–30; public schools
and, 70–75; recruitment of, 80–83,
92, 98–99; retaining, 84–90, 98–99;
types of, 70, **71**
teaching profession: during 18th and
19th centuries, 5; during 1960s
through 1980s, 24; during Civil
War era, 9; during Cold War era,
20; during colonial era, 4; during
Gilded Age, 12; pluralistic system
and, 228–30; during Progressive Era,
15–16; during top-down reform
era, 28
technical education, 166–67
technology: COVID-19 and, 51–52;
educational materials and, 27;
instruction and, 57; pluralism and,
228
Tenth Amendment, 5
thematic instruction, 49
Thompson, Tommy, 133
Thorndyke, 68
Tigerland, 171
TIMSS, 61, 62
Tirozzi, Gerald, 92
Title I, 22, 120, 200
Title IX, 22
top-down education reform, 24–29
transfer options, 130–31
transparency, 222

Trends in International Mathematics and
Science Study (TIMSS), 29
Tri-Rivers Career Center, 166
Troops to Teachers, 74
truancy, 126, 132
Trump, Donald, 121, 163–64
trust visits, 161
Tucker, Marc S., 143, 220
turnover, teacher, 84–85
Twenty-First Century Skills, 27

unions, 20, 24, 88, 89–90, 118–19, 120,
124
universal public education, 107–8
Urban, D., 29
urban districts, teacher recruitment and, 81
U.S. Constitution, 182, 205, 235
U.S. Department of Education, 23, 25,
200
U.S. National Commission on
Excellence in Education, 76

Veteran's Administration (VA), 112
Village School Downtown (Schrag), 23
Vocational Education Act (1963),
37–38
vocational schools, 130
Voinovich, George, 187
Volunteers in Service to America
(VISTA), 21
voucher programs, 118, 119, 121,
133–37, 138–39
Vygotsky, Lev, 18, 69

Wagoner, J. L., 29
Walker, Watson, 114
Wallace, George, 186
War on Poverty, 21, 22–23, 199
Washington, Booker T., 12
Webster, Noah, 5, 39, 207
Whigs, 7–8
white flight, 205
White Hat Ventures, 124–25
Whittle, Chris, 125

"whole child" development, 36
whole child individualized learning,
    36–37
whole language approach, 36, 38
*Why Johnny Can't Read and What You
    Can Do About It* (Flesch), 35
Whyte, William, 17
Williams, Annette "Polly," 133
Winter, William, 187

working conditions, poor, 84

XPRIZE Foundation, 242, 243

Youngkin, Glenn, 43

Zelman, Susan, 124, 136
Zelman v. Simmons-Harris, 223
Zimmerman, Jonathan, 249

About the Authors

Over their lifetimes, the authors of this book have experienced firsthand many dimensions of the American educational system. They have witnessed education's triumphs and struggles and may have contributed to some of its failures. They have been students, parents, schoolteachers, researchers, and policy analysts. They have the range of experience from working with small children in a settlement house to teaching graduate students. They have engaged in the education system from a personal point to view to the state and federal vantage point. They not only have the big picture state-level view into the politics and inner workings of education but also have the up-close and personal view of students they care about deeply.

Of interest, both authors wrote dissertations, years apart, looking at the role of parents in education. Both affirmed that parents and other community "outsiders" must be included in any arena of reform. Lasting reform also requires knowledge of history, where we have come from as well as a vision of where we can go.

The latter part of the authors' careers has been in Ohio, which is a microcosm of the United States with its eight large urban areas, inner ring suburbs, affluent suburbs, and rich and very poor rural areas. In Ohio, as in the entire United States, diversity is our greatest asset.

ABOUT SUSAN TAVE ZELMAN

Susan was born and raised in the Bronx and is a product of New York City Schools. Many of her teachers entered the profession during the Depression when teaching jobs were hard to come by. She graduated from an all-girls high school and Hunter College. At Hunter, she majored in history and

275

minored in political science. Following graduation, she taught high school social studies in the New York City schools, and then received a fellowship funded by the U.S. Department of Education to the University of Michigan to pursue a doctorate in education. She spent the next fourteen years of her career as a college professor, teaching and doing research. She then pursued a career in state government as the associate commissioner of education in Massachusetts, deputy commissioner of education in Missouri, and state superintendent for public instruction in Ohio. She is the recipient of three honorary degrees and numerous awards and grants.

Dr. Zelman, who retired from the Ohio Department of Education at the end of 2018, is also the president of the Zelman Education Consulting Group. She recently served as senior vice president for education and children's programming at the Corporation for Public Broadcasting where she developed policies and programs to integrate public service media into a national reform education agenda. Currently she is a consultant to education technology firms on a variety of education issues. She has witnessed firsthand policy negotiations in education at the federal, state, and local levels.

Susan is also the mother of three children and grandmother of seven. As she has observed her grandchildren's education, especially during the COVID-19 pandemic, she has gotten depressed. She feels that their education can be so such more exciting and challenging. She worries whether our current public education system is adequately preparing children for a future that we cannot even imagine and senses that their world will be more difficult than we have experienced.

ABOUT MARGARET ERLANDSON SORENSEN

Peggy Sorensen's relationship to education is nontraditional. Born and raised in Cleveland Heights, Ohio, until her family moved to a small town in Michigan while in high school. She holds a BA in English education from Michigan State University and a PhD in education from Walden University. When Peggy graduated with a degree in education and a teaching certificate, she intended to teach but was diverted by service in Volunteers in Service to America (VISTA). Originally planning to spend a year garnering experience before entering the classroom, her VISTA placement at a settlement house in Columbus, Ohio, working with children in community theater, led to an eighteen-year stay. While at the settlement house, with a value base that stressed experiencing "the richness of human difference," the Columbus City Schools were moving through a desegregation lawsuit and ultimately a court desegregation order. As a consciously integrated agency, the settlement house supported school desegregation.

When Peggy headed back in the direction of traditional teaching, she entered public education as a substitute teacher, as well as teaching adults in the Adult Basic Literacy and Education (ABLE) program. By then she had, as a single parent, adopted two children and was beginning to experience school from the perspective of a parent. She chose to buy a house and live within the City of Columbus because she loathed following the flight of families with means to the suburbs following desegregation. In addition, she feared that her adopted children of color might not be well accepted in a mostly white district.

Her perspective as a substitute teacher, as an ABLE teacher, and as an advocate for neighborhood children and later her own, one of whom had learning difficulties, has given Peggy a practical and realistic view of the American education system. She has personally experienced the humbling challenge of facing a completely unknown group of children, maintaining order, and trying to follow someone else's lesson plans, all the while hoping to teach something worthwhile. As a sub, she also experienced a wide variety of schools, school environments, and students. As an ABLE teacher, she found that many of her students were "push outs" from the public system. Some had been categorized as having vague learning disabilities but little knowledge of what they were or how to overcome them. As a parent advocate, despite years of advocacy experience, she struggled to be heard or to have any sense of impacting the system. She has learned that even when parent issues are valid, they may not align with those of teachers or administrators. She is also aware that parents seldom have a place at the official table to share their issues or to impact policies.

She recognizes that her point of view may not be the same as that of many other more traditional educators, people who also care deeply about children and work very hard at what they do. But she argues that views such as hers are necessary to understand our education system and ultimately improve it. Through her work, she has realized the uniqueness of the parent voice and point of view of education. And she knows all too often that educators simply go through the motions of parent engagement, the perception of control, without actually accepting their influence. This lessens political advocacy and increases political cynicism.

Employing their experiences as lifelong educators, in this book the authors present a primer for individuals wanting to reinvent public education so we can preserve our democracy, promote our economy, and improve the quality of life for everyone.

Made in the USA
Middletown, DE
12 November 2022

14790446R00182